Employment and Work Relations in Context Series

Series Editors

Tony Elger and Peter Fairbrother

Labour Studies Group,
Department of Sociology,
University of Warwick

PRIVATIZATION AND EMPLOYMENT RELATIONS

The Case of the Water Industry

Julia O'Connell Davidson

MANSELL

First published 1993 by
Mansell Publishing Limited. *A Cassell Imprint*
Villiers House, 41/47 Strand, London WC2N 5JE, England
387 Park Avenue South, New York, NY 10016–8810, USA

© Julia O'Connell Davidson 1993

Reprinted in paperback 1994

British Library Cataloguing-in-Publication Data
A catalogue record for this book is available from the British Library.

ISBN 0–7201–2150–7 (Hardback)
ISBN 0–7201–2214–7 (Paperback)

Library of Congress Cataloging-in-Publication Data
O'Connell Davidson, Julia, 1960–
    Privatization and employment relations: the case of the water
industry/Julia O'Connell Davidson.
        p.   cm.—(Employment and work relations in context)
    Includes bibliographical references and index.
    ISBN 0–7201–2150–7 (Hardback)
    ISBN 0–7201–2214–7 (Paperback)
    1. Waterworks—Great Britain—Personnel management.
    2. Waterworks—Great Britain—Employees.   3. Privatization—Great
Britain.   I. Title.   II. Series.
    HD4465.G7D38   1993
    331'.04136361'0941—dc20   92–45067
                                                                CIP

Typeset by Colset Pte Ltd, Singapore
Printed and bound in Great Britain by
Biddles Ltd, Guildford and King's Lynn

CONTENTS

SERIES EDITORS' FOREWORD

The aim of the Employment and Work Relations in Context series is to address questions relating to the evolving patterns of work, employment and industrial relations in specific workplaces, localities and regions. This focus arises primarily from a concern to trace out the ways in which wider policy making, especially by national governments and transnational corporations, impinges upon specific workplaces, labour markets and localities in distinctive ways. A particular feature of the series is the consideration of forms of worker and citizen organization and mobilization in these circumstances. Thus the studies will address major analytical and policy issues through case-study and comparative research.

Tony Elger
Peter Fairbrother

PREFACE AND ACKNOWLEDGEMENTS

This book is concerned with new patterns of employment relations and work organization in one of Britain's newly privatized water service companies. Drawing on research in this company (which has been given the fictional name 'Albion Water' in response to management's request for anonymity) and in a firm of civil engineering contractors (referred to as 'Harrup's', again to preserve confidentiality), the book shows how the pattern of employment relations in the water industry is changing. In the past, Albion Water relied predominantly upon but two types of labour: 'standard' full-time, permanent, direct employees, and contract labour which undertook a limited range of specific activities. Privatization has stimulated diversification, however, making the pattern of employment relations more varied. The labour upon which Albion Water relies is increasingly divided horizontally (into 'standard' direct employees, self-employed workers, temporary staff, part-time employees, freelance workers, contract workers) as well as vertically by occupational status and grade. These changes, and the way in which they have been effected, are of broader theoretical significance and my aim in writing this book is not simply to document developments in a privatized utility, but also to highlight some of the problems which the variability of capitalist employment relations poses for existing theoretical models of that relation.

Variability has always been a feature of capitalist work relations, no matter which stage of development is considered. Maxine Berg has shown that from the eighteenth century on, there were marked differences in production arrangements even within single industries, such as textiles, and that these differences 'were rooted in socio-economic structures: historically established levels of industrial concentration and social inequality, legal and customary regulations, and regional cultural traditions' (Berg, 1985, p. 317). Clearly, such variations created a great diversity of employment relations. As capitalism developed through the nineteenth century in Britain, this variety of relationships between capital and labour persisted. The putting-out system, even in some cases handicraft production, survived alongside large-scale industrial production; casual employment, in agriculture and docking for example, existed alongside indentured labour, particularly in mining areas. Employment 'opportunities' ranged from the most casual, to what amounted to virtual slavery. Employment contracts could tie the worker to an employer on a daily, weekly, monthly or yearly basis. In some industries, payment was made regularly in cash, whilst in others payment was irregular and often in truck; in either case, workers could be paid an hourly rate, or paid by the piece or by some combination of the two. Even within large-scale production, employment relations varied both between and within different industrial sectors, and indeed within any one factory (Pollard, 1965; Littler, 1982).

This historical diversity of capitalist employment relations and work organization has often been presented as a phase of development through which capitalism passed, before more efficient techniques were developed and standardized. For many writers, Taylorist-type direct employment relations marked the end point of this development and were the last word in efficiency. The argument this book advances is that where the purpose of economic activity is to maximize profits, there is no one, ideal form of employment relation which guarantees the employer 'efficiency'. Instead, employers must adjust that relation to a range of economic, political, spatial and institutional factors (such as market demand, local labour market conditions, fiscal policy, the development of financial institutions and trade unions and so on). The book is thus informed by the assumption that employment relations today, as much as those of previous eras, are analytically inseparable from their wider historical setting. This point is well illustrated by the rapid and extensive changes to employment relations instituted at Albion Water in response to privatization – an event which transformed the context in which Albion Water's labour process was organized. The book further argues that the nature and form of the employment relation is affected by political struggle between collective classes. For example, the broad legal framework within which employment takes place is the outcome of struggle, and sets definite limits on both the content of work which people can be required to undertake, and the terms on which they do so. At Albion Water, direct labour levels have been savagely cut, and those direct employees who remain are working harder and longer, often under worse conditions for less money. These changes were imposed by management in a political and economic climate which was especially unfavourable to labour, and this underlines the fact that employment relations, like the rate of surplus value created in the labour process, vary 'according to the relative strength of the combatants within the production process' (Nichols, 1980, p. 35).

The book draws on Economic and Social Research Council funded research into restructuring and change in two public utilities conducted between 1988 and 1991. The ESRC's support is gratefully acknowledged (ESRC award number R000231466). An earlier version of Chapter 7 appeared in the journal *Work, Employment and Society*, and I am grateful for permission to reproduce this material. There are a number of individuals to whom my thanks are also due. I am grateful to all the 'Albion Water' and 'Harrup's' employees who participated in this research; to Frank Rowberry of GMBATU and Ken Terry of NUPE who were extremely helpful; and to Catherine Price for reading Chapter 2 and for her general comments on the economic regulation of privatized industries. I would also like to thank Karsten Grummitt for an eclectic mix of cuttings from the *Financial Times*, satire, conversations about business issues, diversions, financial support (together with Lloyds Bank), and, above all, friendship and encouragement. Jackie West and Paul Thompson read and critically discussed the entire original manuscript, and my heartfelt thanks are extended to both of them. I am also more than grateful to Peter Fairbrother and Tony Elger, not only for their comments on the draft manuscript of this book and for their skill and tact as editors, but also for more general support and encouragement over the past few years. The research was based in the Sociology Department of Bristol University, and I want to thank Jackie Bee and Cheryl Miller for all their help, Rohit Barot for sympathy and light snacks, and, most especially, Wen Bin Sun for her insights, wit and friendship. Finally, and most of all, I owe a debt of thanks to Theo Nichols, who directed the research project. Without his patience, generosity and inspiration, neither this book, nor the research upon which it is based, would have been possible. The book's faults and weaknesses remain,. of course, my own responsibility.

LIST OF ABBREVIATIONS

AEU	Amalgamated Engineering Union
AUEW	Allied Union of Engineering Workers
BMU	Building Maintenance Unit (of 'Albion Water')
BT	British Telecom
DLO	Direct Labour Organization
DOE	Department of the Environment
EC	European Community
EEC	European Economic Community
EETPU	Electrical, Electronic, Telecommunication and Plumbing Union
ESRC	Economic and Social Research Council
GMB	General Municipal Boilermakers' Union
GMBATU	General Municipal Boilermakers' and Allied Trades Union
ICA	Instrumentation, control and automation
ICE	Institution of Civil Engineers
IMS	Institute of Manpower Services
JAWS	Joint Action for Water Services
M&E	Mechanical and Electrical Maintenance
MATSA	Managerial, Administrative, Technical and Supervisory Association
NALGO	National and Local Government Officers' Association
NHS	National Health Service
NUPE	National Union of Public Employees
OFWAT	Office of Water Services
PMC	Period main-laying contract
PSBR	Public sector borrowing requirement
RPI	Retail price index
TGWU	Transport and General Workers' Union
TUC	Trades Union Congress
UCATT	Union of Construction, Allied Trades and Technicians
WAA	Water Authorities Association

1 PRIVATIZATION AND THE VARIABILITY OF CAPITALIST EMPLOYMENT RELATIONS

In Britain, Conservative politicians generally justify their government's privatization programme as a response to the 'over-expansion' of the state sector of the economy and the public sector borrowing requirement associated with it in the post-war years. Between 1945 and 1979, the public sector grew in size under both Labour and Conservative governments until, by 1975, almost 30% of the gross national product was directly consumed by public bodies such as hospitals, schools, police and army (Coates, 1984) and by 1975, around 30% of the economically active population was employed by the state (Therborn, 1984). This expansion was partly a result of the general commitment to the extension and maintenance of a comprehensive system of welfare support and partly a consequence of the nationalization of particular industries, such as fuel, power and the railways. Both Conservative and Labour governments of this period saw public ownership as

> a necessary cost which government would have to bear in order to sustain a profitable private sector. Nationalisation was a strategy for maintaining production in those areas of the economy which much of the private sector depended on but which were insufficiently profitable to attract new private-sector investment. (Dearlove and Saunders, 1984 p. 273)

The growth of the public sector reflected a growing acceptance of the Keynesian notion that 'capitalism cannot be counted on to provide full employment or even socially adequate capital utilization without state intervention' (Schott, 1983, p. 340); that government has a responsibility to bolster the private sector and to ensure 'the "success" of the economy, as defined by the twin criteria of full employment and growth'

1

(Goldthorpe, 1987, p. 364). Nationalization gave government direct control over segments of the economy, and so provided one of the instruments through which Keynesian demand-management economic policies could be implemented. For a time, it seemed that governments were able to manage this so-called 'mixed economy' reasonably successfully. By the mid-1970s, however, Britain faced slowing economic growth, and rising unemployment coupled with rising inflation. New Right political theorists attributed this economic crisis to the 'excessive' state intervention associated with Keynesianism. It was argued that in pursuit of the 'unnatural' goal of full employment, governments had borrowed, bureaucratized and taxed excessively, creating a 'nanny state' which stifled real wealth creation and economic growth and nurtured 'the cancer of inflation'. Margaret Thatcher's commitment to New Right and monetarist theory may not have been clearly evident in the run-up to the 1979 election, but by the early 1980s her government had embarked on a programme explicitly designed to 'roll back the frontiers of the state'. The Thatcher government's privatization programme, which was not fully developed until after the 1983 election, has transferred state-owned assets into the private sector and so clearly contributed to this process of reducing state intervention in the economy (MacInnes, 1987, p. 52).

Privatization is a policy which holds a particular appeal for New Right thinkers. Such people saw the nationalized industries as symbolic of the political strength of organized labour in the post-war years and as epitomizing the evils of state intervention. Insulated from the discipline of market forces, these industries were characterized by the New Right as bureaucratic, inflexible, inefficient and unresponsive to customer demands. Returning these industries to the private sector is therefore not only welcomed as heralding a brave new world of efficiency and consumer responsiveness, but is also celebrated as standing alongside events in Eastern Europe as part of a worldwide rejection of socialist values and practice. New Right rhetoric about privatization tells us that its benefits 'will extend beyond our dreams', even that it is a means of vanquishing 'brutality, ignorance, poverty, corruption and waste' (Clarke, 1987). Privatization has indeed had some dramatic consequences, though none of them fits easily with Clarke's feverish vision of privatization laying the foundations for a society in which all 'human services will be fully engaged and freed' (Clarke, 1987, p. 91).

The most obvious beneficiary of privatization is the Treasury. Between 1979 and 1987, successive Conservative governments in Britain raised almost £15 billion[1] in cash from the sale of state assets, and this despite the fact that these assets were massively underpriced by the government in order to ensure the success of the privatization programme. The TUC estimates that, even by 1984, the loss for taxpayers from such underselling amounted to at least £1.4 billion (Abromeit, 1988). Not everyone lost out, however. The chairmen of newly privatized concerns have seen fit to reward themselves with handsome pay rises, and senior managers now own substantial share capital in their privatized companies. At British Telecom in 1989, for example, the top five executives together held 1.3 million BT shares, worth around £5 million, whilst at British Gas the top seven executives between them owned around £3.5 million worth of shares in 1991. City institutions have also gained from the government's privatization programme on a magnificent scale, and it is argued that from the water sale alone, stockbrokers, merchant bankers, lawyers, advertising agencies and other 'advisers' received £400 million in fees (SCAT, 1989).

The political rhetoric of privatization celebrates the virtues of the free market, and holds that once freed from 'the cobwebs of the state' people and institutions will flourish. Managers will be restored their potency as they regain the 'freedom to manage', while once moribund and sterile organizations will become efficient producers. Conservative MPs have held privatization to be 'a remedy for some of the ills that have beset UK industrial performance in recent years' (Moore, 1983) and a 'new economic creed' (Redwood, 1988). Consumers will benefit from a more competitive and effective service, and workers in privatized concerns will enjoy greater job satisfaction. Clarke concedes that privatization may lead to 'a rapid contraction in numbers employed and a swift reform of antique restrictive practices' but goes on to assert that 'the prospects for employees in organizations removed from the State sector would seem to be enhanced' (Clarke, 1987, p. 81). So far as the rapid contraction in direct employment is concerned, Clarke is undoubtedly correct. SCAT (1990) estimates that more than 70 000 jobs were lost as a direct result of privatization and compulsory competitive tendering in the 1980s. If jobs lost during pre-privatization 'efficiency' drives were taken into account, the figure would be far higher. These job losses are the more significant given that first, public sector workers have been central to the post-1966 growth in trade union membership, and second, public sector employment is fairly evenly geographically distributed. Thus, as Massey (1984, p. 183) observes, such cuts not only represent an attack on one of the fastest-growing parts of the organized labour movement: they also imply a reduction in jobs in one of the few parts of the economy where the spatial structure of employment is not massively reinforcing geographical inequality.

Meanwhile, there is little evidence available to support the claim that employees' prospects are enhanced by privatization. Indeed, most of the claims that have been advanced about the effects of privatization have been made in something of an empirical vacuum, for there has, until recently, been very little independent research in privatized companies. This may be partly due to the fact that it is the public utilities which have occupied pride of place in the government's privatization programme, and despite the fact that over a quarter of a million people are employed in the electricity, gas and water utilities in the UK (roughly the same number as are employed by the motor industry and making up around 5% of employment in production industries as a whole), historically, the public utilities have been largely ignored by the industrial sociology literature. This tendency to neglect the utilities persisted throughout the 1980s, with manufacturing continuing to occupy centre stage so far as empirical research into industrial restructuring, changes in employment relations and work flexibility was concerned; see, for example, the work of Batstone (1984), Daniel and Millward (1983), Millward and Stevens (1986), Edwards (1985a, b), and MacInnes (1987).

This book is based upon research in a public utility, which will be referred to as 'Albion Water'.[2] One of its main aims is to examine patterns of work organization and employment relations in a hitherto neglected sector of the economy, and to document the effects of privatization upon Albion Water's organizational structure, its employees and its subcontractors. Given the political rhetoric which has surrounded privatization, the empirical investigation of its effects is clearly called for, and this book contributes to the growing number of studies which document developments in privatized, or about to be privatized, concerns. But there are also other reasons why studies of work and employment in privatized utilities are worthwhile. It has already been noted that the utilities are major employers, and it is therefore necessary to investigate developments in these organizations in order to acquire a real overview of restructuring across all sectors of the economy. Work organization, employment practices and industrial relations in the utilities have all undergone rapid and extensive change in the 1980s both in preparation for, and subsequent to, privatization. This restructuring has taken place in a relatively compressed period of time, which makes the processes behind change more visible and accessible. It is therefore possible that research in the utilities may provide valuable insights into patterns and processes of change happening elsewhere, especially given that many developments in the utilities appear to be consonant with those reported in other industries (e.g. reductions to direct labour levels, increased resort to various forms of subcontract, the pursuit of various forms of 'flexibility', a shift away from constitutionalist industrial relations and so on). In a sense, there is nothing new about the utilities sharing a great deal of common ground with private sector concerns. To begin with, like all nationalized industries, the utilities were increasingly cash-limited and increasingly pressured to finance their capital investment out of operating profits by governments struggling to contain or reduce the PSBR from the 1960s on. The effects of this on public sector management priorities and practice were similar to the effects of recession and the profit squeeze upon private sector concerns. Moreover, although New Right thinkers like to portray nationalized industries as non-commercial organizations, inspired by socialist principles and pursuing socialist goals, in reality these organizations could hardly be said to depart from the private sector model. The main nationalizations carried out by the Attlee administration in 1945–1951 set the precedent for future nationalizations, and were heavily influenced by Herbert Morrison, who held that 'the best business brains' should be left to run public industry efficiently. As Schott (1983, p. 354) observes:

> Various industries were nationalized, but they were to operate on hierarchical lines like private firms with recognized business talent in charge . . . Consultation between management and workers at various levels within these nationalized industries was envisaged, but the structures for it were not particularly influential.

Of course, the nationalized industries differed from privately owned companies in the sense that they did not have to compete in the capital market, but management's right to manage was not questioned and the boards of nationalized industries were typically dominated by people with a strong commitment to the business ethos. The idea that they were run along totally different lines to private sector organizations is something of a fiction, as those who had hoped that nationalization would constitute a step towards worker democracy soon discovered. It is true that the utilities were, until recently, very much engineering-led, technocratic organizations, but again this was not unique to the public sector. Much of the private sector was also modelled on these lines until the late 1970s or early 1980s, when the lieutenants who generated the white heat of the technological revolution were increasingly squeezed out by a new breed of 'intrapreneurial' and upwardly mobile accountants.

The public utilities did, however, have three really singular features. First, they were monopolies. Second, virtually every industry and every household was dependent upon their products and services. Third, governments were in a position to shape industrial relations in the nationalized industries far more directly than could be achieved in the private sector, and industrial relations in the utilities of the 1960s and 1970s certainly bore the stamp of the broader political commitment to some form of corporatism. (It is also significant that, so far as the utilities were concerned, it was widely believed that any serious industrial relations problem would carry equally serious electoral consequences for the government of the day.) These last two features gave the utilities their distinctive character. On the one hand, employees' awareness of the social usefulness of their product led to the development of a very strong public service ethos within the utilities (at British Gas, for example, workers traditionally took pride in their safety record, in the quality and impartiality of advice offered to consumers, in the fact that, until privatization, free servicing of old age pensioners' gas appliances was routinely undertaken, and so on). On the other hand, government involvement meant that the utilities were characterized by constitutionalist and fairly harmonious industrial relations. They were densely unionized, with well-established national bargaining machinery through which relatively good packages of job security, working conditions and employment benefits (if not high wages) were negotiated. It was in this context that the notion of the state as a 'model employer' emerged.

However, privatization and the restructuring of the public sector through the 1980s has, as Fairbrother (1991, p. 71) notes, given 'an entirely new meaning . . . to [the idea of] the state as a model employer to be emulated by other sectors'. It can be argued that in terms of dismantling the industrial relations machinery and practice of the post-war era, and of pursuing workplace flexibility and labour intensification, the state has led the way both through legislation, privatization and its own practice as an employer. This is another reason why studies of privatized utilities provide especially fertile ground for exploring the dynamics that underpin industrial restructuring in Britain. It is not that they are unique in their greater reliance upon various forms of contracting out, or in their search for flexibility and new techniques for cutting labour costs. What is of particular interest is the way that these changes have impacted on the nature and pattern of employment relations within the utilities. In the past, the utilities were characterized by a certain uniformity of employment relations (with all direct employees from canteen staff through to managers enjoying the same degree of employment security, similar rights to fringe benefits, seniority rather than performance-based progression through grades, and so on). Privatization has stimulated diversification, making the pattern of employment relations more varied. The labour upon which the utilities rely is now divided horizontally (into 'standard' direct employees, self-employed workers, temporary staff, part-time employees, freelance workers, contract workers) as well as vertically by occupational status and grade. These changes, and the way in which they have been effected, are of broader theoretical significance, and a further aim of this book is to explore the implications of developments at Albion Water for theories of the capitalist employment relation.

Theoretical Models of the Capitalist Employment Relation

The term 'employment relation' refers to the set of explicit and tacit bargains struck over the exchange of pay, benefits and conditions on the one hand, for work on the other (Brown, 1988, p. 54). It therefore embraces two main features of work in a capitalist economy: the nature of the tasks that workers undertake and the terms on which workers' labour power is procured. Distinctions can thus be drawn between, say, the self-employed electrician and the electrician directly employed by a firm, even though the content of their work may be exactly the same, as well as between electricians and unskilled labourers both directly employed by the same firm. The employment relation represents the web of tacit and explicit bargains struck between a unit of capital and the labour it uses over a range of issues concerning what work is to be done and how, and what payments and other benefits will be ceded in exchange.

At a theoretical level, this book is concerned with the nature and determinants of capitalist employment relations, and above all with the source of their variability. Even the most cursory glance at production past and present immediately reveals the diversity of possible forms of employment relations under capitalism. In terms of contractual rights and obligations, capital has made use of, and does make use of, both free and unfree labour, the labour of subcontractors, self-employed individuals, outworkers, freelances, casual labourers and direct employees. Direct employment itself has taken, and can take, a number of forms. Capital has, and does, set direct labour to work on tasks ranging from the most complex and highly skilled, through to the most routine, simple and standard. Likewise, capital can provide direct labour on a multiplicity of terms; employers can directly employ workers on full-time or part-time, permanent or temporary contracts, and can make use of any one of a number of forms of payment system. Direct employees may be offered a variety of perks and non-statutory fringe benefits; they may be provided with training and offered a substantial degree of job security. Conversely, they may be offered none of these things. This list is by no means exhaustive.

Neither the observation that employment in capitalist societies can take many forms, nor the idea that different groups of workers undertake different tasks and experience very different conditions of employment, is especially startling or original. Yet despite being a constant and highly visible feature of capitalist production, the range and diversity of employment relations poses theoretical and empirical problems. At an empirical level, it is extremely difficult to map either the extent or pattern of this variability in any one country or even industry, and this is illustrated by recent debates about trends in 'non-standard' employment; see, for example Beechey (1985), Casey (1987), Creigh et al. (1986), Hakim (1987a, b), Meager (1986) and Dale and Bamford (1988).

At a theoretical level, the source of this variability is equally problematic. An explicit model of the capitalist employment relation has rarely been articulated in the academic literature on work, and historically this may have been because a stress on the range and diversity of employment relations was incompatible with other key theoretical assumptions. For, as Kumar (1986, p. 110) observes, 'in the development of sociology, certain central inferences about the nature of industrial society were lifted from the general body of thought of the early sociologists, and fused into a "model" of industrialism'. This model was essentially an evolutionary one.

Marx had provided a theory of the long-term dynamics of capitalism, which identified the contradiction between the expanding forces of production and the institution of private property as the motor of social change and economic development. Although Weber rejected any general 'law of motion' underpinning capitalist development, he also identified processes which inevitably shaped industrial development in the modern world: rationalization, mechanization and bureaucratization. Both of these classical sociologists' work could be, and was, used to develop evolutionary models of industrialization, and given that the most striking feature of industrial development in the late nineteenth and early twentieth century was the phenomenal expansion in the scale of production and the size of corporations, it is unsurprising that large enterprises, and the forms of work organization and employment relation adopted by them, were often taken to be the zenith of an evolutionary process.

Marx's discussion of increasing concentration and centralization of capital, of mechanization and of the increasingly specialized division of labour could be used to identify a tendency towards one dominant form of production organization – large-scale production organized along basically Taylorist principles. Weber's work was also compatible with an emphasis on the development of one standard form of work organization, and until the late 1960s, much industrial sociology drew heavily on Weber's conception of 'industrial society' as opposed to 'capitalist society' in order to develop an evolutionary model of industrialization. For Weber, 'industrial society' was:

> A form of society characterized by large-scale industrial production, technological rationality, the inexorable power of material goods, bureaucratic administration, and a pervasive 'calculating attitude'.
> (Bottomore, 1985, p. 26)

Weber was ambivalent about modernism, referring to rationalization and intellectualization as a process of 'disenchantment' and to the 'iron cage' of rationality, and distinguishing between formal and substantive rationality. Many later theorists of industrial society were less cautious, however. Bell (1960), Kerr (1960) and Blauner (1964), for example, all provide evolutionary models of development, and the 'logic' of this process is to arrive at *substantively* rational, harmonious, pluralist, conflict-free social order. Liberal theorists of industrial society identified the technological exigencies of production, rather than the social relations of production, as the motor of social change. Like many other industrial sociologists of the 1950s and 1960s, they used a linear model of technological development, dividing technical systems of industrial production into three basic stages: batch production, mass production, and automation (Mann, 1973, p. 54). Contemporary diversity in terms of organizational structure and size was likewise explained through reference to differences in production technology. It was often assumed that job content and employment conditions could be read off from the technical system of production, and, of course, liberal theorists claimed that employment in the final stage of automation would be both materially and psychologically enriching. Empirical evidence to counter claims about work in automated process production plants was provided, most notably by Nichols and Beynon (1977) and by Gallie (1978). But the important point is that, as Goldthorpe (1984, p. 332) observes, liberal theorists assumed

> that in order to meet requirements, of reliability and predictability, production would increasingly be carried out according to one standard pattern: namely, that of the large-scale, bureaucratically organized enterprise, run by a professional management team and regulating its work-force through a complex 'web of rules' that are in substantial part negotiated 'constitutionally' with union representatives.

Both economic recession and industrial and social unrest in the advanced industrial nations during the late 1960s and early 1970s represented a profound challenge to such views. It was the beginning of what eventually came to be seen by many as the crisis of Keynesianism, the dissolution of the post-war political settlement, a fundamental break with the historical trajectory of industrialization. There was growing concern with both the limits of corporatism and the limits of Fordist production techniques. Recession and protest both served to draw the division of labour back into the spotlight, sparking off what Rose (1988, p. 311) terms the 'New Wave' of industrial research, theories and ideas. On the one hand, strikes, particularly those in the motor industry, led to a resurgence of interest in workers' alienation as a consequence of minutely subdivided, machine-paced production. On the other hand, the uneven impact of economic recession brought sectoral and labour market divisions more sharply into focus. In this sense, industrial sociologists, labour market economists and labour process theorists from the 1970s on have been more directly concerned with the nature and determinants of direct employment, and the variability of employment relations. The remainder of this chapter briefly outlines the main approaches to these issues, and the problems that such analyses raise.

The Nature of Direct Employment

Through the 1970s, new analyses of the nature and determinants of direct employment which drew on Marxist theory emerged. Where liberal theorists of industrial society had identified a historical tendency towards ever more satisfying and fulfilling work, Marxist commentators drew attention to the widespread existence of employment relations characterized by minutely subdivided, closely specified work, combined with deeply authoritarian control structures. They not only pointed out that such employment relations were the norm, but also argued that these employment relations were the inevitable corollary of a system driven by the need to maximize capital accumulation and that they therefore could not be transformed without first transforming the social relations of capitalism.

The finest exposition of such a view is provided by Braverman (1974). Braverman argues that, put crudely, the process of accumulation was inhibited so long as capital attempted to treat labour as a simple commodity, using a variety of forms of subcontract and putting out which enabled the capitalist to purchase labour power after it had already been incorporated in the product, or part of a product. In order to maximize accumulation it was necessary to sacrifice the security of buying finished labour at a fixed cost, and take on labour as a variable cost, since it was only by entering into an employment contract that living labour could be systematically controlled and organized in pursuit of profit.

However, human labour power is a commodity of indeterminate value, and since the social relations of capitalist production are antagonistic, workers will not voluntarily surrender the 'full usefulness' of their labour power. Consequently, control over the variability of labour power becomes *the* critical problem for management in capitalist enterprises. Since it is the craftsman's skill that allows him to control the work process, capital can only gain control by deskilling the workforce.

For Braverman, then, there is a historical movement towards direct employment relations, because only by directly employing labour can capital gain control over the organization of the labour process and so ensure that this process is directed towards accumulation. The nature and terms of direct employment are a function of this same imperative for control. There is a tendency for workers to be employed to undertake increasingly subdivided, routine and unskilled tasks, because deskilling transfers control from labour to capital and cheapens labour. So long as workers design, plan or pace their own work, they retain the power to prevent capital from extracting the full potential value of their labour power. Capital thus has an interest in reducing this power. The project of scientific management in the late nineteenth and early twentieth centuries was essentially to transfer knowledge about production from skilled workers to managers, so that management could take over the design, planning and pacing of work, and ensure that the labour process was organized in such a way as to maximize the production of surplus value. This entailed curtailing the worker's power to pursue ends other than that of accumulation through the process of deskilling. Braverman (1974, p. 86) argues that 'Taylorism . . . is nothing less than the explicit verbalization of the capitalist mode of production'.

In short, Braverman suggests that accumulation depends on capital acquiring greater control over the labour process by deskilling labour in a specifically Taylorist fashion. Deviations from the standard Taylorist form of employment relation in the era of monopoly capitalism are the vestiges of a former age, surviving in specialized, and unspecified, instances. Similar (though not identical) analyses are to be found in the work of Marglin (1976), Stone (1973) and Clawson (1980), all of whom argue that capital's need for control over the labour process is the fundamental dynamic behind work organization and employment relations. 'Control' is a slippery concept, however (Littler and Salaman, 1984; Burawoy, 1985; Bray and Littler, 1988), and simply to say that capital must control production tells us very little about the particular ways in which control can be exercised in the workplace, or how general control over the production process can be achieved. What is distinctive about these authors is that capitalist control of the production process is synonymous with Taylorist techniques of direct control. Coercion can be openly manifested as a brutal dictatorship, or, alternatively, capital can seek to disguise its domination behind a battery of ideological devices, but it necessarily leads to one, single form of work organization, namely, direct supervision combined with the close specification of work. For these writers, there is only one way to skin a cat.

Other writers in the labour process tradition have taken issue with this view, and explored a range of alternative and additional strategies which can be adopted by capital to secure control over the labour process (Thompson, 1983). This leads to a recognition that direct employment does not have a uniform profile, and, indeed, that this diversity can be functional to capital rather than being simply a relic of a former age. The stress on the managerial problem of realizing the full usefulness of labour power is retained by labour process writers such as Burawoy

(1979, 1985), Edwards (1979) and Friedman (1977a, b, 1990), but greater emphasis is placed on the historical and contemporary variability of work organization and employment relations. To explain this variability, both Friedman (1977a, b) and Edwards (1979) make use of a centre/ periphery model. But, as will be seen below, the use of such a model to accommodate the diversity of capitalist employment relations is not exclusive to Marxist analyses.

The Problem of Variability

The idea that industrial societies were developing along convergent lines towards one, standard form of production organization came under attack from a number of quarters in the 1970s. It was becoming increasingly obvious that small-scale production and vulnerable, insecure employment were persistent, rather than transitory, features of capitalist economies, and, in this sense, the variability of capitalist employment relations became part of the agenda for most theorists of work and employment, and remains so today. Dual labour market theory, segmentation theory, the new institutional economics literature, and the flexible specialization and flexible firm literature are all concerned with this issue at one level or another.

The dual labour market model is concerned with the distribution of economic uncertainty. The model holds that investment strategies are shaped by patterns of demand. Where demand for a product or service is relatively stable, heavier and more specialized capital investment can be amortized than where demand fluctuates. This creates a dual economy, in which a capital-intensive primary sector – or centre – caters for the stable portion of demand, and a labour-intensive secondary sector – or periphery – serves more volatile markets (Doeringer and Piore, 1971; Piore, 1979; Berger and Piore, 1980). Differing investment strategies in each sector lead to 'substantial segmentation in . . . labour markets' (Sabel, 1982, p. 11).

The model clearly owes much to Adam Smith's discussion of the determinants of the division of labour. For Smith (1986), both the social division of labour and the division of labour within production is limited by the extent of the market. What dualist theory adds to this is a recognition that it is not only the absolute volume of demand which affects production organization, but also the pattern of demand. By emphasizing the significance of fluctuations in the volume of demand, the model offers an explanation for the persistence of variability in employment relations in advanced capitalist economies.

The problem with the model is that it posits what Lever-Tracey (1984) describes as a 'triple fit' between firms, jobs and workers. Primary firms are said to provide primary jobs (well paid, secure, with good training and promotion prospects) for primary workers (typically semi-skilled or skilled, white, male workers). Secondary firms conversely are said to provide secondary jobs (poorly paid, insecure work without training or promotion prospects) for secondary workers (typically unskilled, female, immigrant or 'black' workers). The idea of a neat fit between firms and jobs has been challenged by a number of commentators. Blackburn and Mann (1979, p. 28), for example, observe that 'all firms contain some "bad" jobs, even if the firm is itself in the primary sector', whilst Sabel (1982, p. 48) comments that 'skilled and unskilled workers in the same firm are likely to belong to different worlds'. Dualist theory was also strongly criticized by Marxist commentators, particularly for its tendency to ignore the relationship between the social relations of production and economic and technological rationality. As Gordon et al. (1982) point out, segmenting a homogeneous labour force can be a highly effective control strategy.

While the notion of a triple fit between firms, jobs and workers has been largely abandoned, there is a continued tendency to attempt to match core jobs with core workers, and peripheral jobs with peripheral workers. The 'flexible firm' literature, for example, argues that unstable and saturated product markets combined with economic recession have greatly increased management's desire for a number of forms of flexibility. Functional flexibility is sought in order to adjust to changing product markets and to enhance labour utilization; numerical flexibility in order to adjust labour-power levels to match demand; and pay flexibility in order to match rewards more closely to individual performance (Atkinson, 1984). The flexible firm literature identifies a tendency for firms to separate out core and peripheral activities. Management is thought to pursue functional flexibility with core workers, who undertake the organization's 'key, firm-specific activities'. In exchange for offering functional flexibility, such workers are more likely to enjoy not only better wages but also better promotion prospects, training opportunities and working conditions and greater job security than peripheral workers who undertake 'marginal' activities and provide the firm with numerical flexibility (NEDO, 1986).

Though the flexible firm model explains the tendency to pursue differential strategies at the core and periphery through reference to unstable product markets, the difference between employment relations at the centre and at the periphery is essentially presented as a function of job content. Core workers undertake more skilled or more crucial tasks, or simply a broader range of tasks, using new, more flexible technologies or new forms of work organization, and their jobs therefore differ qualitatively from those at the periphery. These qualitative differences in the nature of their work and the manner in which it is undertaken forces management to make certain concessions to core workers, and forge a relationship with them very different from that entered into with peripheral workers. Much the same line of analysis is to be found in the flexible specialization literature, which holds that in the 'post-Fordist' era, characterized by unstable, highly differentiated markets, a new 'production paradigm' is called for, one which facilitates 'permanent innovation'. Flexible specialization is such a paradigm. Sometimes this refers to industrial districts such as those found in the 'third Italy', or in parts of Baden-Württemberg, Germany. Here, a flexible network of small to medium-sized firms are said to use highly adaptable, advanced technology to cater for rapidly changing markets. This type of technology and interdependence between firms is said to necessitate new forms of employment relations; cooperation becomes more important than control, and 'high-trust' work relations and the reskilling of the workforce are essential (Sabel, 1982; Brusco, 1983; Piore and Sabel, 1984).[3]

At other times, flexible specialization appears to refer to restructuring within existing, large, mass-production plants, for example the introduction of team working and new technology in the motor industry. Once again, changes to the technical organization of work are seen to augur well for labour. Katz and Sabel (1985) state that in the US auto industry 'concern with the flexible use of labour . . . has led to a preoccupation with . . . the distribution of rights within the factory'. In either case, it is assumed that changes to the technical organization and content of work are necessarily are accompanied by changes to the nature and substance of employment relations. Though the flexible specialization thesis has been challenged on both empirical and theoretical grounds (e.g. Williams et al., 1987; Hyman, 1988; Smith, 1989; Amin, 1991), this assumed link between technical change and changes to employment relations has not received the same degree of critical attention. This may be because, as Batstone et al. (1987) note, the idea that job content is the primary determinant of employment relations is a feature of a wide range of literature on work.

Many radical and Marxist authors stress the relationship between job content and employment relations. Fox, for example, argues that the more closely specified work is, the less workers will need to exercise discretion, and, consequently, the less employers will need to 'buy' their commitment and loyalty. Unlike high-discretion workers, low-discretion workers 'need not . . . be expensively wooed' (Fox, 1974, p. 61). Others focus on the fact that unskilled workers are more readily substituted than skilled workers, and the degree of expendability is the key to variability in employment relations (Littler, 1982; Friedman, 1977a, b). Highly consensual models of work and employment, such as that provided by the new institutional economics literature, also accord primacy to job content (Williamson, 1985). This approach focuses on the transaction costs associated with different types of employment relation and asserts that good employment packages will be associated with skilled, firm-specific work, and more minimal employment relations with unskilled, non-firm-specific work.

In short, then, the variability of employment relations has largely been explained in terms of diversity in job content. An implicit model of the employment relation is widely adopted which suggests that the more routine, fragmented and/or unskilled work is, the less the employer is concerned with either retaining labour or winning its active cooperation and ingenuity. Conversely, when workers undertake tasks which require multiple and/or firm-specific skills, or when market success rests more on quality of output than speed of throughput, it is assumed that employers must attempt to 'buy' labour's active cooperation, reliability, loyalty and ingenuity with better pay, conditions, training, fringe benefits and job security. At a theoretical level, this one-dimensional model places conceptual limits on the variety of possible employment relations. At one end of the spectrum are essentially coercive employment relations, associated with close task specification and low worker discretion. At the other end of the spectrum, where work is characterized by loose task specification and high worker discretion, lies a more integrationist approach. At one pole, labour is seen as a commodity to be controlled, and at the other as a resource to be harnessed:

Close Task Specification	Loose Task Specification
Non-specific skill	Firm-specific skill
Insecure	Secure

Minimal compliance	Commitment/innovation
Direct control	Responsible autonomy
Numerical flexibility	Functional flexibility
Neo-liberal	Status-oriented
strategies	strategies
Coercion	**Integration**

When this unidimensional model is used in conjunction with a centre/periphery model the tendency is to assign peripheral workers to the left-hand side and core workers to the right-hand side of the continuum. This is problematic since, first, core operational activities are not always undertaken by a 'core' workforce enjoying the kind of employment relations found at the right-hand pole of this continuum, second, it is possible to subcontract highly skilled work, as well as closely specified, routine work, and, finally, as Wood (1989a, p. 6) points out, subcontractors' employees are at the same time 'core' employees for the subcontractor and 'peripheral' workers for the contractor's client.

If job content is taken to be the critical determinant of the employment relation, it is difficult to account for the fact that employment relations can be substantially altered without any changes to job content being made. Yet, as Fevre's (1986, 1987) study of British Steel shows, in the real world this can happen. British Steel made large numbers of direct employees redundant, whilst simultaneously extending its use of sub-contract. Firms of subcontractors then employed British Steel's former employees, who often undertook exactly the same jobs they had pre-viously carried out, only under far worse conditions of employment. The contingent nature of the link between job content and employment relations is further illustrated by the fact that it is also possible to make changes to job content without transforming the terms and conditions of employment. The introduction of new technology, or multi-tasking or functional flexibility, for instance, may alter the range and type of tasks performed, but is not *automatically* accompanied by concessions to labour. As Tomaney (1990, p. 44) observes, 'benefits from the process of change . . . have been won by labour and are not simply the consequence of technical change as some researchers imply'. Winning such benefits is, in turn, contingent upon wider political, institutional and economic factors.

This book is concerned with the changing pattern of employment relations in one of Britain's newly privatized water companies. At Albion

Water, tighter government financial control of the industry and subsequent privatization proposals through the 1980s spurred management into making substantial changes to the nature and pattern of employment relations; there is now greater diversity, tacit wage–effort bargains have been altered as labour has been intensified, and, for many groups of workers, direct employment has been degraded. This degradation of employment and intensification of labour has not been effected primarily through changes to the technical content of work, however. An examination of the changing pattern of employment relations in Albion Water thus serves to underline the fact that the link between employment patterns and conditions and job content is by no means a direct or unmediated one.

The book is structured as follows. Chapter 2 outlines the impact of Conservative government policies since 1979 upon Albion Water's organizational structure, and Chapter 3 examines the effects of privatization proposals on management strategies and industrial relations. Much of what is described will be familiar to workers and managers in the other nine water companies, and indeed to employees in other privatized utilities. While there are demographic, geographical and climatic variations which create regional differences in terms of operating costs, direct labour levels, capital expenditure and output, as public authorities are subject to national planning and policy, all the water companies share fairly similar histories as organizations and as employers. In this sense, geographical and spatial factors did not exert an especially powerful influence over the structure or nature of employment in the water authorities. Albion Water's experience of, and response to, privatization is also reasonably typical. All the authorities received the same advice from the government on how to go about restructuring in preparation for privatization, and all are now subject to the same form of economic and environmental regulation.

Chapter 4 explores why the water industry has been partitioned up into a number of different firms and organizations and looks at how this social division of labour is changing as a consequence of Albion's privatization. In recent years, many economists, management theorists and industrial sociologists have increasingly drawn on transaction cost analysis to explain the nature of modern corporations, talking about the firm as a nexus of contracts or treaties (Aoki, *et al.*, 1990). With critical reference to this emerging literature, this chapter considers why Albion chooses to draw the boundaries of the firm where it does, and why it chooses to enter into both direct and indirect employment relationships. Chapter 5 focuses upon Albion's relationship with the labour deployed in the function of water supply. Here Albion employs labour indirectly and directly, and employment relations with direct employees are further subdivided. The chapter examines the rationale behind Albion's three-pronged labour strategy, and argues that the variability of employment relations does not stem primarily from skill, job content or features intrinsic to the production process, but has to be explained in relation to wider political, institutional and economic factors. The spatial structure of employment also impacts on labour strategies in the water industry, since regional variations in unemployment levels and local labour market conditions further constrain management's choices over whether to use contract or direct labour.

Chapter 6 turns to the nature of direct employment in Albion Water's sewerage function. It examines how management is attempting to transform the traditional wage–effort bargain by changing payment and work allocation systems. The focus of this chapter is on the limits of Taylorism. It argues that whilst Taylorist-type work organization is not the ultimate or only form of work organization that can benefit capital, a shift towards greater 'flexibility' does not automatically augur well for labour. Chapters 7 and 8 look at the commercialization of employment relations in Albion Water. They describe how labour has recently been intensified not through further degrading the work itself, but through the degradation of employment.

Overall, the most conspicuous feature of these changes is that the social organization of work has been manipulated in an attempt to reduce labour porosity and intensify working.[4] This has implications not only for an understanding of the particular experience of utilities privatized in the 1980s, but more broadly for models of the capitalist employment relation, and the book therefore concludes with a discussion of these broader theoretical issues.

Notes

1. This figure is based on Treasury information presented by Abromeit (1988) and is net of costs in floating the share issues. Abromeit notes that it 'does not include sales of the British Technology Group and of North Sea Oil licences, nor mergers and the Phoenix projects in the steel industry. The Trustee Savings Bank was not floated by government and hence does not come under the heading of privatization.'

2. The company remains anonymous at the request of its management. The research undertaken at Albion Water involved around 80 in-depth, unstructured interviews with Albion Water managers and manual employees, managers and manual workers from one of Albion's main civil engineering contractors, and trade union officials from GMBATU, NALGO, NUPE and the EEPTU. The interviews were taped (except in four cases) and transcribed. A two-day training session for 30 craft workers and a number of team briefings were also attended and detailed notes on the proceedings were taken.

The research further involved searches of management and trade union documents, contract documents, Albion's annual reports and accounts and *Hansard* records.

Because the research adopted a case study approach, the sample of employees interviewed was selected pragmatically rather than systematically. However, since the interviews were primarily designed to obtain information about working practices, employment patterns and work organization, rather than attitudinal data, the reliability of the research does not rest on obtaining a sample that is representative of all Albion Water workers. Where attitudinal statements have been quoted (e.g. those about the threat of contractors and about union power) and more subjective judgements (such as statements about intensity of working), these were all expressed by a majority of the manual employees interviewed. The same patterns of attitudes were also revealed by a survey of employees from Albion Water and another privatized public utility, which took a larger and more representative sample from Albion Water (O'Connell Davidson *et al.*, 1991). This suggests that data from the fieldwork which is reported in this book are reliable.

3. As Lever-Tracey (1984) points out, this represents a strange twist to the ideas of dual labour market theorists. Sabel (1982) and Piore and Sabel (1984) switched their attention from immigrant, 'black' and female workers in the secondary sector of the USA to a new breed of craft workers in the secondary sector of the Emilia-Romagna region of Italy. The secondary sector, previously the source of worker vulnerability, low pay and poor conditions, was suddenly celebrated as holding the key not only to industrial renewal and economic prosperity, but also to 'reskilling' and worker autonomy. It was the greater emphasis on the technical content of work which enabled them to make the transition. They 'discovered' that work in the

secondary sector was not always closely specified, unskilled work requiring little or no training, and took this as evidence of worker autonomy.

4. The impact of privatization upon clerical work at Albion Water is not described. This is because the research at Albion focused exclusively upon the manual workforce. However, research undertaken by the same author in another privatized utility suggests that privatization may have similar effects on patterns of employment and work organization for clerical workers, namely greater use of non-standard employment contracts, particularly part-time contracts, the individualization of employment relations, the introduction of new accounting practices designed to allow management greater control over labour costs and direct labour levels and the intensification of labour through the introduction of various forms of 'flexibility' which reduce porosity in the working day (O'Connell Davidson, 1990, 1993).

2 ALBION WATER: CREATION, PRIVATIZATION AND REGULATION

Albion Water serves an area of several thousand square kilometres. It is responsible for more than 10 000 kilometres of pipes, supplying over two million people with water and sewerage services. A number of statutory water companies also supply water within Albion Water's boundaries. It was created by the 1973 Water Act, along with the other nine regional water authorities of England and Wales, and the structure imposed on the water industry by this Act can be seen as the culmination of a long historical process through which water services were gradually brought together under regional management, subject to national policies and central government financial control. Until its privatization in 1989, the water industry was seen to include three key functions – water supply, sewerage and sewage treatment (recovery) and environmental functions – for, as Rees and Synott (1988, p. 180) note, water is a 'multi-purpose resource':

> Provision is not simply a matter of constructing the storage reservoirs, bulk water transmission facilities, water-treatment plants and the distribution networks needed to serve final consumers; it involves the management of an entire, interdependent water-use cycle. To the basic supply function must be added the removal of sewage and trade effluents, the treatment of sewage, the maintenance of river water quality, the control of coastal pollution, flood protection, land drainage, river navigation, the regulation of river flow, protection of aquifers from depletion and pollution, the management of water-based recreation, and the protection of aquatic flora and fauna.

Between 1945 and 1973 there was a growing recognition of the inter-dependence of these three water functions. With rapid population and industrial expansion, there was increasing concern that existing supply sources might not be able to match demand for water. Investment in water abstraction and reservoir construction became a more urgent question: so also did pollution control and investment in water treatment, since the pressure on conventional supply sources could be reduced if polluted water was treated and reused. The 1973 Water Act addressed such concerns through the creation of ten regional water authorities for England and Wales which were to take responsibility for all aspects of the water industry. It replaced a patchwork of hundreds of different local authorities, water undertakers and sewerage agencies, all serving areas defined by political boundaries, by these ten authorities, whose boundaries were drawn on the basis of hydrological and geographical criteria, around a river basin or river basins, giving them control over the entire water cycle (Mitchell, 1971; Colling, 1987). Albion Water, for example, took over responsibility for three river authorities, six water undertakers and 86 sewerage and sewage disposal authorities at its inception in 1974. Thus, for the first time, rivers, estuaries, aquifers, ground and surface waters, drainage systems, water works, sewage works, the water supply system and sewers in one area were combined to make up a total, integrated system. As Colling (1987, p. 23) observes, 'the concept of Integrated River Basin Management was . . . enshrined at the heart of the water industry at its birth in 1974'. Integrated river basin management represented the full recognition of the interdependence of the three water functions. It was unique to Britain and admired by water professionals all over the world. The system was seen as improving efficiency and effectiveness by facilitating optimum use of resources, especially in emergencies such as drought, floods or major pollution incidents (Watts, 1987).

The 1973 Act also continued the historical trend towards the centralization of control over the water industry. It gave central government a key role in the financial control of the industry; the regional water authorities had to conform to government directives on charging, long-term planning and borrowing. Two separate water authority budgets were specified, a revenue budget for the day-to-day operation of services and a capital budget for their investment programmes. The stated objective of financial control was to balance the needs of the community with regard to water against competing claims within the public sector (Department of the Environment, 1973a, b). The regional water authorities had to raise the revenue budget through charges to domestic and industrial consumers, charges for water abstraction, licences for trade effluent discharge and so on. It was also hoped that authorities' replacement investment would eventually be self-financing, so that current revenue would maintain the existing system intact. Repayments on loans inherited from local authorities and on new loans were likewise to be funded through the revenue budget. The capital budget was raised through borrowing and through government grants.

The newly created Albion Water was structured as a number of departments (such as finance, personnel, scientific services) and 16 operational divisions, defined on the basis of their functional activities. There were three rivers divisions, seven supply divisions and six sewage disposal divisions. Gradually over the next ten years these divisions were rationalized. Strict functional demarcations were replaced by geographical divisions, until finally there were just three operational divisions, each of which incorporated supply, recovery and environmental functions and served a particular geographical area. The organization had a pyramid structure. At the apex was the board and chief executive, and beneath them were the heads of the various functions (finance, operations, personnel, secretariat, information services, public affairs, scientific services and fisheries). The largest and most significant function, both in terms of direct labour levels and revenue, was operations. This meant that engineers played a leading role in the organization, and this emphasis on engineering reflected the underlying philosophy of the 1973 Water Act. As Colling observes, the 1973 restructuring of the water industry mirrored reorganizations taking place in local government and the National Health Service at that time: 'they instituted a substantial shift in prerogative from political agents to professional and technical experts . . . the management structure emphasised the ascendancy of technical criteria in the new industry' (Colling, 1987, p. 23). Colling argues that although this restructuring of the water industry is 'often presented as a simple victory of technocracy over political and sectional interests', in reality, political and sectional interests were not totally excised by the 1974 reorganization. Local government was given majority representation on regional water authority boards, and agricultural and industrial interests continued to exert pressure on the industry. The authorities' control over the water cycle was also constrained by the continued presence of the 28 private water supply companies.

Under the head of the operations function were managers responsible for various aspects of operational activities, including the managers of the three geographically defined operational divisions. Divisional managers each had responsibility for the day-to-day running of all aspects of water services in their areas, but within the divisions there were strict functional demarcations. Beneath each divisional manager, then, were functional managers responsible for the three different elements of water services. In other words, Albion Water had a functionally demarcated and hierarchical management structure; a chain of managers each directly responsible to an immediate superior.

When Albion Water was created it inherited over 2500 employees (the regional water authorities as a whole were bequeathed some 59 000 employees in 1974). These workers were brought together from many disparate agencies and authorities. Albion therefore inherited, in the words of one manager, a 'real mess'. Like the other water authorities, it was confronted by a multiplicity of different forms of work organization and employment practices, and a workforce represented by many different trade unions. However, the majority of water employees were organized by seven of the ten largest unions in the TUC: NALGO, GMB, NUPE, TGWU, UCATT, EEPTU and the AEU. The regional water authorities adopted industrial relations based upon the Whitley Report, with two-tier negotiating machinery. National negotiating procedures were established, with national-level councils making broad agreements on pay and conditions for manual and clerical employees, and regional-level joint industrial councils negotiating the details of work organization, job descriptions and bonus schemes. There was a general consensus that the water industry and its employees should come to share the sort of pay and conditions enjoyed by other utility workers (Colling, 1987, p. 46). In the 1970s, Albion Water was very much a model public sector employer. Like the other regional water authorities, Albion agreed to national terms and conditions such as a no-redundancy deal, inflation-proof pensions, and what were generally perceived to be reasonable sickness and holiday entitlements. Between 1974 and 1979, Albion Water's direct labour force grew, and industrial relations were fairly harmonious. Both sides were keen for the industry to dispense with schemes and procedures inherited from local authorities, and Albion management is reputed to have maintained a high level of communication and good relations with the unions through the 1970s.

Although industrial relations were stable during this period, the industry was under financial pressure in terms of capital investment as the Labour government sought to reduce the PSBR. Since the water industry is highly capital intensive, the extent of cuts during this period is perhaps best illustrated by the declining ratio of capital to revenue expenditure. Where in 1974, capital expenditure was over £100 million more than revenue expenditure, by 1978 capital expenditure was £146 million *less* than revenue expenditure (Water Authorities Association, 1988). Thus the Thatcher government did not initiate the process of cutting capital expenditure in the water industry. However, since 1979 the state has significantly tightened financial control over the industry and encouraged a move away from the service principles embodied in the 1974 reorganization towards a new commercialism. This process reached its zenith with privatization in 1989.

The Commercialization of the Water Industry

In line with general macroeconomic policy and policies towards all nationalized industries, the prime objective of government financial control over the water industry from the mid-1970s was cost cutting rather than infrastructure development. Between 1979 and 1983, the Thatcher government continued and increased cuts to regional water authorities' capital budgets. The government also devised new forms of financial control for the industry, which 'precipitated the introduction of commercial criteria into a wider range of regional water authority activities' (Colling, 1987, p. 26). The first was to introduce an external finance limit from 1981 which limited the amount regional water authorities could borrow from external sources. This limit has been progressively reduced (Figure 2.1), which has forced regional water authorities to fund long-term development 'internally'. Second, in 1981 regional water authorities were instructed to switch from historic cost accounting (where assets are valued at their original cost) to current cost accounting (where assets are valued at current replacement costs). This meant that regional water authority assets appeared considerably larger. From 1983 onwards, water authorities were instructed to make a percentage return on these assets, or a 'notional profit'. Again, in recent years this device has been used by government to increase pressure on regional water authorities to cut costs and to encourage them to operate on commercial principles. Most water authorities not only met, but consistently exceeded, these financial targets (Figure 2.2).

Finally, from 1983, the government instigated a system of financial targets for regional water authority water supply and sewerage services. The government agreed performance aims whereby authorities pledged themselves to reducing operating costs to a fixed target over a cycle of three years, with 'signpost' targets for intermediary years. For instance, in 1986–1987 the actual operating costs of all regional water authorities were £1233 million, and the target for 1989–1990 was £1205 million.

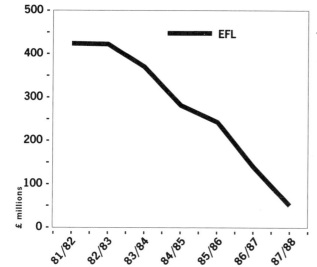

Figure 2.1 *External finance limits for the water industry 1981–1988. Source: WAA (1988).*

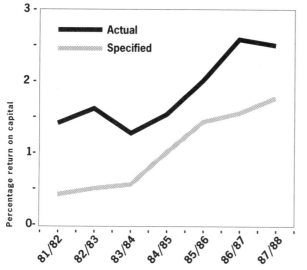

Figure 2.2 *Specified and actual rates of return for regional water authorities 1981–1988. Source: WAA (1988).*

Performance aims had to be met by improved efficiency and economy and not simply through price increases. Colling (1987, p. 27) notes that:

> In effect, though, they require cuts too. Performance aims are applied to those services separately and demand that each one is self financing with no 'unfair' cross subsidisation. This severely restricts an authority's

flexibility in balancing its books and has led directly to reductions in staffing levels.

Thus, throughout the 1980s, regional water authorities have not only been squeezed in the sense of having capital budgets cut, but more importantly financial controls, such as the rate of return directives, pushed the authorities into a more commercially orientated world, where effectiveness was measured against financial returns rather than against achievements in terms of developing the infrastructure, planning for future demand, pollution control, conservation or the like. These changes came at a time when the existing infrastructure of the water industry was badly in need of capital investment. It is estimated that more than a third of water mains are corroded and need replacement, which means that, on average, 30% of the water supply never reaches the tap. The condition of water mains also poses risks to public health, as corroded lead pipes mean that many homes are supplied with water containing dangerous levels of lead. In 1986, 10% of the 150 000 miles of sewer pipes under regional water authority control was over 100 years old, and there were 3500 sewer collapses and 1500 blockages requiring excavation (NALGO, 1988). Incidents of water pollution rose from 1980 onwards. The most horrific of these was the Camelford incident, in July 1988, when a relief driver for a chemical firm poured 20 tons of aluminium sulphate into the wrong tank at an unmanned water treatment works. Over 20 000 people were affected by water containing aluminium levels 6000 times above the World Health Organization safety limit (Cook, 1989). Less dramatically, but more insidiously, many of the regional water authorities' own sewage treatment plants' effluent discharge consistently failed to meet standards set by the authorities themselves, and around 20% of the sewage works in England and Wales were so defective by the mid-1980s that they broke the law (Cook, 1989). Perhaps equally significant, the European Commission revealed its drinking water directive at this time, which laid down stringent standards for water purity, setting parameters for 66 substances (in place of the 11 specified by UK standards), including lead, nitrates and pesticides. These standards were to come into force in 1985, and virtually all of the UK's drinking water fell far short of them (JAWS, 1989). It was estimated that billions of pounds would need to be spent in order to reach this level of water purity. The new financial controls led to price increases, capital investment cuts and cuts to standards of service (Colling, 1987; JAWS, 1987, 1989; NALGO, 1988; Cook, 1989). Tighter finan-

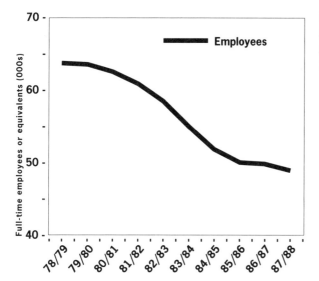

Figure 2.3 *Regional water authority direct labour levels 1978–1988. Source: WAA (1988).*

cial control also led to organizational change within the regional water authorities themselves, e.g. reductions in direct labour levels (Figure 2.3), increased resort to various forms of subcontract, reduced out-of-hours services and so on.

In 1983 the government reorganized aspects of the water industry with a new Water Act. These reorganizations were important in paving the way for subsequent privatization. The Act was concerned to give more autonomy to individual water authorities. It replaced the National Water Council, which had until then planned and coordinated national water policies, with the Water Authorities Association, and gave water authorities the right to withdraw from this body's proceedings. The Act also attempted to make the authorities resemble private, commercial bodies more closely by changing the structure and composition of water authority boards. For example, local authority representation was replaced by ministerial appointees, and these appointees typically represented business interests (Cook, 1989, p. 73), often the interests of major polluters, such as ICI, Rio Tinto Zinc, English China Clays and Associated Lead (Colling, 1987, p. 30). Finally, the Act pushed regional water authorities towards the private sector by reducing their public accountability and abolishing the right of press and public to attend water authority meetings (Cook, 1989, p. 73).

In keeping with its general policy for the public sector, then, the Thatcher government began by extending and tightening central government's financial control of the water industry, the aim being to gradually eliminate all government funding of the industry through the National Loans Fund, and to make regional water authorities self-financing. It then replaced local government-style boards of management with the intention of creating a more commercial style of management by water authorities. Commercial management was then combined with greater autonomy for individual authorities.

The Impact of Tighter Financial Control on Albion Water

Like other regional water authorities, from 1983 on Albion Water was set performance aims, or financial targets, which had to be met through improved efficiency rather than through price increases, and this forced the authority to focus on how to cut costs and achieve productivity gains. Albion responded to these demands by setting itself targets for reducing manpower levels by between 2% and 3% a year. Since Albion had to honour the no-redundancy agreement negotiated at national level, this had to be attained through a 'natural wastage' policy and by encouraging early retirement. It is the manual workforce which has been hardest hit by the policy – it has been reduced by over 18% between 1983 and 1989 (Figure 2.4). In Albion's Annual Reports, these reductions in staffing levels are presented as indicators of rising productivity levels. Whilst it would appear that labour productivity has risen through the application of new technology and increased work intensity for many employees, the claim hides the extent to which such cuts have been supported by lowering standards (for example, routine maintenance of plant, equipment and buildings has been cut back) and by increased resort to contractors. Financial targets have also been met through cuts in other areas. Overtime working has been and continues to be reduced, and this has been achieved partly through cutting the out-of-hours services that have traditionally been provided. For example, where previously almost any leak or burst pipe was treated as an emergency to be dealt with immediately, now only those 'causing nuisance' to customers or road users are covered by the out-of-hours service. Departments are also now financially penalized for sending workers out on overtime.

The Thatcher government's push for more commercial-style management, combined with the pressure to meet financial targets, also led to the restructuring of some of Albion's activities. In 1980, the Local

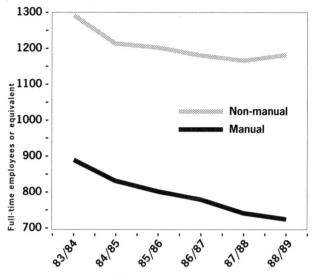

Figure 2.4 *Albion Water direct labour levels 1983–1989. Source: Albion Water Annual Reports and Accounts 1984–1990.*

Government Planning and Land Act had introduced compulsory competitive tendering to local authorities, forcing them to turn certain sections of their direct labour force into direct labour organizations (DLOs), which had to compete against outside firms for highways and building maintenance and construction work (Walsh, 1989, p. 10). Although this legislation did not cover water authorities, Albion Water began to reorganize certain groups of workers along the lines of the DLO model, hoping to cut costs by so doing.

In short, then, tighter financial control and the general commercialization of the industry led to changes in employment practices and work organization. Albion Water drastically reduced direct labour levels, increased its use of 'non-standard' labour, and refashioned its relationship with certain targeted groups of direct employees. The government's privatization proposals therefore did not initiate the tendency to transform employment relations; this process was already under way. But, as will be seen, the proposals for post-privatization environmental and economic regulation, combined with a new responsibility to maximize profits for the shareholders, were responsible for organizational changes which consolidated this tendency.

The Privatization of the Water Industry

Government think tanks and ministers who initiated the call for water privatization were joined by many regional water authority chairmen and senior executives who welcomed the idea of privatization as liberation from 'unpredictable, short-term and politically motivated' financial control of the industy. Initially the government was cautious. In January 1985 Mrs Thatcher proclaimed that 'The water authorities are natural monopolies . . . and we need to be particularly careful when considering replacing a public monopoly by a private one' (*Official Report*, 31 January, Vol. 72, c292). But the government's subsequent proposals demonstrated a singular lack of careful consideration. Discussion papers on privatization were produced in 1985, followed in early 1986 by a White Paper. It proposed that the regional water authorities be privatized almost intact, since, as the White Paper explicitly pointed out, 'the principle of integrated river basin management . . . has worked well and will be retained' (Water, 1986). Nicholas Ridley, the then Secretary of State for the Environment, announced that the regional water authorities were 'fit and ready to join the private sector' (*Official Report*, 5 February 1986, Vol. 91, c288), and that government intended to legislate that autumn. However, problems with the White Paper's proposals meant that rather than legislating in the autumn of 1986, and floating the industry soon after, it took three years to push through.

Plans to sell off water highlighted the problems with the government's privatization policy perhaps more sharply than the privatization of any other utility. Critics were quick to agree with Mrs Thatcher's description of water authorities as 'natural monopolies'. Customers are unlikely ever to be provided with a choice between competing suppliers bringing water of different quality and/or price to their homes. Privatization, far from exposing the 'winds of competition', would therefore make consumers captives of private, rather than public, monopolies. Such arguments fell on deaf ears. The government had not baulked at privatizing monopolies in the past, and proponents of privatization insisted that a private monopoly can be regulated as effectively, if not more effectively, as a public one, through strict government controls on prices charged, profits earned and costs incurred. It was also argued that privatization would expose the industry to competition in capital markets. The argument that the water industry is inherently monopolistic did create a pressure to sharpen up the proposals for the post-privatization economic regulation of the industry, but did not affect the government's commitment to this course of action. The second set of problems proved more troublesome. Because public and environmental health is inextricably linked with the extraction, treatment and distribution of water, the government was actually proposing to entrust private monopolies with control over a unique commodity. Critics asked whether a water industry governed by the profit motive could seriously be expected to act as a guardian of public health and the environment. For example, in times of drought, would water companies act to protect the environment by encouraging the public to limit consumption, or would their prime concern be to maintain turnover and so profitability? Such questions were barely addressed by the 1986 White Paper. Furthermore, as they stood the proposals would create ten private companies with awesome powers, and would generate conflict between a private water industry and other vested interests. Because of this, the 1986 White Paper faced criticism from unexpected sources. Amongst the critics were two powerful lobbies, the National Farmers Union and the Country Landowners' Association.

The White Paper proposed to privatize all water authority functions except land drainage and flood protection, which would have left private water companies responsible for all other environmental functions (e.g. the protection of river systems, pollution control, fisheries). Since the regional water authorities granted licences to various industries to abstract water or discharge effluent, and had a role in policing agricultural and industrial users of the water environment, the 1986 proposals would have given private bodies the power to license other private bodies, and potentially restrict or deny them use of a resource vital to their activities. Obviously, the farming community and such industries as would be affected were fiercely opposed to the plans. Equally problematically, the proposed water companies would be both polluters (through their sewerage functions) and pollution regulators, both poacher and gamekeeper in effect. The National Farmers Union and the Country Landowners' Association expressed fears that commercial water companies would exercise their regulatory functions with more zeal in respect to other bodies than to themselves.

Finally, the argument that commercial water companies could not and would not manage water resources in such a way as to both extract maximum profit from *and* protect and safeguard them came to be seen by government as the most potentially damaging to the idea of water privatization. The trade unions and other critics made effective use of this issue in their campaign against privatization. (For a detailed account of the response of organized labour to the privatization of the water industry, see Colling (1987).) The government's proposals had to be revised; methods of both economic *and* environmental regulation of the industry had to be devised.

In November 1988, the government published its Water Bill. It was primarily concerned with the post-privatization regulation of the industry; both economic and environmental. It struggled to balance too much regulation (which would make the industry unattractive to investors) against too little (which would lay the government open to criticism from both consumers and the agricultural and environmental lobbies). As will be seen, the proposed environmental and economic regulation of the privatized water industry had an enormous and immediate impact upon the water authorities, creating an imperative for organizational change in preparation for privatization.

Environmental Regulation and its Effects

Following the 1987 General Election, Ridley unveiled the government's new proposals for water privatization. Apart from suggesting the introduction of water metering to replace the rates system, the most significant change was the proposal to create a National Rivers Authority, which would undertake the regional water authorities' environmental and regulatory functions. These changes were designed to deflect the kind of criticisms that had been levelled at the 1986 proposals. However, even with these amendments, the progress of the water privatization legislation was arduous, and continuously brought the government into conflict with a variety of different groups. Under the revised proposals, the National Rivers Authority was to take over all the regional water authorities' environmental functions. Ridley explained to Parliament that:

> After further consideration . . . I came to the conclusion that these functions are essentially a public responsibility. I could not accept the principle that one private body should determine what another can take out of a river or put into it or how much it should be charged for so doing . . . The business of protecting the environment and the conservation of rivers, and of ensuring that all the disparate interests, including those of the utilities, are protected, is essentially a public sector regulatory function.(*Official Report*, October 1987, Vol. 21, c770)

In effect, this represented an admission that no suitable regulatory machinery could be designed for the water industry as presently structured. In order to facilitate privatization, the much-prized principle of integrated river basin management was to be jettisoned. The water companies would undertake water supply and sewerage functions, and their activities would be subject to both economic and environmental regulation. The National Rivers Authority as a regulatory body would assume the overall management and resource planning of the water environment. Up to this point, integrated river basin management had been fully endorsed by the government. By May 1987, however, Ridley had made a U-turn, arguing that the government's commitment to extending share ownership and reducing the size of the public sector must take precedence over the desire to maintain integrated river basin management. Other commentators (Dr Cunningham, *Official Report* 1987, Vol. 21, c788) suggested that it was not only commitment to privatization *per se* which led to this revision, but also pressure from the National Farmers Union and the Country Landowners' Association (one of whose officeholders happened to be Nicholas Ridley's elder brother).

Whereas regional water authority chairmen and senior management had greeted the 1986 proposals with cautious approval, the 1987 proposals excited virtually unanimous hostility. Of the ten regional water authority chairmen, only John Bellak, Severn Trent's Chairman (who has in the past stood as a Tory candidate), did not oppose them outright (*Financial Times* 14 September 1987). Roy Watts, Chairman of Thames Water, spoke for the other eight chairmen when he argued that nothing could justify a departure from integrated river basin management:

> The government . . . should not . . . sacrifice what is right for what they believe to be politically possible. You don't strip and rebuild a car that is running well. You don't change your child's school if he is progressing. You don't divorce if you are happily married . . . to accept privatization at any price is simply irresponsible. (Watts, 1987, p. 4)

Perhaps not surprisingly, within months there were hints from the Department of the Environment that Nicholas Ridley would not be renewing Mr Watts's contract when it expired in September 1988 (*Financial Times* 25 January 1988). Gradually, the individual authorities broke ranks with each other and made conciliatory moves towards the government. Threats to withdraw their support from the privatization programme came to nothing, and a shadow National Rivers Authority was duly created in

1988, and prepared to take over environmental functions on privatization. This move had a profound impact upon the water authorities.

By transferring the regional water authorities' environmental and land drainage functions to the National Rivers Authority, the government slashed the size of regional water authorities at a stroke. At Albion Water, some 350 employees (about 18% of the workforce) were transferred to the National Rivers Authority. The loss of environmental functions also meant a loss of turnover (on average, regional water authorities lost 10% of turnover to the National Rivers Authority). In itself, this is enough to significantly impact on any organization. But the creation of the National Rivers Authority also had other organizational implications. The principle of integration enshrined in integrated river basin management had dominated every level of the regional water authorities. As has been seen in the case of Albion Water, until 1988 the authorities broke their region down into a number of geographically defined operational divisions, each of which was responsible for all three of the core functions (supply, recovery and environmental functions). Since the environmental functions were to be passed on to the National Rivers Authority, it was necessary to sever the ties between this function and the supply and recovery functions. The regional water authorities responded to these changes by rationalizing and merging divisions. Albion Water, for example, merged its three operational divisions into one.

One consequence of environmental regulation has therefore been to encourage a shift towards more highly centralized organizational structures. In what initially appears as something of a paradox, however, the centralization of control within the organization has been accompanied by a devolution of responsibility as Albion, on advice from the DOE has shifted towards a variant of 'profit centre management'. This shift cannot be fully understood without reference to the form of economic regulation proposed in the 1988 Water Bill, and its impact upon the organizational structure of the water authorities.

Economic Regulation and Its Effects

One way in which the government attempted to justify its privatization programme was to claim that private firms are more efficient than public sector organizations. Since in privatizing water, it was privatizing a number of monopolies, normal market mechanisms could not be relied upon to discipline them. In the absence of competition, the industry had to be economically regulated in such a way as to promote greater efficiency. However, the government could not be seen to measure the efficiency of a monopoly in terms of profitability alone. It had to design a regulatory structure which would be perceived not only to provide incentives to cut costs, but also to compel private water companies to invest adequately, and to keep charges down.

The main instrument of economic regulation of the water companies is a price limitation formula, based upon the RPI minus or plus X formula devised by Professor Littlechild to regulate other privatized utilities.[1] The system governs how much the privatized concerns may put up their prices to meet the government's pre-fixed efficiency goals. It is designed to limit average prices in real terms, and provide maximum incentives for cost cutting, while imposing no limit on profitability. In water, this form of regulation will be applied only to core activities, i.e. supply and recovery. Enterprise activities, such as consultancy or any other business into which the water companies may diversify, will not be subject to economic regulation. Known as the 'K price limitation formula', the system allows the Director General of OFWAT to control charges for water services as follows:

> This formula limits increases in a basket of principal charges made by Water Service Companies for water supply and sewerage services. The percentage weighted average annual increase is limited to the sum of the percentage movement in RPI plus an adjustment factor, K, which may be positive, negative or zero. K is a number set for each Water Service Company individually and may be a different number in different years.
> (Secretary of State for the Environment, 1989, p. 38)

The application of the formula to the water industry provoked much controversy (Carsberg *et al.*, 1986; Herrington and Price, 1987; Rees and Synott, 1988).[2] Most problematic was the question of what kind of costs should be included in the K factor, for it is this factor which prevents or enables water companies to pass on costs to the consumer through price increases. Most commentators were agreed on the fact that in the water industry, the K factor was unlikely to be a negative one. On the one hand, as Colin McMillan, Director of Finance at Severn Trent pointed out, it is unlikely that charge increases for water services would come below the rate of inflation in the foreseeable future because 'In the water industry we are not expecting new technology to come to our aid' (Carsberg *et al.*, 1986). On the other hand, the water industry desperately needs to embark upon a massive capital investment programme to repair its decaying infrastructure and to meet the new environmental standards required by EEC law. Any K setting which prevented these costs from being passed through on a cost plus basis to the consumer would positively discourage investment. This is particularly troubling, given that OFWAT has not been given the power to dictate investment decisions, merely to 'discuss' them (Glynn, 1987). As Herrington (1989, p. 11) notes:

> Investment requirements dictate that 'K' will be positive and real prices for regulated services will rise rather than fall. Price regulation will be a matter of containing increases rather than enforcing decreases. The level at which 'K' is set will, therefore be central to the financial performance and profitability of the industry . . . Any underestimates in setting 'K' would leave the Water Companies under-financed, while any overestimation would generate surplus profits.

The Department of the Environment set the initial K levels individually for each of the water companies. The settings were made on the following basis. Ten-year forecasts for capital expenditures, operating costs and target efficiency gains were provided by each regional water authority. Model profit and loss accounts and financial projections assuming different K settings were examined to select the K setting which would be most likely to satisfy potential investors, potential debt-providers, the Treasury and consumers (Herrington, 1989, p. 11). Because K is a number set for each individual water company, it is possible for the regulator to take into account geographical, demographic and climatic variations between companies, in an attempt to 'level the pitch'. Moreover, the government allows for adjustments to the K setting through periodic reviews. Ian Byatt, Director General of OFWAT, states:

> The industry is facing many changes and a new operating regime. At a 5 year review it would be opportune to consider the extent to which the arrangements for implementing the regulatory regime had achieved their objectives and to examine any deficiencies which may have emerged. It would provide an opportunity for reviewing the available evidence on the rate of return which investors and creditors would require, and on the performance . . . which it would be reasonable to expect from a company, with the same characteristics as an Appointed company, which was well regarded by the City. A review could involve adjustment of K factors . . . in the light of events. (Secretary of State for the Environment, 1989)

What is most striking about the K price limitation formula, then, is that despite its superficial appearance as a precise and scientific instrument which takes into account a host of objective economic criteria, ultimately the K setting is the outcome of a social bargaining process between the company and the government. It is affected by the Director General's perceptions of the rate of return *required* by investors and creditors, and of what would constitute *reasonable* expectations about company financial performance and so on.

Critics have argued that the water companies will not be as profitable as government led investors to believe. Vickers and Yarrow (1988) claim that if capital expenditure in the industry rose by 10%, in order to maintain profitability either charges would have to rise by 60% or operating costs would have to be reduced to zero. They continue, 'Although water authority charges have, in real terms, been steadily increasing in the pre-privatization period, it is unlikely that the Government will be politically attracted by price hikes of [this] magnitude' (Vickers and Yarrow, 1988, pp. 411-12). Herrington (1989, p. 16) points out that the initial K setting produced ten-year capital programmes which entailed annual rates of investment far higher than had been achieved in the water industry in the 1988-1989 period, and that, further, the initial K setting failed to take into account all the capital expenditure that will be required through the 1990s. For example, the costs of meeting more stringent EC directives on water quality were excluded from financial profiles. Others claimed that the controls were so stringent as to defeat the whole object of privatization. A *Financial Times* leader commented:

> In arranging these very tight controls the Government has wisely responded to public anxiety about the effect of unleashing a profit motive into a vital industry where customers will remain captive to one supplier and where water charges are essentially the same as a tax . . . However [the regulation] is not very different from the monitoring which is done within the Government machine at present . . . As a result of these controls and the extensive general powers retained by Government . . . [the water industry] . . . will be very different from the Conservative paradigm of private sector enterprise . . . [Investors] will have safe, high controlled businesses which are likely to provide a commensurately modest rate of return not far from that of gilt edged stock. Then what is the point of selling them? (*Financial Times* 25 November 1988)

However, the Director General's comments, quoted above, show that the government is willing to adjust the K factor to bring profits into line with

City expectations, and suggests that it will be prepared to agree to such price increases as are necessary to ensure that shareholders are satisfied. The government had argued that there was nothing dangerous about privatizing a monopoly, since a private monopoly could be as effectively regulated as a public one. Yet though the K price limitation formula may promise to protect the shareholders' interests, it seems singularly inadequate to protect the consumer. Concern about this was fuelled in early 1989 when the existing private water companies threatened to raise their charges by between 30% and 50% before privatization legislation (which would apply the price limitation formula to the statutory water companies as well) was enacted. Disinterested observers were also predicting price rises of 30% by regional water authorities after privatization (*Financial Times* 7 December 1989).

However, even though massive price increases seem inevitable, it does seem unlikely that OFWAT's Director General will allow water companies to increase profit margins *solely* through price increases. He will also put pressure on water companies to make 'efficiency' gains. The K setting can be used to discipline the water companies, as well as to bail them out. The Director General notes that since there is little scope for direct competition, he will compare the performance of the ten water companies. Geographical, demographic and climatic differences between water companies as well as expenditure arising from EC directives (which may have a greater impact on some companies, e.g. those with bathing beaches, than on others) are supposed to be taken account of in the individual K settings, so that in theory the companies are evenly matched. Thus the Director General states that he will compare the costs, efficiency and return on capital of the water companies:

> Such comparisons can reveal significant differences which can be pointers to ways in which some companies may be performing relatively weakly . . . In competitive markets, competition brings prices down to those of efficient firms. In the case of water I must set the charges limit to have a similar effect. (Secretary of State for the Environment, 1989, p. 45)

In other words, water companies now have a strong incentive to cut costs and improve labour productivity, in order to avoid being penalized when their K setting is reviewed. This pressure from the Director General to make 'efficiency gains' was one of the factors which spurred Albion Water management to make the changes to employment relations and work organization which are described in this book.

The proposed economic regulation also had an effect on the organizational structure of the water authorities. The price limitation formula was only to be applied to the core activities of the water companies (supply and recovery). This made it expedient for regional water authorities to restructure in preparation for privatization by separating out two organizational strands – 'core business' and 'enterprise activities'. All regional water authorities began to devote time and resources to developing the unregulated 'enterprise areas' and this could be achieved in two ways. First, many existing 'core' activities, particularly various forms of maintenance work, offer the potential for profitable commercial work. These activities, which had previously been integrated into the operations function, were stripped out and reorganized as distinct units. Where in the past, the three core functions had not only cross-subsidized each other, but also other regional water authority activities, now all activities are being separated out, and transformed into notionally autonomous and separately accountable units. Each unit must contribute to revenues and profit independently of the others, so that, as has been the case in British Telecom since privatization, the principle of cross-subsidization upon which the service had previously been based is undermined (Hallet, 1990). Second, the regional water authorities began to think seriously about branching into new fields such as plumbing, septic tank emptying, and disposing of industrial waste.

Albion Water plc is now a holding company with a number of subsidiaries (Figure 2.5). It has diversified into plumbing and international construction contracting, and both of these new ventures are organized by separate subsidiary firms, PlumbCare (a wholly owned subsidiary) and AlbionConstruct Ltd (a joint venture with a major construction company). Albion Water Services Ltd (which now undertakes the core activities of water supply and sewerage) is now organized as a number of departments and 'profit centres', and the board plans to further separate some of the 'profit centres' in future, turning them into subsidiaries if they prove successful.

In short, both environmental and economic regulation have led to changes in organizational structure, and these changes are characterized by both centralization and fragmentation. Environmental regulation in the form of the creation of the National Rivers Authority involved savage cuts to turnover and direct employment, which precipitated the merging of small operational divisions and a centralization of authority. At the same time, the proposed form of economic regulation combined with advice to adopt profit-centre-style management encouraged water authorities

Albion Water PLC		
Albion Water Services Ltd	Albion PlumbCare Ltd (plumbing)	AlbionConstruct Ltd (construction)

Figure 2.5 *Albion Water plc and its subsidiaries.*

to separate out regulated and non-regulated activities, and fragment them into numerous, separately accountable units. These organizational changes facilitated the changes to work organization and employment relations described in later chapters; changes which have enabled management to cut labour costs, and which, for many workers, have degraded employment and increased work intensity. To understand why management has instituted such changes, it is necessary to examine briefly the relationship between privatization and managerial concern with labour costs.

Privatization, Profits and Labour Costs

As a private sector organization, answerable to shareholders, Albion Water is now obliged to make, and to continually increase, profits. Given that water companies are monopoly suppliers, facing stable and (very) gradually increasing demand, this may not appear to be a very challenging brief. However, government economic regulation is supposed to constrain the way in which profits can be raised from core activities. It has heen seen that one way in which water companies have responded to this dilemma is by diversifying into non-regulated areas. Despite management zeal for such projects, some economic analysts (e.g. Herrington, 1989) argue that the significance of these diversifications is likely to be negligible for two reasons. First, revenue from non-core business prior to privatization was negligible (less than 0.2% of total revenue in 1987–88), and second, in the context of increasingly stringent EC water purity standards and a dilapidated infrastructure, all spare cash will have to be used to fund a massive capital expenditure programme, and 'This means a zero or very limited capacity for acquisitions' (Herrington, 1989, p. 15).

Many commentators further argue that the potential for profits from core activities is also limited. It is claimed that 'the water industry has already been forced by financial constraints to make substantial economies and now has little operating fat. The need to generate profits for shareholders can only be met by decreasing investment or by large rises in water charges' (Rees and Synott, 1988, p. 202). Herrington also argues that efficiency savings and cuts in manning levels through the 1980s were so great that profits are unlikely to be further raised in this way, and concludes that 'there is almost no scope for increases in operating efficiency' (Herrington, 1989, p. 4). Of course, Herrington's *Deep Water: Investors Beware* was written for NALGO as part of its political campaign against privatization, and he is therefore primarily concerned to demonstrate that shares in water will not be the lucrative investment that the government would have investors believe. But his analysis does raise some important issues. First, it argues that diversification will not quickly generate high profits, and so suggests that developing non-core activities will not be of vital concern to management. Second, it argues that water companies have already reached their limits in terms of cutting direct labour levels and raising worker productivity. Finally, it raises the question of whether, in a highly capital-intensive business like water supply and recovery, reducing labour costs will be seen by management as the key to increasing profitability. These points need to be considered in relation to Albion Water.

In 1990, Albion Water's residual profits amounted to £23.5 million, of which just over 80% came from sewerage services, around 18% from water supply services, and only just under 1% from other trading activities. Thus, in absolute terms, non-core activities have not produced large profits. However, one of the attractions of the 'enterprise initiatives' for management is that few of them require substantial new investment. For example, the plumbing service uses self-employed workers, who initially started work using their own tools and vehicles. It is administered from existing office space, using existing administrative staff and facilities. The set-up costs were very low. 'Core' services which are being hived off and required to win commercial work, such as the Mechanical and Electrical Maintenance Unit, likewise make use of capital which is invested for core business purposes, and do not require major new investment to get off the ground. Moreover, Albion has entered into a joint venture with a major construction company in order to develop other non-core activities, so that, again, its own investment is limited.

This means that although (measured in absolute terms) profits appear quite low, in terms of the rate of return, non-core activities appear attractive. Albion is therefore looking for ways of exploiting the commercial potential of existing resources. As the chairman states, 'We shall build on the success we already have by using known skills and not wandering into adventures we do not understand' (Annual Report, 1990). Thus, it is probable that the developing of both non-core and core-related services will continue. Acquisitions seem an equally likely route to diversification, despite the fact that, as Herrington observes, investment programmes may starve the organization of cash, for not all acquisitions require cash. Takeovers can be funded through share issues, and this is an especially simple route to acquiring non-quoted companies such as small industrial waste disposal concerns. Herrington may be right that in the short term no dramatic increase in profitability will arise from such activities. But Albion is not only interested in dramatic increases in profitability. The chairman states that Albion aims to reward shareholders with 'steady growth and progress' (Annual Report, 1990), and the development of non-core business is seen as playing an important part in this.

What of the notion that labour costs have already been cut to the bone, and that no more efficiency gains can be made? At Albion Water, direct labour levels have indeed dropped dramatically through the 1980s, as was seen in Figure 2.4. Employment costs as a percentage of operating costs have also fallen (Figure 2.6). But even if the pace of change through the 1990s proves less drastic than it was throughout the 1980s, it is arguable whether the workforce will feel any direct benefits from this. To begin with, cuts cannot be assumed to be once and for all gains by management. If efficiency targets have been met by cutting direct labour levels and increasing the work rate of those who remain, then pressure must be maintained to hang on to those gains. To continue to function with a manual workforce of only 576, management will have to continue to pay attention to squeezing labour productivity.

Leaving this aside, there is really no reason to suppose that the process of cutting direct labour levels has come to an end since there is almost no limit to the amount of work that can be contracted out. As will be argued in Chapters 4 and 5, whether or not management chooses to do so is determined by a number of economic and political factors, not by any factor intrinsic to the work process itself. Moreover, as will be seen in Chapters 5, 6, 7 and 8, Albion management does not accept that no more efficiency gains can be made, and is seeking to further intensify the labour of manual workers.

Finally, it is necessary to address the question of why management should remain so concerned with labour costs, if efficiency targets can only be met through capital investment. As can be seen from Figure 2.6,

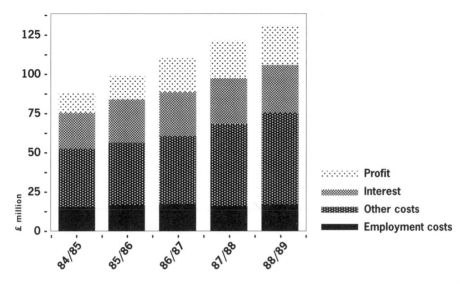

Figure 2.6 *Albion Water – employment costs, other operating costs, interest payments and profit 1984–1989. Source: Secretary of State for the Environment (1989).*

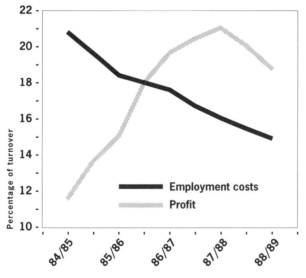

Figure 2.7 *Albion Water employment costs and pre-tax profit as a percentage of turnover 1984–1989. Source: Secretary of State for the Environment (1989).*

Albion's operating costs, as well as its turnover, rose sharply between 1984 and 1989, yet employment costs remained at much the same level. At the same time, profits were rising. In 1985, employment costs represented 20.6% of turnover. If they had remained at this level in 1989, then employment costs would have been £26.9m as opposed to £19.2m, i.e. £7.7m greater than they actually were (Figure 2.7). Since £7.7m actually represents around 32% of Albion's pre-tax profits for 1989, there seems little doubt that management had a strong incentive to squeeze labour costs. This incentive to cut labour costs remains, for even though a fall of 2% in labour costs would cut operating costs by only 0.5%, it would raise margins by 2%, and the effect on profits is much greater. Even steady but undramatic growth is more attractive to shareholders than no growth at all.

In short, the new obligation to produce profits for shareholders, coupled with the constraints imposed on Albion Water by government economic regulation, has made the control of labour costs of vital importance to management. This, then, is the backcloth against which the changes to management structures and strategies, industrial relations, work organization and employment relations described in this book were set.

Notes

1. Littlechild was one of the government's foremost privatization advisers, and has now been appointed the regulator-designate for the privatized electricity industry, a task which he himself describes as 'the most important appointment available in this field at the moment' (*Financial Times* 23 May 1989).

2. It is interesting, in the light of Littlechild's earlier comments on the RPI – X formula, that objections did not also come from him. In 1986 he argued that this type of formula

> 'holds the fort' until competition arrives, and is inappropriate if competition is not expected to emerge. It is a temporary safeguard, not a permanent method of control. The one-off nature of the restriction is precisely what preserves the firm's incentive to be efficient, because the firm keeps any gains beyond the specified level. Repeated 'cost-plus' audits would destroy this incentive and, moreover, encourage 'nannyish' attitudes towards the industry. (Beesley and Littlechild, 1986, p. 42)

Since there is no hope of competition arriving in the water industry, it seems odd that he recommended this type of regulation.

3 PRIVATIZATION: MANAGEMENT STRATEGIES AND INDUSTRIAL RELATIONS

The historical development of the water industry from the mid-nineteenth century up to the 1970s was characterized by the increasing integration of the three key water functions (supply, recovery and environmental functions) and by increasingly centralized control over planning, resource management and finance. These historical trends reached their zenith in the 1973 Water Act, which created the ten regional water authorities of England and Wales. Privatization turned these authorities into a number of private monopolies, and it divided the three key functions of the water industry, which had been integrated from 1974 onwards. For the first time in the industry's history, all water supply and sewerage services were the responsibility of privately owned organizations. But while privatization represented a profound break with the water *industry's* historical development, the Thatcher government's privatization programme should not be seen as representing a fundamental transformation of the nature of the capitalist state. Neither the municipalization of the public utilities from the late nineteenth century on, nor their privatization in the 1980s, can be fully explained except through reference to both the political *and* the economic climate in which they occurred. Municipalization of the water industry took place during a period of rapid economic growth. This economic expansion both required improved urban amenities, and provided local government with the funds to assume greater responsibility for their provision (Stern, 1954; Hassan, 1985). Privatization took place in the context of economic recession when capital was neither willing nor able to support public sector spending on the same scale. Privatization was thus driven by economic exigencies, and was not *merely* an expression of political dogma. In general, capital has benefited materially from moves to reduce the PSBR, and certain factions (particularly City institutions) benefited from privatization on a stupendous scale. While privatization may ultimately prove to have been a disastrously short-term expedient, in both municipalizing and privatizing the public utilities the state developed policies which furthered the interests of dominant groups.

For water industry managers, government legislation from 1981 onwards created immense practical problems. It starved them of cash and required them to operate in a pseudo-commercial world. Privatization presents an equally formidable scenario. Bequeathed an ageing and dilapidated infrastructure, they must find ways to meet higher EC water standards. They may soon face the possibility of hostile takeover bids, especially from French-based multinationals.[1] Lord Hanson's recent interest in PowerGen (Labour Research, 1990) demonstrates that the newly privatized utilities are of interest to asset strippers, and certainly top management in the new water companies are conscious of the need to 'milk' their companies before someone else does.

Above all, the water companies now face the problem of how to fulfil obligations to their shareholders without antagonizing OFWAT. The form of economic regulation devised for the privatized water industry provides water companies with a powerful incentive to cut costs and improve labour productivity, in order to avoid being penalized when their K setting is reviewed. Meanwhile, proposals for both the post-privatization economic and environmental regulation of the water industry forced organizational change upon the water authorities. Environmental regulation in the form of the creation of the National Rivers Authority precipitated the merging of small operational divisions and a centralization of authority. Furthermore, in destroying the much-prized system of integrated river basin management by transferring the water authorities' environmental functions to a separate body, the government simultaneously destroyed the management principle around which regional water authorities had been organized for some 15 years. The industry therefore had to restructure around a different set of management principles. This chapter provides an overview of the impact of these changes upon management strategies and industrial relations in Albion Water.

'Profit Centre' Management: Centralizing Control, Decentralizing Responsibility

In 1988, the Department of the Environment began offering the water authorities advice on how to go about restructuring in preparation for privatization, and it strongly favoured a shift to some form of 'profit centre' management. Albion Water sought the advice of the management

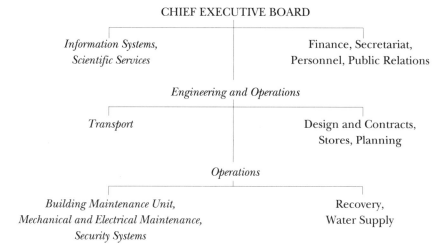

CHIEF EXECUTIVE BOARD

Information Systems,
Scientific Services

Finance, Secretariat,
Personnel, Public Relations

Engineering and Operations

Transport

Design and Contracts,
Stores, Planning

Operations

Building Maintenance Unit,
Mechanical and Electrical Maintenance,
Security Systems

Recovery,
Water Supply

Figure 3.1 *Albion Water Services Ltd: departments and profit centres. Note: independently accountable 'profit centres' are italicized.*

consultants Coopers & Lybrand on how to implement this directive, and a new management structure was finally put in place in 1988. Profit centre management both facilitated and intensified the more general shift away from a public service style of management towards a commercial, profit-maximizing approach. Albion Water plc is now a holding company with a number of subsidiaries (Figure 2.5), and Albion Water Services Ltd, which undertakes the core activities of water supply and sewerage, has abandoned its former pyramid structure and is organized as a number of departments and 'profit centres' (Figure 3.1).

The profit centre approach is an accounting exercise designed to provide a variety of incentives and penalties for managers which will force them to adopt a commercial, private sector style of management. Various activities have been separated out and turned into independently accountable units which must 'buy' and 'sell' services from and to other departments or profit centres within the organization, and engage in commercial ventures outside the firm. Each profit centre is allocated a budget by the board. The term 'budget' smacks of traditional bureaucratic control, however, and so a new jargon has been coined by Albion Water managers – the profit centre's budget is referred to as a 'pot of gold', or 'pot' for short. The size of the 'pot' is determined on the basis of three main factors:

1. The profit centre's income from charges or sales

2. The level of revenue and capital expenditure proposed by the profit

centre in the business plan that it has submitted to the board (criteria concerning expenditure and profit levels which the plan must conform to are laid down by the board)

3. Corporate goals and the competing claims of other profit centres for funds

For example, Mechanical and Electrical Maintenance (M&E) might submit a business plan which involved investment requiring £X000 above its income from charges. The board would consider whether or not the investment proposed in the plan was necessary or desirable in terms of corporate aims. The board might then decide that Transport had a more urgent need for investment, and allocate M&E less. M&E would then be instructed to cut back on revenue expenditure and fund the proposed capital expenditure out of such savings as could be made. Having been allocated its 'pot', the profit centre uses it to implement its business plan. Each profit centre operates a profit and loss account, and once allocated a budget it should behave almost as an independent firm, pursuing output and profitability specified in the plan. The profits generated by individual profit centres are ploughed back into the corporate whole. However, there are a range of rewards which are supposed to act as an incentive to profit centre managers, including profit-related bonus payments, company cars, expansion of successful profit centres and so on. Sanctions for failing to meet profit and performance targets are also directed at the individual managers. They can be financially penalized, and ultimately face demotion or dismissal if they consistently fail to meet the targets agreed in the business plan.

The aim of this model of profit centre management is to propagate market forces *within* the organization. Until 1988, the relationship between different divisions and departments was regulated bureaucratically. For example, every department relied on the finance department for payrolling, and finance was allocated a budget to cover the costs of providing this service bureaucratically. Under profit centre management bureaucratic relationships are commercialized. Divisions and departments must 'buy' and 'sell' services from and to each other. The assumption is that this enables the invisible hand to perform its wonders within the organization, rationing resources and optimizing efficiency. A finance manager explains:

> The problem with the sort of public sector domain we were in previously
> is that as a user of things like computing services, I didn't get charged

anything, and therefore my appetite was infinite. We all wanted more and more. If you offer a free service the demands are enormous, whereas if you charge for those services, people actually begin to think about whether they need them. Should they be using the mainframe, or would it be more economical to buy a personal computer? . . . It focuses attention on costs far more.

Profit centre management is, then, supposed to equal good management for the following reasons. First, profit centre managers know how much their 'pot' contains, and 'good sense' dictates that they will not spend more than is available. Second, because other departments are charging for their services, the manager's voracious appetite for the organization's resources is curbed. The system ensures that managers use their 'pots' wisely. Third, because they have to make a profit by 'selling' their services either to other departments or profit centres, or to outside firms, who may choose to go elsewhere if the service is shoddy or overpriced, the system forces profit centre managers to keep costs to a minimum and standards at their highest. Finally, because profit centre managers have been given both 'freedom to manage' and personal responsibility for outcomes, there is great pressure on individual managers to perform effectively.

Like much Thatcherite economic thinking, the ideological power of the model lies in its simplicity and its focus on individuals rather than structures. It is informed by a kind of homely wisdom about human behaviour, and rests on the idea that bureaucracies provide individual managers with perverse incentives to expand their realm instead of maximize efficiency, and that individuals will not perform effectively in a framework without personal rewards and penalties. Yet when profit centres are considered in relation to the whole organization, rather than to individual managers, they appear to have rather less potential as a radical, efficiency-maximizing force.

The idea is that when departments face each other across markets, instead of enjoying a hierarchical relationship, competitive pressures are injected into the firm and efficiency will improve. As will be seen in Chapters 7 and 8, Albion Water's senior managers make much of this notion of competition, and continually emphasize the need to cut costs and improve efficiency in order to 'win' work from other departments or profit centres. Yet in reality, most departments are monopoly suppliers to other departments, because no profit centre or department is given absolute freedom to choose its suppliers. The notion that a profit centre (e.g. Operations) could decide that the finance department provided an inefficient and costly service and go to a cheaper outside firm for payrolling instead is fanciful since it would slash the volume of work for Albion's payrolling unit by about 40%. Likewise, if Operations found that it could save money by going outside for vehicles instead of going to Transport (another profit centre), the cost to Albion as a company would again be high. The finance manager comments, 'There is this conflict between the profit centre and the corporate whole, but that is very much the responsibility of the corporate whole to make sure that profit centres . . . do toe the line of the corporate good.' In other words, the board would not allow a profit centre to make such decisions.

Without freedom to choose between suppliers, the notion of a market between different units is a fiction. Profit centres are not disciplined by competitive forces if there is no real likelihood of losing custom, and so in reality it is still the board which must exert pressure for cost cutting and greater efficiency. Moreover, profit centres do not only lack independence in terms of their choice of supplier. They are closely controlled by the board in other ways. The board vets profit centre business plans, and also constrains them through the allocation of overheads. Profit centres have to 'pay' for overheads out of their 'pot'. The charge includes a nominal sum for office space, heating, cleaning, the billing process through which water rates are collected, and so on.

The allocation of central overheads provokes a great deal of controversy. Profit centre managers tend to believe that they are forced to shoulder an unduly large share of Albion's costs. Once again, they have little choice. As one profit centre manager pointed out, it is unlikely that the board would allow him to work from a Portakabin to reduce his costs, if this meant that Albion was left paying for unused office space. The board also constrains profit centres by imposing corporate policies on such matters as overtime and staffing levels. Profit centres are not free to take on more employees without permission and are penalized for allowing their employees to work overtime. Profit centres are also unable to negotiate their own contracts with employees; they cannot negotiate wage levels and cannot even implement bonus schemes without the board's approval.

In short, although profit centres are exhorted to think and act like independent firms and to conceive of other departments and profit centres as their 'customers', in practice they have virtually no autonomy at all. They must negotiate a business plan with the board; capital and revenue expenditure is set by the board; their overheads, manning levels and employment practices are imposed from above; performance and profit targets are set by the board; and finally, they are constrained by the board in their choices of suppliers and customers. What is there left for market forces to act upon? Under the old regime, departments were bureaucratically allocated budgets, and their efficiency and profitability was determined by decisions taken by the board. Under the new system, budgets are replaced by 'pots', but the profit centre's efficiency and profitability are still crucially determined by the board's decisions.

Profit centre management has not entailed any decentralization of power or authority, nor has it genuinely created market forces within the organization. Why then was it recommended? It might be argued that this is an illustration of the gap between formal and substantive rationality, that the civil servants and management consultants who advocated this model of profit centre management simply failed to appreciate its limitations. Yet much the same model was imposed upon British Telecom and British Gas on privatization, and upon the universities through the Rayner Report, and the DOE therefore had plenty of opportunity to see the model in action. It might be tempting to think that profit centre management is merely an ideological device.

Wood (1989b) has observed that a distinctive feature of the 'new wave' management literature of the 1980s (typified by Peters and Waterman's *In Search of Excellence*) is the insistence that managers must shift from 'reactive' to 'proactive postures', from a bureaucratic to an entrepreneurial style of management. New Right politicians in Britain have also argued that economic (and social) regeneration will be facilitated by the development of an 'enterprise culture' in both private and public sector organizations (Gamble, 1988; Du Gay, 1991). The form of profit centre management advocated by the DOE for newly privatized concerns is clearly intended to contribute to the creation of an 'enterprise culture' within organizations which have, for so long, languished under the dead hand of state bureaucracy. Managers are thrust from somnolent structures of a bureaucratic hierarchy into a bracing new world. No matter if the markets across which departments meet are illusory, the rewards and sanctions that managers face are real enough. In this respect, the policy could be judged as relatively successful. It generates an almost ecstatic response from many senior managers, who see it as allowing them greater freedom (they talk about being able to control their 'pot') and bringing them into a commercial world where they can be 'real' managers (they talk about enjoying 'the challenge'). Profit centre management is described as 'a breath of fresh air', and 'a window of opportunity'. Senior managers have already benefited materially from these changes, with company cars, BUPA membership and substantial profit-related bonus payments.

But profit centre management is more than an ideological device, and it does more than simply flatter and reward managers' pretensions to entrepreneurialism. As will be seen in Chapters 7 and 8, profit centre status is used by managers to justify cost-cutting exercises, changes in working practices and demands for increased productivity. Indeed, it is here that an answer to the question posed earlier (namely, after the board has set performance and profit targets, direct labour levels, overheads and employment practices and so on, what is there left for market forces to act upon?) may be found. Labour is all that remains to be disciplined, and this is effected through new forms of labour organization, recruitment, retention and, above all, intensification.

Though profit centre management serves fairly obvious ideological functions, it is also a necessary response to the government's proposals for post-privatization economic regulation of the water industry. As noted before, the core activities of the water companies, supply and recovery, are subject to economic regulation, and the price formula is intended to impose limits on the level of profit that can be extracted from these core activities. A senior Albion manager commented:

> If we make profits on the core side, then the Director General of OFWAT is going to say, 'Well, you've made a lot of money here, you don't need to put your charges up. Indeed you might even have to put them down.' Now that might be good for the consumers in one respect, but the shareholders, which is who we have to answer to, will be down on it.

As a private company, Albion Water is under pressure to sustain its profit levels and to improve them in relation to those of other enterprises. When the proposals for post-privatization economic regulation were announced, the board saw diversification as an important means of achieving these ends. It therefore split its operations into two separately accountable areas; the 'core', which is subject to economic regulation, and 'enterprise activities', which are not. From 1998 on, Albion sought to keep as many activities as possible separate from the core business, and so from regulation, and to develop and expand the enterprise area. To this end, a variety of commercial initiatives are being established. Some are entirely new departures for Albion, e.g. the plumbing service and the septic tank emptying service. Others involve turning existing services into commercial ventures. Albion's construction group, its M&E Unit and its Building Maintenance Unit (BMU) all now seek commercial work as well as providing services to the core functions of supply and recovery. Similarly, Albion now engages in various consultancy projects on a commercial footing.

New initiatives which are totally functionally independent of Albion's core operations, such as the plumbing service, are simple to separate out and, as noted above, have been organized as subsidiary firms. It is not so easy to separate out those areas which exist primarily to serve the core business. The M&E Unit is a case in point. Albion is transforming this function into a separately accountable profit centre which will 'sell' a service to the core business, and also engage in commercial ventures outside. The finance manager explains that such units can then make a profit 'so long as you can show that they are not charging the core exorbitant rates in order to generate profit, so long as they are in line with market forces'.

This raises enormous problems for the regulator, e.g. defining what would constitute 'exorbitant rates', demonstrating precisely how and where profits were generated, and determining whether the core might not be able to obtain a cheaper service through vertical integration. OFWAT's Director General has recently expressed concern about precisely these questions, and is currently undertaking a study on transactions between core businesses and associated companies within the groups (Freeman, 1991). Yet it is clearly in the water companies' interests to disaggregate core activities in order to generate profits from commercial ventures (of course, it is also in their interests to make the regulator's task harder). An Albion finance manager comments:

> A decision has been taken that the bulk of these activities within the
> core, if they can earn some money by doing something which is
> associated with that core activity for third parties outside, and earn some
> profit then we should encourage that to take place because obviously it
> increases the wealth overall.

Profit centre management is clearly consistent with this objective of expanding commercial activities. Because they are separately accountable units, profit centres will have an incentive to pursue commercial ventures which will generate income and expand their 'pot'. Again, Albion's senior management are enthusiastic about such ventures. Again profit centre employees are exhorted to improve productivity and accept changes in working practices so that their unit can compete effectively for commercial work against outside firms. Again, as will be seen in Chapters 7 and 8, the reality is that each unit's competitiveness is constrained far more by board decisions and directives than by the flexibility or motivation of its employees.

To summarize, profit centre management has sought to commercialize relationships between different units and departments within Albion Water, and these departments and units have, in turn, sought to commercialize their relationships with employees. In this sense, it is consistent with the philosophy of privatization, which in itself constitutes the wholesale commercialization of water services. The new accounting practices are used to provide incentives and sanctions for managers, and as a way of intensifying the pressure for changes to working and employment practices. They also make it easier to reduce the amount of activities which fall under the control of the regulator. Profit centre management thus fulfils both ideological and practical functions.

So far, this chapter has been primarily concerned with the shift towards profit centre management. Alongside this structural change in preparation for privatization went an almost continuous reshuffling of senior executives and management. Many of those managers who were unsympathetic to privatization were gradually shunted through a number of posts across to the National Rivers Authority, or effectively demoted through the new structures that were emerging. There are several anecdotes circulating in the company about managers arriving at work to find their desks cleared, and a note telling them they had been transferred to offices 50 miles away. Other managers experienced meteoric rises through the organization, with supervisors and junior managers being promoted to new posts as heads of freshly established profit centres, and old divisional managers finding themselves amongst the senior executives. For Albion's manual and clerical employees, restructuring meant uncertainty and disruption as their place in the organizational structure changed; it meant changes to working practices and a general intensification of the pressure that had been exerted on them to improve productivity ever since the Thatcher government began to impose tighter financial controls on the industry. It also meant changes to their collective bargaining institutions.

Privatization and Industrial Relations

The government claimed that privatization would enhance industrial relations in the utilities in a number of ways. The White Paper for the privatization of the water industry states that as a consequence of privatization, 'employees will benefit from shareholdings, closer identification with their businesses, greater job satisfaction, better motivation, and the prospects of the rewards that enterprise has brought to those who work for other industries that have been privatized' (Cmnd 9734, 1986 Paragraph 7). This is in line with government's more general claims about the virtues of privatization, which is said to eradicate 'old fashioned distinctions between workers and owners' and offer employees the opportunity to benefit 'from higher salaries and bonuses earned by the possibilities of higher productivity' (HM Treasury, 1990, pp. 4–5). In general, then, privatization is supposed to lead to more 'cooperative' industrial relations. Yet as Nichols (1986, p. 176) points out, though New Right politicians use the rhetoric of cooperation, their 'achievements' in terms of changing shop-floor behaviour owe more to reducing trade unions' powers to protect their members and to fostering fear and anxiety, than to nurturing 'cooperative' sentiments amongst the workforce. The public sector has been an arena in which successive Conservative governments have been most anxious, and most directly able, to refashion industrial relations. As Heald and Morris (1984, p. 32) observe, 'the "good employer" tradition has died and the official promotion of public sector trade unionism as one of the bases for sound industrial relations [has been] abruptly reversed'.

Aside from the fact that public sector unions played a key role in the downfall of governments in both 1974 and 1979, government ministers in the early 1980s were hostile to them because of their rapid growth and success. Thus, John Moore MP argued in 1986 that 'Public sector trade unions have been extraordinarily successful in gaining advantages for themselves in the pay hierarchy by exploiting their monopoly collective bargaining position' (Moore, 1986, p. 78). Public sector unions have been attacked not just by a comprehensive legislative assault on unions in general, but also by the privatization programme (Ascher, 1987, p. 101). Privatization reduces the power of public sector unions 'not only by removing access to Exchequer funds, thus making management more cost conscious in responding to trade union claims, but also by providing opportunities to dismantle national agreements. The latter are seen as a strategic factor underpinning trade union bargaining power in the Public Sector' (Ogden, 1990, p. 4).

In virtually all the industries and services which have been privatized, or which are subject to privatization plans, there has been a movement away from national-level negotiating, away from a 'constitutionalist' approach towards industrial relations. Beynon et al. (1991) and Winterton (1990) discuss this trend in the coal industry, Upham (1990) describes the same pattern in British Steel, Ascher (1987) in the NHS, and Ferner (1987) in British Rail. The regional water authorities have proved no different. In 1986, Thames Water gave notice to withdraw from the national pay bargaining machinery. Northumbria Water soon followed suit, and in August 1988 the other eight regional water authorities collectively gave the unions 12 months' notice of their intention to end national negotiations on both pay and conditions (*Financial Times* 26 August 1988; Ogden, 1990). The electricity unions were successful in persuading the government to include a clause in the legislation which prevented companies from withdrawing from national agreements until after flotation, and in obtaining a 'gentleman's agreement' that no company would give the statutory 12 months' notice to leave the national machinery until after all the electricity companies had been floated (Ferner, 1990), but the water unions did not enjoy the same degree of power and influence.

For water employees, then, the period before the first round of local negotiations was particularly worrying, since they had no written guarantee from the water authorities that national agreements, such as the no-redundancy agreement, would still be honoured. Thames Water's actions provided little reassurance to the unions. Despite its original insistence that it wished to withdraw from national negotiations in order to have the freedom to pay more, in the second non-national pay settlement in 1989, its offer was worth less than the national deal (*Financial Times* 24 May 1989). Since, as Fairbrother and Waddington (1990, p. 40) observe, 'state sector unions have traditionally been highly centralised with workplace organizations centrally sponsored and controlled', the trend away from national bargaining alone poses very real organizational problems for most unions; see also Fairbrother (1991). Add this problem to those created by successive Thatcher governments' legislative assaults on trade union powers in general, and to the fact that the increasing substitution of contract labour for direct labour in many privatized or about to be privatized industries reduces union membership and control in the workplace (Winterton, 1990; Fevre, 1986), and it becomes clear that unions face enormous difficulties in this sector. How these problems manifested themselves at Albion Water are now considered in more detail.

Union Organization at Albion Water

When the regional water authorities were created in 1974, a patchwork of organizations and their employees (rivers authorities, local authorities,

Table 3.1 *Union Density in Albion Water 1990*

	Union	Non-union
Manual	81.3%	18.7%
	(490)	(113)
Clerical, technical	68.5%	31.4%
and supervisory	(653)	(299)
Senior management	75.6%	24.2%
	(34)	(11)

Source: GMBATU (1990)

water boards) were brought together almost overnight. The regional water authorities therefore inherited a disparate workforce, and those who did enjoy representation were represented by a large number of different unions. A closed shop agreement was negotiated at national level, and, as a consequence, regional water authorities have, since their inception, had a well-unionized workforce. With the withdrawal of the closed shop agreement in 1983, union membership has fallen, but still the vast majority of Albion Water employees are unionized (Table 3.1). However, despite being well organized in terms of numbers, this organization was very much imposed from above, and there has never been a strong tradition of membership involvement. As a GMBATU regional official observed:

> The unions haven't been that strong within water. We've always been a closed shop and all the rest of it, if that is the measure of strength, yes, but whether that means industrial strength is another question. The national water strike showed up the weakness. We had to get people back to work before it crumbled . . . It wasn't a victory at all, it was an orderly retreat before we had a disorderly retreat . . . Overall, it showed up not the strength of the unions in the water industry, but the weaknesses.

The weaknesses are, in part, structural. To begin with, the employing organizations cover huge geographical areas, and the workforce (particularly the manual workforce) is therefore geographically dispersed. The majority of manual employees only have immediate and daily contact with between two and ten other manual workers. Clearly this presents organizational problems. As one NUPE steward commented:

> The water industry, it's not like a factory, there's no time when you're all together and can talk to each other. The water industry is . . . three or four men here, two or three there, three or four somewhere else. We're all scattered around.

For administrative purposes branches will include substantial numbers of members, which means that they tend to cover large geographical areas. Again, this militates against active participation by members, who cannot simply attend a meeting at their place of work, but may have to travel up to 20 miles to attend. The same steward noted that at branch meetings, 'We're lucky if a dozen turn up, and that's out of a branch membership of 140.' This in turn leads to inadequate communication between different levels of the union. Regional and branch officials may exchange information, but low turnout at meetings, combined with the fact that branch officials cannot possibly maintain contact with all the branch members who are spread across perhaps 30 depots in their area, means that branch officials do not always have information about members' concerns and grievances.

Regional officials are therefore highly dependent upon local representatives in each depot or workplace to maintain a flow of communication between the union and the membership. Unhappily, not every depot has a shop steward. Another GMBATU regional official noted:

> A lot of the time I think changes in working practices and the like are being introduced, and we don't hear about it. If there isn't a shop steward in the depot, it just gets slipped in. I'd like to get a steward at every depot, but unfortunately they just won't come forward . . . They just want to keep their heads down.

Because the water industry produces a geographically dispersed and predominantly rural labour force, several regional officials argue that these problems are endemic, and that had it not been for the top-down imposition of the closed shop and national bargaining, it is unlikely that water unions could ever have become so well established. As one remarked, 'If [union organization] begins to collapse, I don't know how you'd go about rebuilding it. Just trying to find people, let alone recruit them, would be almost impossible.'

Table 3.2 *Albion Water Employees by Union*

	Manual	Clerical*	Managers	Total
NALGO	1	607	34	642
TGWU	46	1	0	47
NUPE	282	16	0	298
GMBATU	121	20	0	141
MATSA	0	3	0	3
EEPTU	2	4	0	6
UCATT	9	0	0	9
AUEW	28	0	0	28
Others	1	2	0	3

*Clerical, Technical and Supervisory workers.

Source: GMBATU (1990)

If the geographical dispersal of members creates problems, so too does their dispersal amongst a number of different unions (Table 3.2). All of the Albion Water unions are major, national unions. None is solely or even primarily a water union, and each union has its own internal structure, being divided into regions with different geographical boundaries. Each region is further subdivided into divisions, again on the basis of different geographical boundaries. NUPE differs from other unions in Albion in as much as it bases its own structure upon the employer's structure. Thus, because Albion had three operational divisions, NUPE likewise adopted this form. The separation of the National Rivers Authority and the merging of these three divisions into two clearly makes this pattern redundant, and NUPE now plans to reorganize around the new Albion structure.

Not all of these unions model themselves on the employer's structure, however, which means that their internal structures correspond neither with each other nor with Albion Water's organizational structure. As a consequence, regional union officials can represent water workers employed by up to three different water companies, whilst employees in any one water company are not only divided between different unions, but are often also divided between different divisions of the same union. With unions such as GMBATU, which are organized along federal lines, this is particularly problematic. Each area has a degree of autonomy from the national union, and is administered separately. The union's boundary is drawn right through the middle of Albion Water's geographical territory, so that Albion Water workers in neighbouring depots fall into two different GMBATU regions, both of which are 'run very much along their own lines'. Though regional officials try to 'relate to each other . . . and mirror what we're doing in regard to Albion', it is not always possible to coordinate effectively.

In the early days of Albion's existence, when relations between management and unions were relatively harmonious, these organizational problems were not perceived by the unions as a major problem. Their activities were coordinated by the regional joint industrial council, and this sufficed in a context where management took a basically constitutionalist approach. In the run-up to privatization, however, this approach has changed, and the lack of coordination is now felt to be more worrying. Albion management has not only withdrawn from national negotiating machinery, but has also withdrawn from conditions that were negotiated locally. It has instigated team briefing for employees with the express intention of bypassing the unions as a channel of communication with employees, and its Director of Personnel explicitly states that he sees no role for trade unions in future.

As yet, this anti-union sentiment has found little practical expression. At the same time as withdrawing from locally negotiated conditions and national machinery, management has stated that it will continue to honour national conditions, such as the no-redundancy agreement. Apart from the introduction of team briefings, there has been no overt attempt to undermine the unions' position. As yet, there is nothing substantial for the unions to organize around, despite the fact they feel their position is being eroded. As one regional official said soon after privatization, 'We are in limbo still, waiting to see what they'll do . . . I don't think they want to take us on, I think they're just playing a waiting game.'

Continuity + Change.

Unions, Work Organization and the Wider Political Climate

Government policy has directly affected the unions' position in Albion Water in three main ways. First, tighter financial control forced Albion to shed labour, and this clearly impacts on the unions. Union density has always been greatest amongst manual workers, and it is the manual workforce that has been hardest hit by the policy (see Figure 3.1). Albion is making far more extensive use of contract labour than ever before (see Chapter 5), and so it is partially replacing a well-unionized workforce with totally non-unionized labour. GMBATU has made unsuccessful attempts to recruit contract labour, and given that the firms of civil engineering contractors Albion uses refuse to recognize any union, it is unlikely that such attempts will ever prove effective.

Second, privatization and the dismantling of national bargaining machinery have forced regional-level union officials to deal with new issues. For example, they must now enter into negotiations over pay with Albion management directly. This makes the organizational problems outlined above of far more critical importance, but it does also open up certain possibilities previously denied to local and regional-level unions, and may ultimately encourage the development of more active workplace union structures (Fairbrother, 1991).

Finally, privatization and economic regulation, which force Albion to diversify and develop the non-regulated enterprise area in order to increase profits, also impact on the unions. New initiatives, such as the plumbing service, are staffed entirely by self-employed, non-unionized workers. In the new profit centres, workers are organized along the lines of DLOs, and though they are still direct employees, their working practices and bonus payments are determined at the level of the work unit. All this means that instead of organizing a large, relatively homogeneous direct labour force, unions are facing an increasingly fragmented workforce: contract labour, self-employed workers, direct employees whose pay and conditions are linked to the performance of their particular work unit, as well as 'standard' direct employees. To organize such a disparate body of workers is obviously a far more difficult task than that faced in the past. As one regional GMBATU official observed:

> This is our dilemma in the public sector. Every water authority, every local authority, every district council, they're all doing it every day, breaking the work-force down into smaller and smaller groups, putting out more and more services. We need to be everywhere at the same time. Every deal with every worker is different, there is nothing corporate about it, it's all fragmented. This is the unions' problem. How do you monitor all that, how do you keep it together?

The task is made more difficult by the geographical dispersal of this workforce described above, which means that if there does not happen to be a steward in a particular depot, work units can be restructured without regional union officials knowing anything at all about it (see Chapter 7). All these problems are exacerbated by the wider political context in which they are set. Union officials argue that privatization has transformed the nature of industrial relations at Albion:

> In the past, we did have common interests to provide clean water and take away sewage for the benefit of the customer, whilst at the same time maintaining our own job security and wages and conditions . . . With privatization of course, there is a conflict of interests. We are looking to protect our members' job security and wages and conditions, management is looking to put money into the hands of the shareholders . . . They've got to make a profit however they can, no matter what the cost to the consumer or those employed in the industry.

Yet they now have to protect the membership in a climate which is particularly unfavourable to them. Throughout the 1980s, fewer and fewer people came forward to act as stewards (although one regional official believed that this was beginning to change), which makes communication with the membership more difficult. Albion management enjoys the explicit backing of the government, and is eager to experiment with its new-found 'freedom to manage'. This freedom is also seen as freedom from the obligation even to inform, far less to consult with, the unions about planned changes. As one official said, 'In the past, changes of this kind of magnitude would have been discussed, and wouldn't have got off the drawing board without our agreement. Now we're lucky if we even find out about them after the event.' Finally, and perhaps most damaging of all, rank and file members are so demoralized that they often do not bother to inform union representatives about changes to working practices or even threats of redundancies.

So far, it has been argued that both the government's new and tighter financial controls on the water industry through the 1980s and its subsequent privatization proposals led to change on a dramatic scale in Albion Water. These policies provoked changes to organizational structures, corporate strategies and industrial relations. The new obligation to produce profits for shareholders, coupled with the constraints imposed upon Albion by economic regulation, has made the control of labour costs of vital importance to management, and management is seeking to exercise this control in an economic and political climate which is especially unfavourable to organized labour. The changes to work organization and employment relations described in the following chapters cannot be understood except in relation to these changes.

Notes

1. The question of mergers and takeovers within the privatized water industry was problematic for the government. Almost from the moment the possibility of privatization was first raised, French water and construction companies showed increasing interest in acquiring stakes in the 28 statutory water companies. Between 1987 and 1988, for example, Lyonnaise des Eaux spent £145m in the UK water business, acquiring 6% of the British water market. Their French competitors, Générale des Eaux and SAUR, also began launching offers for UK water companies (*Financial Times* 7 April 1989). Fears of predatory takeovers were expressed by the statutory water companies, and there was growing concern that the water authorities, once privatized, would be subject to the same fate. The government came under increasing pressure to act. In January 1989 Nicholas Ridley announced that the Water Bill was to be amended to safeguard the ten authorities from takeover by a special government shareholding for the first five years following privatization (*Financial Times* 12 January 1989), thereby giving the water companies temporary protection against hostile bids. A further amendment was included to refer takeovers of water companies with assets of more than £30m to the Monopolies and Mergers Commission. These amendments undermine the government's rationale for privatizing the water authorities. Initially, the government claimed that even though water was a monopoly, the consumer would benefit from the increased competition in capital markets that privatization would bring, and this line of argument was emphasized by many of the government's acolytes (e.g. Letwin 1988). The threat of takeover would discipline the water companies, and force them to perform more efficiently in order to survive. The problem is that without competition, the only way to prevent a monopoly from satisfying shareholders at the expense of customers is tight regulation of prices, quality and output, and this type of state regulation can easily lead to distortions in the capital market. Share prices may communicate information about the

effectiveness of regulation, rather than about the talents of management. Moreover, in the water industry profits can be affected by questions of geography and demography and by weather conditions. An authority like Thames, for example, would have to be stupendously mismanaged before capital market mechanisms acted to 'discipline' it. Again, visionary management and organizational efficiency will not necessarily be rewarded. The government's dilemma is that if curbs are not placed on takeovers and mergers, the industry might well become consolidated into a small number of large monopolies. These would be even more insulated from market forces than ten smaller monopolies are (for example, OFWAT's Director General could hardly discipline through performance comparisons if only two water companies existed). They could only be controlled through still more extensive state regulation. Yet if the Monopolies and Mergers Commission protects the ten larger companies in years to come, it will effectively remove the only market discipline available, a discipline which government ministers themselves had vaunted as *the* guarantee of the public interest.

4 BOUNDARIES, CONTRACTS AND GOVERNANCE: RELATIONS BETWEEN ALBION WATER AND CIVIL ENGINEERING FIRMS

Albion Water relies on the labour of thousands of workers in order to supply its customers with clean water and to take away and treat their dirty water. It not only depends upon the workers who operate water treatment works, who lay and repair pipes, who process bills and so on; it also relies upon the labour of workers who construct reservoirs, pumping stations and office buildings, and even those who manufacture the pipes, shovels, JCBs, computers and everything else which is vital to Albion's day-to-day activities. Because the social division of labour in capitalist economies is so advanced, most of this latter type of labour can be bought across markets, after it has been incorporated into a product. If Albion requires a new fleet of vehicles, it does not have to (nor would it be economic for it to) directly employ workers and organize them to manufacture those vehicles. This work is arranged by other units of capital, and Albion Water can simply buy the vans and so the 'dead labour'[1] incorporated in them, without entering into a complex contractual relationship with either the firms or the labour involved in producing them. But what of the labour which engages in activities that are specific to Albion alone? No firm is likely to buy land and build a reservoir or a water treatment works on the off-chance that Albion Water, or some other company, will want to buy it. Albion must therefore choose between directly employing specialist construction workers to undertake this work or entering into some kind of relationship with another firm or firms which will marshal the labour to construct these idiosyncratic items on Albion's behalf.

This chapter is concerned with precisely such relationships. It asks why Albion chooses to contract work out and explores the contractual problems which Albion encounters in so doing. These issues are significant in relation to employment relations for two reasons. First, the problems associated with relationships between Albion Water and firms of contractors (particularly those of specification, control and governance) have many parallels with those associated with relationships between Albion and its direct employees. Second, there is nothing final or irrevocable about the balance a firm strikes between its dependence on direct labour and on outside contractors. Firms can become less reliant upon other firms, e.g. through vertical integration. They can move in the opposite direction by subcontracting out more work. Such changes have repercussions for the nature and pattern of employment relations within the organization, and it is therefore important to understand why firms make decisions to contract out parts of their production process. The new institutional economics literature addresses these questions and will therefore be taken as a starting point for the analysis of relations between Albion and the civil engineering firms upon which it relies. However, this literature explains these decisions primarily through reference to the properties of the transaction (arguing that the more frequent and the more idiosyncratic the transaction is, the less likely it is to take place across a market), and largely ignores the economic, political and institutional context in which the transaction takes place. This chapter is concerned with why Albion Water draws up the boundaries of its operations where it does, and with the contractual framework employed by Albion to regulate its relationship with contractors. It also explores how these boundaries and governance structures are changing as a consequence of the privatization of the regional water authorities and argues that relative preferences for market and hierarchical relationships cannot be understood independently of broader historical factors, such as booms and slumps, the relative bargaining power between firms, unemployment levels, trade union density and labour legislation.

Transaction Cost Analysis and the Boundaries of the Firm

One facet of the academic debate about restructuring in the 1980s has focused on the changing boundaries of the firm. For example, it has been argued that the decade witnessed a trend away from vertically integrated organizational structures (Blyton and Morris, 1991), and some surveys have indicated a growing reliance upon subcontractors (Marginson *et al.*, 1988). There are those who have welcomed increasing resort to various forms of subcontract and decentralization of production as an antidote to industrial decline in the advanced Western economies. Pop management theorists have exhorted companies to 'stick to the knitting' (Peters and

Waterman, 1982), and the same basic message (though in rather more grandiose language) is to be found in the new institutional economics literature:

> [O]nly core skills of high asset specificity should be governed internally. Complementary skills of medium asset specificity can more efficiently be obtained through strategic alliances, and are governed bilaterally, while all low specificity assets are most efficiently contracted in the market, and no specialized governance structure needs to be set up. (Reeve, 1990, p. 142)

What is innovative about the new institutional economics literature is precisely its concern with the variability of organizational forms. Oliver Williamson's much acclaimed work uses transaction cost analysis to explain the range and diversity of both economic institutions and employment relations in capitalist societies. He argues that what underpins both standard and non-standard forms of economic organization is the drive to minimize the contracting costs (both *ex ante* and *ex post*) associated with complex transactions between different parties. The economic institutions of capitalism may be diverse, but all are efficient in terms of minimizing transaction costs. Thus differential transaction costs are the source of variance in the organization of production and the 'efficient boundaries' of the firm, as well as of work and employment (Williamson, 1985, 1989, 1990). Issues of power are held by Williamson to be of secondary importance. Contrasting his 'efficiency hypothesis' with the 'power hypothesis' of radical commentators such as Stone and Marglin, Williamson (1985, p. 237) asserts that:

> Vertical integration will occur selectively rather than comprehensively . . . mistaken vertical integration can rarely be sustained, and . . . more efficient modes will eventually supplant less efficient modes – though entrenched power interests can sometimes delay the displacement . . . [H]owever . . . *large* efficiency differences place entrenched interests under great strain.

Williamson's opposition between power and efficiency is problematic since efficiency in terms of extracting and accumulating surplus value generates social and economic power. What is of more concern here, however, is the way in which the institutional economics literature assumes that transaction costs derive solely from the transaction itself, and fails to consider the effects of the wider economic, social and political context in which the transaction takes place. For example, Reeve's discussion of the construction industry is useful in that it highlights the fact that a firm's 'strategic core' is variable, rather than absolute. However, he asserts that:

> [P]roperties of the transaction determine what constitutes the efficient boundary of the firm . . . Thus the efficient boundaries vary by transaction class as defined by the various subdimensions of asset specificity – site, physical assets, human assets, and dedicated assets. (Reeve, 1990, pp. 144–5)

Where the transaction entails low asset-specific investment, it is efficient to subdivide the 'value chain' of the construction industry (that is, concept, design, project management, construction and service) amongst a number of specialist firms. Where the transaction involves a complex construction project of high asset specificity, it will be efficient to integrate all five stages of the chain within one firm's boundaries (Reeve, 1990, p. 144). Clearly, the properties of a given transaction are an important variable affecting make or buy decisions. A construction firm kitting out a new office is hardly likely to decide to vertically integrate the production of filing cabinets instead of buying them across a market. But if the same firm found itself continually turning to specialist design consultants to draw up designs, it might consider vertically integrating the design process. This much appears as common sense.

The problem comes when we turn to high asset specificity transactions and find that, despite having identical properties, the same transactions can be organized differently in different countries. Japan's industrial structure, for example, cannot be fully understood except in relation to wider economic and political factors. The origins of Japanese dualism can be traced back to the Meiji government giving Zaibatsu conglomerates preferential access to modern technology and finance capital in the late nineteenth century, and it is also necessary to consider the role of the state and financial institutions to explain relational contracting in Japan today (Ueno, 1980; Littler, 1982; Sako, 1988). Moreover, the 'efficient boundaries' of the firm change over time. Work previously undertaken in house can be contracted out and vice versa without the properties of the transaction changing. Schneiberg and Hollingsworth argue that transaction cost analysis cannot readily explain the existence and form of trade associations since 'state policy . . . plays a central role in generating variation in the extent and rate of associational formation' (Schneiberg and Hollingsworth, 1990, p. 331), and there are similar problems in applying transaction cost analysis to the boundaries of the firm. Even the fact that employers are legally obliged to make national insurance contributions, statutory sickness payments and the like affects firms' choices between direct and contract labour, for example.

A description of how the boundaries between Albion Water and various firms of civil engineering contractors have vacillated over the past decade illustrates their historically contingent nature. Moreover, locating these transactions within a particular economic and political climate highlights difficulties with Williamson's (1985) assertion that it is the properties of the transaction (particularly the frequency with which it occurs and the degree of asset-specific investment it entails) which determine the appropriate and efficient form of governance structure (Williamson, 1985, pp. 68–84). As Wright notes, Williamson suggests that non-specific transactions are always best regulated by market mechanisms, but that:

> [R]ecurrent transactions involving a high degree of asset-specificity are preferably handled through internalisation. Occasional transactions involving at least some degree of specificity lend themselves to trilateral governance structures, whereby third parties (arbitration) may be used to resolve disputes between the main parties. Bilateral governance (obligational contracting) deals with instances of frequent transactions involving only some degree of specificity. (Wright, 1988, p. 195)

However, the nature of relationships between firms and the governance structures used to regulate those relationships are also affected by factors external to the transaction itself. Williamson recognizes that it is the incompleteness of formal contracts which creates the need for governance structures, and in this sense, he could be said to be elaborating the consequences of Durkheim's analysis of the non-contractual elements in contract for industrial structures. But again, Williamson is concerned to downplay the significance of power and does not discuss how power differentials (which often stem from wider economic, political and institutional factors) impact on the way in which parties deal with these non-contractual elements of their relationship. However, as Macauley (1963, p. 55) observes, in the real world business people 'fail to plan exchange relationships completely, and seldom use legal sanctions to adjust these relationships or to settle disputes', and the relative bargaining power of the two business units affects the degree to which contract is used. Evan (1963, p. 68) comments:

> [T]he greater the bargaining position differential between the organizations, the more likely their transactions will be contractual in nature. In addition, the greater the power differential between the organizations, the less likely conflicts between them arising out of a contract will be settled by legal methods, whether by litigation or arbitration, unless the organization that has less power is capable of pooling its resources with other organizations similarly disadvantaged by the power of the party in question.

Fox (1974, p. 169) makes similar points about the significance of power in determining whether high-trust or low-trust business relations are adopted. Again, an examination of relations between Albion Water and the various firms of civil engineering contractors it employs develops this theme, and shows how the wider political and economic climate affects the relative power of firms, and so affects both their relations and the governance structures which they adopt to regulate their exchange.

Albion Water's Boundaries: The Case of Supply

The supply of clean water is one of Albion Water's two core functions. In 1990 this accounted for approximately 32% of its turnover, and 19% of its profits (Figure 4.1). Water supply basically consists of extracting, treating and distributing water, which involves the construction, maintenance and operation of a supply system. It therefore entails three main types of work. First, there are major construction projects, such as building reservoirs or water treatment works. Second, there are smaller projects, such as laying new trunk mains and service pipes, making new connections and undertaking work commissioned by outside agencies (for instance, British Gas might ask Albion to move existing water pipes in order to lay a new gas pipe in a street). Third, operating a supply system involves the routine and emergency maintenance of pipes, treatment centres, pumping stations and so on. These basic activities are supported by a range of technical, administrative, clerical and ancillary labour, and also rely on the 'remote labour' embedded in the tools, machinery and plant that they use.

Though the construction, maintenance and operation of the supply system are all critically important to the water supply function, not all of this work is undertaken in house by directly employed personnel. Since its inception in 1974, Albion Water has contracted out the bulk of its major construction projects, such as the construction of new reservoirs, pumping

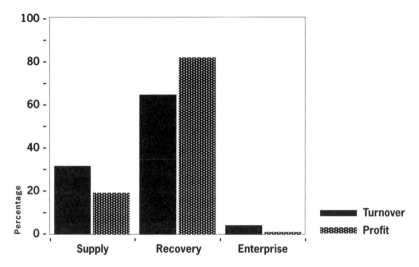

Figure 4.1 *Albion Water: turnover and profit by function. Source: Albion Water Accounts 1990.*

stations, water towers and so on. Albion has also always used contract labour on smaller capital projects and to undertake a portion of its routine pipe-laying and maintenance work. In contracting out work, Albion enters into relationships with outside firms, and these relationships vary in nature and form. In particular, there are differences between relationships with major capital works contractors and those who are contracted to undertake smaller schemes and routine pipe-laying work. These are considered in turn.

Formal Contractual Relationships with Firms undertaking Major Capital Projects

In the water industry, major capital works projects involve basically the same five stages as those identified in the construction industry by Reeve (1990, p. 143):

1. Initial concept

2. Design

3. Project management

4. Construction

5. Operation

Of these five stages, only the first always falls, and has always fallen, exclusively within Albion Water's boundaries. Only the fourth stage, that of construction itself, virtually always falls outside Albion boundaries. The other three stages are sometimes contracted out and sometimes undertaken in house. The rationale behind contracting out the actual construction stage of major capital works projects is straightforward. On the one hand, demand for such work is infrequent and on the other, major construction projects require plant, skills and expertise that were not typically found within regional water authorities, and are not available in the new water companies. Albion does not generate a sufficient volume of such work to warrant the vertical integration of specialist construction units. The construction of new water treatment works, water towers, reservoirs and so on requires specialist skills, plant and equipment of a type found in the civil engineering industry. Since the demand that most water companies make on these assets is unpredictable, infrequent, and/or fluctuating, it makes sense for the companies to buy them in as and when necessary, rather than paying all the overheads that would be involved in keeping these assets on tap. Because these assets can also be deployed in construction work outside the water industry, it is possible for a number of competing civil engineering firms to offer a specialist service to, and yet exist independently of, any given water company. Traditionally, then, water authorities have entered into relationships with civil engineering contractors, and these relationships are regulated by a formal contractual framework.

The contract system has a long history in civil engineering. Such contracts have been used for major capital works, such as canals, irrigation schemes, roads, docks and bridges since at least the eighteenth century. Haswell and de Silva (1989, p. 1) note that the contract plays a crucial role in coordinating the key stages of such projects:

> The carrying through of a civil engineering project requires that its object should be first identified; then the scheme has to be planned and thereafter implemented . . . [the project's] ultimate realization requires the synthesis of three fundamental parties, namely the promoter, the engineer and the contractor. The creation of a contract requires the responsibilities, obligations and duties of these parties to be defined clearly and set out in such a manner that the project is brought into reality properly and with true economy.

After a water company has identified the need for a given project, the next stage is to design it. Before a reservoir can be built, for example, it must first be designed and specifications for building it must be set out. The design and specifications form the backbone of the contract between the water company and the civil engineering contractor. It can either be undertaken in house or contracted out. In Albion Water, this stage of the project takes place in three different ways. Sometimes the design and specifications of major capital projects is undertaken by an independent consulting engineer. Sometimes it is undertaken by Albion's in-house group of design consultants and project engineers. Sometimes the design of the project is contracted out to specialist firms along with the actual construction work. Reeve's (1990) discussion of the construction industry would lead us to predict that these variations would be a function of the different properties of the transaction. However, whilst this is the case in some instances, there are also historical reasons for this diversity, and these are set out below.

Before the 1974 Water Act, water supply and sewerage were the responsibility of a large number of disparate bodies – district and parish councils, private water companies and so on. At this time, the design of such things as new reservoirs, dams and water treatment works was contracted out to consultants since councils and municipal authorities did not generally employ engineers or design consultants capable of undertaking this work. Thus, independent consulting engineers were used to design new works such as water towers or new treatment works. The consulting engineer would then also draw up contracts, which began with what is known as a performance specification (in the case of a water treatment works, for example, the contract would specify the quality of water which should leave the works). The consulting engineer would then go on to specify everything he or she felt was relevant to attaining that performance level. So, for example, the contract might go on to specify the depth, breadth and length of tanks, the materials to be employed and so on. This contract would then go out to tender as a bill of quantities, and contractors would price each item and come up with a fixed price quote for the work.

After their creation in 1974, the regional water authorities gradually developed in-house design departments to undertake this type of work, but a lot of design work is still contracted out. At Albion Water, the existence of an in-house design unit has not meant that independent consulting engineers are no longer used. Sometimes outside consultants are used because they have expertise in a specialist field which in-house consultants lack. A project engineer explains that 'We would not, for example, design an earth dam in this office, it would have to go to a specialist consultant.' But on the whole, outside consultants are used simply for peak lopping:

> If we have too much on and work needs doing, or if it happens to be a very large scheme that would take up too much of our resources to get out in a sensible time, then we use a consulting engineer . . . So [the scheme] might be within our experience, but we don't have the staff to actually do it, or if we did it nothing else would get done . . . We use outside consultants because we don't have the resources in manpower here to do all the work necessary.

The in-house group of design consultants and project engineers design new works and prepare contracts in the same way as outside consultants, and again, these contracts are then put out to tender as a bill of quantities. Albion compiles a list of contracting organizations with adequate financial and technical resources, and invites them to submit fixed price quotes for the work. The price of the job is thus determined through competitive tendering. Competition between large numbers of firms for the work means that, in theory, prices are set by market forces, so that even though Albion is buying something idiosyncratic, without a market value as such, it is protected against the contractor's opportunism.

As well as these two methods of contract design, Albion also uses what are known as 'design and construct contracts', where both the design and the construction of new works is contracted out. Albion began to use these contracts in the early 1980s. An Albion Water project engineer explains:

> It all started off with a reservoir which was designed by a consulting engineer and put out to tender. One contractor came back with an alternative tender, where he promised to design the box and build it and it would save us £60,000 . . . So it seemed (a) it was cheaper to build, which wasn't a very good comment on the design . . . and (b) we would spend less time in the design office, because we wouldn't actually be drawing the designs up, just checking someone else's design.

Albion defines the scope of the project, giving the contractor a performance specification, design criteria, and even perhaps outline drawings, and then allows the contractor to draw up the design details. The contractor bears more risk on a design and construct contract than he does on detailed specification contracts, because should the design fail to meet the performance specification it is his liability, rather than Albion's. However, because the work is not priced on a bill of quantities, and because fewer firms of contractors are in a position to enter into such contracts, the tendering process exerts less of a downward pressure on prices.

Just as the design stage of a major capital works project is sometimes within Albion's boundaries and sometimes the province of an outside agency, so also the project management stage is sometimes carried out by Albion personnel, and sometimes given to the contractor. But regardless of where new works are designed, and by whom they are managed, when Albion contracts out the construction of capital works schemes to a civil engineering contractor both parties enter into a transaction which is fraught with potential problems. The legal contract between the two parties is intended to guard against conflicts and problems by setting out clearly in advance the rights and duties of both sides.

The formal conditions of contract set out to coordinate and safeguard the interests of both the contractor and Albion Water. Albion contracts conform to the conditions of contract laid down by the Institution of Civil Engineers or the Institution of Mechanical and Electrical Engineers or the Joint Contract Tribunal, all of which are nationally recognized bodies. These bodies produce booklets which set out general conditions of contract which are supposed to be fair to both parties. Both Albion Water and the contracting firms agree to abide by these conditions. These conditions represent an acknowledgement by both parties that their transaction is a complex one, and that the terms of exchange can be affected by various contingencies. The contractor submits a fixed price tender, and this price is based upon a set of assumptions about the conditions under which the work will be executed. However, these conditions can sometimes change in a way which substantially raises the costs of carrying out the work, but which could not have been predicted in advance. Rather than penalizing the contractor for failing to predict the unpredictable, the conditions identify various 'unforeseen circumstances' under which the contractor can claim payments over and above that agreed in the contract. Contractors commit themselves not only to carrying out work for a fixed price, but also to completing that work within a given period. Again, they commit themselves on the basis of certain assumptions about the conditions under which they will work. The conditions of contract also contain a clause which states that contractors may apply for extensions if unforeseen circumstances delay the progress of a job. These conditions also benefit Albion Water. If they did not exist to protect the contractor, he would be forced to build the risks into his price. By Albion's agreeing to such conditions, the transaction can be carried out more cheaply. Moreover, there are clauses which specifically protect Albion Water's interests. They set out the conditions under which a contractor should pay liquidated damages to Albion, e.g. if Albion incurs costs because the contractor is late in completing work.

The conditions of contract lay down the procedure to follow when disputes arise. To facilitate the adjudication of disputes, both parties are directed to keep records of job times, and contractors are instructed to keep detailed records of labour, materials and plant employed on a job. Where contracts have been designed by outside consultants, disputes are first referred to the consulting engineer involved in the design of the contract. Where they have been designed in house or by the contractor concerned, disputes must first be examined by senior managers from both firms. If initial discussions fail to resolve the dispute to the satisfaction of both parties, the conditions of contract specify what type of dispute can or should then be referred to outside arbitration.

To summarize, contracts specifying work are put out to tender, and both parties agree to abide by a formal code of contract which sets out when and how the terms of exchange between them may be varied. Likewise, procedures for dealing with any dispute between Albion Water and the contractor about the interpretation of contract, or conditions of contract are formally prescribed. However, as Durkheim (1960, p. 211) observed, 'everything in the contract is not contractual', and problems arise because the conditions of contract themselves are open to inter-pretation and dispute. And though formal structures exist to adjudicate over such disputes, in reality there are often reasons for side-stepping such structures. The costs of arbitration or litigation are often prohibitively high, and in any case, if there is an imbalance of power, the weaker party is unlikely to resort to tactics which will destroy the relationship. Therefore alternative means of resolving disputes must be sought. In other words, though in theory these formal procedures govern the relationship between Albion and its contractors, in practice, because of the limitations of the formal framework, the relationship is also regulated by informal conven-tions and procedures. The following section explores these limitations in more depth.

The Limits of the Formal Framework

Even where a contract gives detailed specification on the one hand, and a fixed price quote on the other, there is room for dispute and dissatis-faction on both sides. Sometimes this is simply because specifications are incomplete. The consultant might, for instance, have failed to recognize the significance of a particular aspect of the construction. He may not specify precisely which make of pump should be installed in a works, and the contractor might then install a pump which he considers appropriate, but which Albion does not. The contractor might argue that the suitability of the pump is a subjective judgement, and besides, it is Albion's liability, since Albion failed to make precise specifications. Albion might retort that the pump installed by the contractor stops the works from conforming to the overall performance specification, and that therefore the contractor has failed to deliver his side of the bargain.

The same sorts of problem can arise with design and construct contracts. Albion gives the contractor a performance specification and it is then up to him to design and build the works. Albion, however, includes various provisos about the design. It might, for example, specify the depths of foundations, or the type of materials to be used. If Albion does not make such detailed specifications, it is up to the contractor to interpret the overall performance specification as he thinks best. The contractor's view does not always coincide with Albion Water's. A project engineer comments:

> We had a case of a reservoir where the contractor came up with a floor thickness of only five inches of concrete. It was designed according to the contract because the contract hadn't specified the thickness, so it was down to him to interpret. He was designing it, he was taking the risk supposedly. But five inches, you know intuitively this is too thin. So Albion had to spend a lot of money checking the foundations, getting different opinions in and so on.

Because the conditions of contract can only give general guidelines about where it is legitimate for the client to adjust or vary specifications, rather than identify all possible eventualities, interpreting the conditions is often a subjective process. Even where specification of the works itself is adequate, unforeseen circumstances can intrude, making the construction of that works a lengthier or more expensive process than was anticipated. The contractor will then want to renegotiate payment, for he will argue that the job is significantly different from the job he contracted to do at the given price. Thus he will make claims for payments over and above the agreed price. The project engineer observes:

> The classic one you get is what we call a Clause 12 claim, and that is one that relates to unforeseen circumstances. Before you commission the work you do a site investigation, and to the best of your knowledge you

tell the contractor what sort of ground is there, what he's going to have
to dig out. Then he comes across something which is different.

The contractor then argues that if he had known how bad the ground
was, he would have submitted a higher tender, and that if Albion had
known how bad the ground was, it would have accepted it. Therefore,
Albion should make good the difference. Whilst the conditions of contract
give guidelines about which circumstances are to count as 'unforeseeable',
because not all possible contingencies can be specified in advance there is
room for debate as to whether or not the contractor should have predicted
a given eventuality.

The conditions of contract are similarly open to interpretation when
it comes to claims for extensions. Because the contract commits the contractor not only to a fixed price, but also to a set deadline, there is a
clause which allows the contractor to claim an extension if he is delayed
by unforeseeable circumstances or circumstances beyond his control. The
most common (and the most contentious) claims rest on abnormal weather
conditions. There is room for debate as to how bad weather has to be
before it affects work, and as to how long bad weather has delayed the work
by. Once again these conditions have to be interpreted. Moreover, even
if it can be demonstrated that the delay occurred through the contractor's
negligence, Albion has to prove that loss has been incurred before it can
claim liquidated damages. This is also problematic and rests as much on
subjective judgements as on objective criteria.

In short, because the conditions of contract cannot specify every possible contingency, and must therefore be interpreted, contracting is as much
a social process of dispute and negotiation as it is a formal, legalistic one.
The subjective element of the transaction cannot be written out by the
contract, and a reference book for civil engineers clearly illustrates how,
in the final instance, claims are evaluated subjectively: '[O]ne can have
no sympathy with spurious claims: cupidity for its own sake is unaccept-
able. Genuine claims are, of course, a different matter' (Haswell and de
Silva, 1989, p. 4). Albion's judgement as to whether a claim is 'spurious'
or 'genuine' and whether a contractor is acting with cupidity is hardly
likely to coincide with the contractor's view. This means that as soon as
a contractor submits a claim, a conflict of interests exists which often
cannot be arbitrated through reference to the formal rules alone. An
Albion Water project engineer notes that some firms are more likely to
submit claims than others. Where some firms are prepared to build for
the price that is in the document, others 'look for every excuse possible'

to claim payments over and above those agreed in the first place. These 'claims-conscious' firms 'come in with a low price and then they make their profit on the claims'. The more claims a contractor submits, the more adversarial the relationship between the two parties becomes:

> Once he starts, you start getting your little black book out and thinking you'll play swings and roundabouts. You think, 'If he claims for that, I'll claim for this', and it's a silly way to go on . . . The paperwork alone costs a lot of money.

Indeed this is partly why a claims-conscious contractor is such a thorn in Albion's side. Although the conditions of contract specify a procedure to follow if Albion agrees, in principle, that a contractor can claim for extra time, or for payment over and above that agreed in the contract, actually settling a claim is a difficult process. One problem is that the conditions of contract direct the contractor to produce detailed records of time, materials, labour, plant hire and so on, to justify the claim. Yet, in the words of an Albion project engineer:

> Needless to say records are seldom perfect, they're seldom adequate. So at the end of the day you have to form a judgement. You sort of say, he's claiming £60 000 for something, and you've done your own sums and come up with £40 000, so you end up in a bizarre bargaining process, where you might end up allowing £42 500 or £47 000 or £50 000.

Prior to privatization, like other public sector bodies, the regional water authorities relied heavily on outside agents to assist with disputes over claims. Since their inception, local authorities and public utilities have contracted out a great deal of work to civil engineering firms, and a method of resolving disputes evolved over the years, which, though not laid down in the conditions of contract, has generally been regarded as the accepted procedure. It was noted above that because the various bodies responsible for water services did not have their own 'in-house' design engineers the design of new works was contracted out to consulting engineers. The consulting engineer continued to play a role after the contract he had designed had been put out to tender, giving advice on the interpretation of the contract, and adjudicating disputes. Typically, the consulting engineer was well respected and trusted by client and contractor alike, yet still he was in a 'curious position', whereby, as an Albion Water manager explains:

> On the one hand he was designing something for and on behalf of a client, and yet when it came to actually adjudicating on the contract he had to play honest broker between the client and the contractor. The contract would be between the contractor and the client to construct work designed by the engineer, and he had to sit on the fence and play honest broker. So if he had made a mistake and it was going to cost his client say £50 000 he was in a very difficult position.

The informal and arbitrary way in which the consulting engineer settled disputes is illustrated by the following apocryphal tale:

> There's a story about a fellow who was the well-respected engineer of the London County Council. This was pre-war, when things were much more gentlemanly. There was a contractor who made a claim. Fine. So they had a meeting. The contractor came in and the engineer said, 'OK Charlie, what's this you're on about?' The contractor says, 'I want £100 000.' The engineer says, 'You can have £50 000.' The contractor says, 'All right Bill, you're on.' And they shake hands and go and have lunch.

Although consulting engineers still do sometimes play this role in the public sector, the system is changing. The Department of Transport, for example, has virtually eliminated the role of the consulting engineer in its highway contracts. Previously, the consulting engineer was authorized to vary the contract on behalf of his client. He would be unwise to commit his client to any substantial increase in expenditure without first having consulted, but he was within his legal rights to do so. This right to vary the contract has been withdrawn by the Department of Transport, which now retains control. An Albion engineer argues that the consulting engineer's role has changed 'because people were beginning to distrust the engineer, to question whether anyone could really sit on the fence and arbitrate fairly between the two parties'. But within Albion Water, the decreasing reliance on consulting engineers is not simply a consequence of distrust. It has also been facilitated by the organization's growing capacity to design contracts in house.

When water supply and recovery were under the control of numerous district councils, there was no one qualified to check the overall design of a scheme, or to determine whether or not contractors' claims were justified. With the formation of the regional water authorities, larger and larger design groups were developed which enabled the authorities not only to design schemes themselves, but also to make better informed judgements as to the validity of contractors' claims. The role of the consulting engineer has not yet been totally eclipsed, but the trend is in this direction and increasingly it is the client, rather than an independent engineer, who says whether or not the contractor's claims will be accepted. Albion managers and engineers argue that this trend is partly a consequence of the increasingly competitive economic environment for contractors and increasingly tight financial control over the regional water authorities throughout the 1980s. Contractors are said to have become more 'claims conscious' throughout this decade. Albion Water, on the other hand, has not only become better informed about the nature and validity of claims, but has also been under far greater pressure to keep costs down. An Albion project engineer describes the current situation as a 'dog eat dog world', and argues that in such a world, it is imperative that Albion should make its own decisions about whether or not to accept claims. This role can no longer be left to an outside consulting engineer. But without the consulting engineer to umpire, disputes over claims must either be referred to arbitration, or else be resolved through informal discussions between client and contractor.

It might be predicted that with increasingly 'claims-conscious' contractors, and with the loss of the consulting engineer as independent referee, Albion and its contractors would have increasing resort to legal arbitration. However, the cost of arbitration is prohibitive to Albion and contractors alike. As an Albion manager puts it, 'arbitration is extraordinarily expensive, it's an absolute nightmare, costs a fortune and . . . the only winners are the legal people'. If Albion goes to arbitration over a claim and loses, it has to pay not only the claim itself and its own legal fees, but also the plaintiff's legal fees. Obviously, a contractor who went to arbitration and lost would have to pay Albion's legal fees, and the same manager comments that whilst the large construction companies could bear the risk, 'for small and medium firms, it could wipe them out'. High costs exert a powerful pressure on both client and contractor to seek a settlement outside court, through informal channels. An Albion manager suggests that for contractors, the costs of arbitration can amount to an inducement to write the claim off, 'even if Albion were being evidently unreasonable'.

Albion Water managers and engineers argue that this does not mean that Albion has *carte blanche* to resist reasonable and justifiable claims, for if Albion refused to negotiate, contractors would not tender for future work. With certain types of highly specialist capital works projects, this provides a strong incentive to Albion to moderate its behaviour. There is not a limitless supply of firms with the technical competence and wherewithal to build reservoirs, for example, 'So there are checks and balances, unreasonable behaviour doesn't pay either side.' What is striking is that these checks and balances are not, and cannot be, built into the formal contractual framework. Instead they are the outcome of informal agreements and negotiations, and a tacit understanding of the balance of power between the two parties.

It was noted above that the institutional economics literature explains the nature of relationships between firms, and the governance structures used to regulate those relationships, through reference to the properties of the transaction alone. This is in part because propositions are generally advanced on a *ceteris paribus* basis. In the real world, however, wider economic, political and institutional factors impact on the way in which parties deal with non-contractual elements of their relationship and the governance structures they employ, and this point is well illustrated by recent changes to the relationship between Albion Water and the firms of civil engineering contractors they employ.

Changes to Contractual Relations

It has already been shown that the formal and informal procedures for arbitrating contracts are changing, with Albion Water relying less and less upon outside consulting engineers to draw up contracts and to arbitrate disputes, and that this is primarily because the economic climate for both Albion and civil engineering contractors is less favourable than it was until the early 1980s. Recession in the civil engineering industry shifts the balance of power between Albion and contractors, and this affects Albion's relative preference for different types of contracts. In the past, design and construct contracts were seen as a way of tapping specialist design knowledge and minimizing problems with interpretation of specifications. These contracts were given to large civil engineering firms, which had their own in-house design groups, so that those designing the project and those actually constructing it were working for the same organization. The attractions of this type of contract are now decreasing, for the following reasons.

First, in recent years, civil engineering firms have made changes to their own internal organization which have made design and construct contracts a less appealing option to Albion. As in other sectors, recession and increased competition in the civil engineering industry have led firms to decentralize their activities. Increasingly, civil engineering firms are putting the design part of the contract out to smaller firms of design consultants, rather than undertaking the work in house. This means that the continuity between design and implementation, which made design and construct contracts so effective, is lost. Albion therefore finds it increasingly necessary to examine designs closely and to try to anticipate any possible problems of interpretation itself, rather than leaving these tasks to the contractor.

Second, the contracts become more expensive when both client and contractor are under financial pressure, because the client has to devote more resources to 'covering its back' when money is tight. Initial specifications have always been important, since design and construct contractors have full responsibility for the design of the system and the client can only intervene if the contractor is perceived to be engaging in bad engineering practice. During relatively prosperous periods, both parties are prepared to allow a little leeway. The contractor is willing to make adjustments, and does not stick to the letter of the contract, and likewise the client is prepared to be more flexible. When both parties are desperately trying to keep their costs down, no quarter can be shown. In such circumstances, the only way to ensure that the contractor comes up with exactly the design of the client's choice is to spend a great deal of time producing and checking detailed initial specifications. There comes a point when this is almost as costly as drawing up the entire design. As a consequence, Albion management are increasingly seeing in-house design as the most cost-effective option.

Wider economic trends also affect the relationship between client and contractor in other ways. In times of recession when competition between firms of contractors is high, there is greater pressure on contractors to put in ever lower tenders. One way in which contractors can do this is to stop building so much risk into their prices. They begin to price each item on the bill of quantities assuming that the work will be done under optimum conditions. If they then find themselves undertaking the work in less than optimum conditions, they are forced to try to make good their losses by submitting claims for unforeseen circumstances. The lower the tender, the more likely it is that a contractor will seek *ex gratia* payments, which then leads to a more adversarial relationship between the two parties. Finally, in a less favourable economic climate, contractors seek to reduce their costs and overheads by subcontracting. This trend is also troublesome for Albion. A project engineer explains:

> When the main contractor uses subcontractors it does lead to problems
> . . . I think they've adopted this approach because they had so much
> trouble laying off labour during the lean times. We would too, of course,
> but again we've passed that aggravation on, but it does cause problems
> . . . I've got a firm of contractors from the Midlands working on a little
> pumping station at the moment. They're using subcontractors to do the
> work and they are never on site and they therefore can't control all the
> problems with the subcontractors. It's a lot of trouble for us.

These sorts of problems increase the tensions between Albion and its contractors, as quality of work falls and contractors experience difficulty in meeting deadlines.

Ceteris paribus, the boundaries of the firm may be affected by the properties of the transaction. But in the real world, they are also affected by the broader economic climate in which the transaction takes place. Moreover, the nature of the relationship between the two parties is not simply a consequence of the type of transaction in which they engage, but is also affected by wider economic and political factors. Over the past decade costly and inconvenient disputes over interpretation of contract have increased as both parties have come under increasing pressure to keep costs down. This pressure brings conflicts of interest between client and contractor, which may lie dormant during boom periods, to the fore.

The limits of contracts become increasingly visible when both parties are squabbling over a cake that is diminishing in size. Contracts are necessarily incomplete (Durkheim, 1960; Fox, 1974; Williamson, 1985). The fallibility of those who design the contract means that it often will not cover everything the client wants. Besides which, without $20:20$ foresight, the client is likely to want to make certain adjustments and modifications to the specifications during the course of the contract. The contract cannot cover every single possible contingency which might arise during the course of the contract, so there is always the risk that some unforeseen circumstance will arise that substantially alters the cost of carrying out the work or the time in which it can be completed. This risk is a source of antagonism between the two parties, neither of whom wish to shoulder it without adjusting prices in their favour to insure against all eventualities. During a recession both parties will resist such price adjustments.

Fixed-price tendering represents an attempt to make the contractor shoulder this risk. Other forms of contractual relationships represent different ways of apportioning this risk. Cost reimbursement contracts and project management partnerships, for instance, attempt to spread the risk more evenly between the two parties and therefore encourage less adversarial relationships. Alternatively, disputes over specifications and claims could be avoided through the use of in-house construction groups. As a direct employer, the client would be firmly in control and could make adjustments to specifications with ease. In theory, where the parties are hierarchically organized rather than meeting across a market, there should be no fear of opportunistic pricing (Williamson, 1985). Yet none of these possible ways of minimizing disputes over contracts is seen as cost effective or efficient for Albion. The fluctuating volume of capital works militates against the continual employment of a direct labour group large enough to cope with peaks, and thus expanding the direct labour force is not seen as an economically viable option. Forging a closer relationship with one particular contractor may reduce the costs associated with disputes and make for greater flexibility and speed of 'output', but it also means that the competitive pressure on prices is removed. The chosen contractor is insulated from the full weight of market forces, and can accordingly raise prices. Likewise, cost reimbursement contracts are seen as providing too much insulation from competitive pressures. Albion therefore prefers to use fixed price contracts, despite the inconvenience and expense of claims and counterclaims. Managers accept that the relationship between Albion and contractors is essentially adversarial, and that competition forces contractors to 'cut tenders to the bone' in order to win the contract, and that both these factors increase the likelihood of claims being made and disputes arising. They work on the principle that even with numerous claims, and a great deal of time spent processing and debating them, the lowest tenderer is unlikely to work out as more expensive than the second lowest. As a project engineer points out:

> It goes back to the question of accepting the lowest tender . . . The second lowest is generally at least 5% more than the lowest. Now clearly, 5% on a million pounds is a considerable sum . . . You'd have to have £50 000 worth of claims on the job before you reached the next tenderer, and you can't be certain he won't make any claims at all, so there is that margin.

The theory is that the costs associated with this type of transaction are less than would be incurred by any alternative, and in the context of tighter financial control throughout the 1980s and of the new pressure to make and increase profits, cost cutting is Albion Water management's prime concern. Whether this approach is efficient as a long-term strategy is another question. The point is that Albion is not only constrained by the properties of the transactions it makes; it must also choose where to define its boundaries and how to conduct its relationship with contractors in a specific economic and political setting. This point is even more clearly illustrated by Albion's relationship with its period main-laying contractors.

The Period Main-laying Contract

When Albion contracts out capital works schemes, it is handing whole, discrete chunks of work over to the contractor. Though contractual specification is incomplete, it refers to an identifiable unit of work, which has been separated out from Albion's 'core' activities, and the contractor has a fairly clear idea in advance how much work he is undertaking. Albion's supply department also contracts out a portion of its pipe-laying work on what is known as a period contract. This is a variant of fixed-term contracting and quite different from capital works contracting. Rather than a period main-laying contractor undertaking a distinct function or part of the production process, his workers work alongside Albion's direct labour on Albion's 'core', firm-specific, recurring activities. The period main-laying contractors essentially sublet labour to Albion on an 'as and when' basis. When a contractor bids for the period main-laying contract (PMC), all he is bidding for is the opportunity to be given the peaks in Albion's workload as they crop up. Just as Albion cannot predict the volume of work that will go to the contractor in a year, neither can it predict the type of jobs that will go to him. Albion therefore specifies in advance all the tasks and jobs that *might possibly* come up during a given period, and asks the contractor to submit a fixed price quote for each one. The contractor does not bid for a predetermined volume of work, nor for a specific job or jobs. Instead he bids for the right to be given work, at a fixed price, as and when it comes up.

The rationale behind the use of the period contract is examined in more detail in the following chapter, but essentially it is designed to give Albion Water three types of flexibility: numerical flexibility in terms of hire and fire; financial flexibility in that it allows Albion to renegotiate prices at fixed intervals ('flexibility to be competitive each year or two years when we change them'); and flexibility of deployment:

Going to tender for every little job, or in an emergency like a drought, takes a lot of time and trouble . . . Using the PMC you can get to work within the week . . . It's labour on tap, and all the rates are agreed.

In short, what Albion wants is to have a pool of labour there for the asking, labour that is sufficiently conversant with the water industry to be able to supplement direct labour, yet which can be taken on and dropped as demand dictates, and the contractual framework which regulates the relationship between the two firms is necessarily a complex one.

The PMC consists of two documents: a schedule of rates, and the conditions of contract. The schedule of rates specifies all the items of work that a contractor might potentially be required to undertake. The detailed nature of the specification is illustrated by the fact that, in all, 152 different items of excavation and pipe-laying work, 190 items of work concerned with fittings and valves, 122 general and miscellaneous items, 94 items concerned with trench reinstatement, and 44 items concerned with laying service pipes are specified. Contractors are required to submit fixed price quotes for each item. The conditions of contract, like those pertaining to capital works contracts, specify how such work must be undertaken and under what circumstances the contractor may vary the fixed prices he has quoted. However, unlike the capital works contracts, the PMC is no longer based upon the Institution of Civil Engineers code of contract. Instead, in 1984, Albion Water drew up its own, tighter conditions. As well as clauses referring to acts of God, riots, and so on, which might prevent the contractor from executing work, Albion's new conditions attempt to guard more closely against inadequacies or shortfalls in specifications by setting out circumstances under which a contractor can make claims for additional payments, over and above the fixed prices he has quoted.

These clauses state that the contractor can claim extra payments if and when 'adverse conditions' prevail. Thus if the contractor encounters 'any condition . . . or any . . . circumstance which . . . could not reasonably have been foreseen by an experienced contractor at the time of tender', and incurs costs because of such conditions or circumstances, he is entitled 'to recover from the employer so much of such cost as is reasonable'. Likewise, if the contractor feels that any aspect of the work he is asked to carry out cannot 'fairly be covered by the rates and prices in the Schedule or by the new rates set by the Engineer', he can request the Albion engineer's permission to carry out work on a day rate, which he will have specified in advance, when tendering for the contract. Negotiations over such claims are carried out between the Albion engineer and the contractor, and the engineer's decision is final. Indeed, the conditions of contract accord the Albion engineer a paramount role in the interpretation of specifications and the supervision of works, and this is where the new conditions differ from those set out by the ICE. The Albion engineer has the authority to direct contractors to make good work he considers unsatisfactory at their own expense, to determine whether or not adverse conditions prevail, to set new rates, the hours of working and extent of overtime and night work, the replacement of any foreman or gang and so on. Moreover, 'the decision of the Engineer that any orders, directions or instructions are necessary or expedient may not be challenged when given and the contractor shall forthwith comply'.

Clearly, contractors are taking on substantial risks when they bid for the PMC. When a contractor tenders for the PMC, he is offering a *willingness* to execute any number of jobs, or parts of jobs, at a given schedule of rates. The contractor commits himself to undertake work at fixed prices; the client does not commit itself to providing him with a pre-set volume of work. If the contractor invests in plant and equipment in the anticipation of a high level of work, and then Albion Water does not provide the work, the contractor will be unable to amortize his investment. If he does not make the investment, and Albion does give him a large volume of work, he may have to get hold of plant, labour or equipment at short notice, and may therefore be unable to negotiate a good deal on it. If he finds that the fixed price he has quoted is too low, he is dependent on the generosity of an Albion engineer to make good his loss.

The period contract is designed specifically to pass the risk of fluctuating demand on to the contractor, and this means that the relationship between Albion and the contractor is characterized by both dependence and conflict. Albion depends on the contractor to undertake work over and above the capacity of direct labour, to furnish it with water-specific skills and knowledge as and when required. The contractor depends on Albion for work. This dependency means that it is in both parties' interests to maintain their relationship. However, their interests also conflict. It is in Albion's interests to get peaks in the workload carried out as cheaply as possible, and it is in the contractor's interests to hedge his bets against fluctuations by pushing his rates up as high as possible. It is in Albion's interests to use contract labour only for peak lopping, and it is in the contractor's interests to get as much work as possible from Albion. It is in Albion's interests to make the contractor shoulder as much risk as possible, and it is in the contractor's interests to resist this.

Given that the service and skills that a main-laying contractor provides cannot easily be redeployed in other industries, barring gas, so that in any given area the water company will be one of only two or three possible employers, there is little chance of competition between clients forcing Albion to adopt mutually agreeable conditions for fear of not being able to find tenderers for future work. Thus, as noted above, the risks taken on by the contractor are substantial. Albion managers acknowledge this, but they argue that the client–contractor relation remains a relation between equals, since the exchange is regulated through prices. Risks should be built into the prices that contractors offer on the schedule of rates – prices should always insure against a shortfall in work and/or problems with specifications. Using the same line of argument, the project engineer reasons that the shift from ICE conditions of contract to Albion's own conditions does not create an imbalance of power:

> If we produced our own conditions and they were totally biased in our favour then the contractor would just turf it out of the window and refuse to tender . . . One could argue that it's loaded in favour of the employer, but at the end of the day, the contractor can express his dislike of the conditions by loading up his rates . . . Whereas if you let him do exactly as he pleased, said 'Here's a job, do it as you like but finish in 20 weeks', he might put in a cheaper price. The more conditions and specifications you hammer him with . . . the higher his price will be.

In the view of Albion managers, the exchange is fair and self-regulating since the more risk that Albion Water makes the contractor shoulder, the higher his prices will be. Contractors do not view the relationship in the same light. They point out that pricing the schedule of rates is far from an exact science, since they cannot see the work in advance, nor are they guaranteed a particular volume of work. They can therefore only guess at the possible economies of scale that can be made. It is because the PMC commits the contractor to a fixed price without enabling him to make an informed assessment of the costs involved that one manager of a firm of contractors calls it 'the most iniquitous contract that anyone could possibly imagine'.

However, the PMC was not always viewed as partial. Period contracts were first introduced during the 1970s when the North Sea gas conversion was carried out, and when there was a boom in the pipe-laying industry more generally. At this time, the contract was seen as lucrative. This encouraged many firms of civil engineering contractors to move into pipe-laying. As the volume of pipe-laying work declined towards the end of the decade, competition between firms of contractors intensified. In this context, small to medium-sized firms of civil engineering contractors were forced to cut their rates in an attempt to win contracts with gas and water utilities. Cutting their rates effectively meant building less risk into their prices, which meant that, once they had secured a contract, their rates were often too low to cover the risks when they materialized. The contract would then get into trouble, yet contractors could not pull out mid-term without being blackballed by the utility. Many firms would therefore struggle along, making a loss, hoping to make good by jacking up the prices in the next round of tendering. With other firms desperate for the work, such a strategy was suicide, and many small and medium firms were driven into receivership.

The contractor's problems were intensified by the fact that the utilities, which were themselves under pressure from government to cut costs, sought to tighten up contracts during the 1980s, sealing up loopholes which had previously operated in the contractor's favour. In this way, throughout the early 1980s, the market winnowed out the weak, and increasingly only subsidiaries of very large construction groups, such as Laing, Wimpey and McAlpines, were left competing for period contracts in both the gas and water industries. As an Albion Water engineer commented, 'only the big companies . . . can carry the troughs'.

Increased competition between firms of contractors coupled with increasingly tight contracts which push contractors into shouldering more of the risk has led to two key sets of changes. First, as with capital works contractors, these developments have intensified the antagonism between client and contractor. Because intense competition encourages contractors to quote rates which provide inadequate insurance against the risks, they are increasingly likely to make appeals to the clauses of the contract which enable them to request variations to the rates, or claim *ex gratia* payments as a response to unforeseen circumstances. To give one fairly common instance, in older streets, where the road's foundations are sometimes made up of huge slabs of stone, the mechanical excavation of trenches can pull up the foundation stones, which then crack the edges of the trench. Reinstatement is then a far more time-consuming and costly business. If a contractor's prices on the schedule of rates have, in the words of a contractor's manager, 'a little fat on them', the contractor will carry the extra cost of reinstatement without complaint. If they have been forced to 'cut tenders to the bone', they will submit a claim for unforeseen circumstances.

Once again, the conditions of contract pertaining to such cases are open to interpretation, since it is impossible to specify against all contingencies. Could the problem with foundations '*reasonably* have been foreseen by an *experienced* contractor at the time of tender'? Does the problem make the 'contract rate . . . unreasonable or inapplicable'? Such questions inevitably lead to disputes, and once again there are pressures on the client and the contractor alike to settle informally. When claims are made on the basis of the adverse conditions clause, the formal contract states that the engineer's decision is final. If contractors do not accept his decision, they have recourse only to legal action. However, in practice neither party would want to totally rupture the contract in this way, or to incur all the costs associated with a legal battle. Thus, if the contractor holds out against the engineer's decision and pursues a claim, it is in Albion Water's interests to attempt to negotiate informally rather than stick to the letter of the contract and take sanctions against the contractor. Disputes begin 'on the ground', between contract agents and engineer's representatives, and if they are not resolved at this level, progressively more and more senior personnel on both sides are drawn in. An area manager of a firm of contractors comments:

> It's a complication and an aggravation you could well do without. We turn over, in one division alone, probably half a million pounds a year, and I have seen me have to get involved in arguments over £15. I've had to go to a meeting over £15. It's hardly worth the petrol, but . . . if we're in the right this time it helps us to negotiate later.

Likewise, if contractors claim compensation when the volume of work is well below that which was anticipated, informal compromises or settlements will be sought by Albion. For contractors and Albion alike, arbitration is prohibitively expensive and this exerts a powerful pressure to arrive at a compromise informally. But more importantly, Albion managers recognize that the power differential between Albion and these civil engineering contractors is so great that a contractor is unlikely ever to take Albion to court:

> It leaves sour grapes, and news would soon travel that this company had done that. Most contractors are very much 'Yes Sir, No Sir', because

they want to come back and get more work. But that doesn't mean they don't set their eyes on the highest profits possible, so they have to argue all the way. When the contracts manager can't get any further, it will be taken up by the directors of the firm. But hopefully it doesn't come to that. We always talk about settlement on the court steps and that is usually what happens. Sometimes it's been known to be 24 hours before the court case and we've called each other's bluff all the way there.

At the tendering stage, and in its terms of contract, Albion Water firmly states that payment is non-negotiable and that contractors must spread risk across the fixed rates in the schedule. In practice, however, the impossibility of specifying against all contingencies, combined with a recognition of the contractor's inability to price effectively in such conditions, means that Albion will enter into *ex post* negotiations. Yet these are negotiations in which Albion has very much the upper hand. Contractors cannot afford to totally rupture the relationship by taking formal action against Albion, and neither party wishes to incur all the costs associated with a legal battle. They thus enter into time-consuming and highly social processes of informal negotiation. In the current economic climate, it is necessary to do this with increasing frequency.

Increased competition and tighter contracts have not only led to a more adversarial relationship between Albion and its period main-laying contractors. These developments have also led to changes in work organization and employment practices within firms of contractors. These firms have adjusted to the new pressures by passing as much risk as possible on to those who work for them. Where civil engineering contractors have, in the past, tended to use their own direct labour, now they increasingly take on workers on a self-employed basis (see Chapter 5), or further subcontract work out to smaller firms. As with capital works contracts, this trend towards subcontract is not welcomed by Albion, and has increased the tensions between Albion and its contractors, as quality of work falls and contractors experience difficulty in meeting deadlines.

From a position of strength, then, Albion can impose conditions that would be impossible to secure during boom periods in the civil engineering industry. Yet taking advantage of this power has unintended consequences. Because civil engineering contractors operate in an increasingly 'cut-throat' world, a contractor's manager observes that their prime concern must be with cost cutting rather than quality of service. Albion's desire to purchase firm-specific skills and know-how and a good, responsive service is seen by contractors to be incompatible with its policy of accepting the lowest tender. As a contractor's manager comments, 'The Chairman of the Water Company wouldn't buy a Sierra and expect to get the same performance as a Jaguar, and it's exactly the same when it comes to contracting.' Again, Albion management accept that the relationship with contractors is adversarial, that competition forces contractors to 'cut tenders to the bone' in order to win the contract, and that both these factors encourage contractors to become 'claims conscious', which leads to frequent disputes. Again, management fiercely oppose any arrangement which protects contractors from market forces, and work on the principle that even with numerous claims, and a great deal of time spent processing and debating them, the lowest tenderer is unlikely to work out as more expensive than the second lowest.

Broader Theoretical Issues

This book is concerned with the variability of employment relations, and this variability is not just a consequence of the firm's decisions about direct employment, but is also a consequence of the firm's choices between direct and contract labour. It is therefore important to understand why firms draw their boundaries as they do; why some activities are undertaken by direct employees and hierarchically controlled whilst others take place across markets. At the start of this chapter it was noted that one of the merits of the institutional economics literature is its focus upon the variability of organizational forms. Diversity is explained through reference to transaction costs. It is argued that the 'efficient boundaries' of the firm are a function of the costs associated with different types of transaction and that these costs can be read off from the properties of the transaction itself. However, in general, this literature advances its claims on 'an all things being equal' basis. The aim of this chapter has been to explore contractual relations and governance structures in the real world. Such an exploration generates some rather different conclusions about the boundaries of the firm.

It would be foolish to deny that the boundaries of the firm are affected, to some extent, by the properties of the transactions in which it must engage. A one-off transaction, or the purchase of mass-market, standard goods, is hardly likely to provoke vertical integration. Yet neither is it always possible to 'read off' the regulation of transactions from their internal properties alone. For example, using Reeve's (1990) model of the construction industry, we would predict that the design stage of major capital works projects would fall outside Albion's boundaries only when the project is highly specialized. Whilst it is true that Albion does contract out highly specialist design work to appropriate design consultants, it is also true that non-specialized design work is contracted out when Albion's own in-house unit is overloaded with work. Staffing levels in Albion's design unit are very much affected by political and institutional factors. As a densely unionized, public sector organization which operates a no-redundancy policy, it has not been possible in the past for Albion to take on and drop design staff in response to fluctuations in the workload. In the run-up to privatization, and since privatization itself, Albion has made more use of temporary and agency workers in the design unit. But its ability to do this also rests on wider economic factors, for the existence of a pool of design consultants and engineers who are prepared to accept such temporary contracts is not a given. In happier times, these workers would be in short supply, so that again Albion would face a choice between offering direct employment, knowing that some design consultants would be underemployed during troughs in the workload, or contracting out peaks in the workload.

It is also important to note that decisions to contract out design and project management are affected by wider economic factors. What seems like an 'efficient boundary' during a prosperous period may become inefficient in a recession, even though the properties of the transaction remain unchanged. Thus, when recessionary pressures encourage contractors to subcontract the design stage of work, or to use subcontractors during the construction stage, Albion begins to consider redrawing the boundaries and bringing work back in house where it is easier to control. As will be seen in the following chapter, these points are even more salient with regard to the PMC, where the choice between contract and direct labour is inextricably linked to the broader economic, political and institutional climate. 'Efficient' governance structures likewise cannot be wholly dissociated from the context in which the transaction takes place. The transactions arising from Albion Water's major capital works projects are characterized, in Williamson's terms, by high asset specificity and occasional frequency. According to his schema, they are therefore most efficiently regulated by trilateral governance structures:

> Once the parties to [mixed and highly specific] transactions have
> entered into a contract, there are strong incentives to see the contract
> through to completion . . . The interests of the parties in sustaining

the relation are especially great for highly idiosyncratic transactions . . .
Rather than resorting immediately to court-ordered litigation – with its
transaction-rupturing features – third party *assistance* (arbitration) in
resolving disputes and evaluating performance is employed instead. (The
use of the architect as a relatively independent expert to determine the
content of form construction contracts is an example.) (Williamson,
1985, pp. 74–5)

Yet, as has been seen, in Albion Water there has been a trend away from
the reliance on third party assistance in resolving disputes and evaluating
contract performance. Once again, this trend cannot be understood except
in relation to issues of power and the wider economic climate. In a relatively gentle climate, when both client and contractor hold equally strong
bargaining positions, it makes sense to allow a third party to arbitrate.
When Albion found itself squeezed, first by tighter government financial
control and then by the need to rapidly increase profit margins in order
to be attractive to investors on privatization, and at the same time saw
civil engineering contractors facing a slump, the attractions of trilateral
governance faded. With more at stake, Albion no longer wished to accept
the decision of an outside consulting engineer. With contractors in a
weaker position, it no longer had to. In certain settings, then, Albion can
rely on economic compulsion forcing contractors to sustain the relation,
and does not need third party assistance to avoid rupturing the transaction.

The PMC is even more difficult to understand in these terms. To begin
with, given that the transaction involves frequent (daily) exchanges of a
highly asset-specific nature, Williamson's schema would suggest that
unified governance structures are most appropriate. Instead, a form of
bilateral governance is adopted. Within this, Williamson's description of
the 'contract as framework' appears to fit (he argues that 'Disputes are not
. . . routinely litigated' since litigation does not help parties to effect
adaptations or maintain continuity (Williamson, 1985, pp. 203–4). But
without a consideration of the relative bargaining power of the two parties,
the contractual framework itself, and the mode in which it is employed,
is incomprehensible. No contractor would take on the risks associated
with the PMC if an alternative source of work was available, and Albion
would not attempt to make the contractor shoulder these risks if it was
not secure in the knowledge that main-laying contractors are desperate
for work. Under these circumstances, the contractors' reluctance to
litigate is a measure of their vulnerability, rather than of the appropriate-
ness of the contractual framework.

It might be objected that none of these criticisms of the institutional economics literature is valid, since it only makes claims about efficiency on a *ceteris paribus* basis. It may well be that all things being equal, Albion Water would make efficiency gains if it did draw its boundaries solely on the basis of the properties of the transaction, and if it adopted the governance structures identified by Williamson as appropriate to particular types of transaction. In the real world, however, all things are not equal, and this is the key weakness of the transaction costs approach. The institutional economics literature challenges classical economic theory by substituting a detailed analysis of the inner workings of firms for the 'black box' model. But this detailed analysis is then located in a black box model of political economy. The properties of the transaction are paramount, and the economic, political and institutional setting in which the transaction takes place is ignored. Make or buy decisions and relations between firms are discussed as though they are unaffected by booms or slumps, bargaining power between firms, fiscal policy, unemployment levels, trade union density, labour legislation and so on.

The significance of the wider political economy for the organization of work and employment is one of the main themes of this book. The following chapter builds on this theme through an examination of manual work in Albion's supply function. It shows that just as the efficient boundaries of the firm and appropriate governance structures cannot be 'read off' from the properties of the transaction alone, neither can the nature and form of employment relations be understood simply as a function of the technical content of work.

Notes

1. Marx argues that in commodity production, any given unit of capital is dependent upon both dead and living labour. All firms are dependent on that previous or remote labour which has been incorporated into products which are necessary to their production process. They buy this labour after it has valorized raw materials purchased by another unit of capital. It is therefore dead labour, but it remains vital to the production process. Marx (1954, p. 182) observes that past and present labour are 'different and successive phases of one and the same process'. Using the example of spinning yarn, he continues:

The labour in the yarn is past labour, and it is a matter of no importance that the operations necessary for the production of its constituent elements were carried out at times which, referred to the present, are more remote than the final operation of spinning . . . [T]herefore the labour contained in the raw material and the instruments of labour can be treated just as if it were labour expended in an earlier stage of the spinning process, before the labour of actual spinning commenced.

This 'remoteness' is clearly a relative category. If the spinning firm vertically integrated the process of yarn production, then the labour in the yarn would also be living labour, valorizing that firm's raw materials. Likewise, what is remote labour to one organization is living labour to another. Marx's observation about products (as use values) can equally be applied to labour as a use value:

Whether a use value is to be regarded as raw material, as an instrument of labour, or as a product, this is determined entirely by its function in the labour process, by the position it there occupies: as this varies, so does its character. (Marx, 1954, p. 178)

Similarly, whether labour is regarded as past or previous, dead or living, remote or proximate to a particular firm is determined by the position it occupies in relation to that firm's labour process. These qualities are not carried by the worker; they simply express the relation between a given firm and the labour upon which it depends. More importantly, the firm's relative dependence on living and dead labour is not fixed but can be adjusted in response to changing circumstances.

5 VARIABILITY AT THE CORE

There is nothing new about the idea that different groups of workers experience very different forms of employment relations. As Hobsbawm (1964, p. 272) observes:

> the phrase 'aristocracy of labour' seems to have been used from the middle of the nineteenth century at least to describe certain distinctive upper strata of the working class, better paid, better treated and generally regarded as more 'respectable' and politically moderate than the mass of the proletariat.

Similarly, there has long been recognition of the existence of peripheral workers, who experience insecure, poorly paid employment often combined with atrocious working conditions. Yet, in the context of the simple evolutionary models of industrial society outlined in Chapter 1, the persistence, or even growth, of a peripheral workforce in the advanced industrial nations towards the end of the 1960s proved theoretically troublesome for both liberal theories of industrial society and labour-market economists. It became necessary to explain why small-scale production and vulnerable, insecure employment now appeared to be persistent, rather than transitory, features of capitalist economies.

Dualist theory linked variability at a macro level to the distribution of economic uncertainty (Doeringer and Piore, 1971; Berger and Piore, 1980; Piore, 1979), and more recently, the IMS 'flexible firm' model (Atkinson, 1984) has argued that dualism *within* organizations can be explained in much the same way. Unstable and saturated product markets combined with economic recession are held to have greatly increased management's desire for a number of forms of flexibility. The 'flexible firm' is said to seek functional flexibility in order to adjust to changing product markets and to enhance labour utilization; numerical flexibility in order to adjust labour-power levels to match demand; and pay flexibility in order to reward individual performance. The flexible firm literature identifies a tendency for firms to separate out 'core' and 'peripheral' activities, and assumes that 'core' and 'peripheral' work can be matched to a 'core' and 'peripheral' workforce. Management is thought to pursue functional flexibility with 'core' workers, who undertake the organization's 'key, firm-specific activities'. In exchange for offering functional flexibility, such workers are likely to enjoy not only better wages but also better promotion prospects, training opportunities and working conditions and greater job security than 'peripheral' workers who undertake 'marginal' activities and provide the firm with numerical flexibility.

The model thus posits a strong link between job content and employment relations; skilled workers undertaking 'core' tasks will enjoy very different employment relations to those experienced by unskilled workers carrying out 'peripheral' work. The institutional economics literature arrives at similar conclusions. Viewing employment as a transaction like any other, Williamson again argues that the properties of the transaction itself determine the form of the exchange and the governance structure appropriate to regulate it. Thus, Williamson asserts that an 'internal spot market' labour relation arises when 'neither workers nor firms have an efficiency interest in maintaining the association' because workers either provide no skills at all, or non-firm-specific skills. In this context, 'Workers can move between employers without loss of productivity, and firms can secure replacements without incurring start up costs. No special governance structure is thus devised to sustain the relation' (Williamson, 1985, p. 245). Conversely, when work entails a 'considerable amount of firm-specific learning', then an 'obligational market' labour relation will emerge. Here:

> Both firm and workers have an interest in maintaining the continuity of such employment relations. Procedural safeguards and monetary penalties, such as severance pay, will thus be devised to discourage arbitrary dismissal. And nonvested retirement and other benefits will accrue to such workers so as to discourage unwanted quits. (Williamson, 1985, p. 246)

Both the flexible firm literature and the institutional economics literature thus explain the variability of employment relations within firms as a consequence of firms dividing their work into 'core' (or firm-specific) and 'peripheral' (or non-firm-specific) activities, and entering into very different relations with the different groups of workers who undertake them. This would lead us to predict that there will be little variability in employment relations at the core of any given firm. It suggests that 'core' workers would provide functional, rather than numerical, flexibility, and would therefore enjoy a good package of wages and conditions. It suggests that the firm has an efficiency interest in maintaining the continuity of its relationship with such workers, and they would therefore enjoy a substantial degree of job security. This chapter takes the form of a case study of employment relations within one of Albion Water's core functions, water supply, and examines the pattern and nature of employment relations in relation to the flexible firm and institutional economics literature described above.

Three Forms of Employment Relation

It was noted in the previous chapter that Albion Water's supply function contracts out virtually all of its major capital works projects, and that its staple, recurrent workload consists of smaller capital projects (such as the laying of trunk mains and service pipes), undertaking new connections, and the routine and emergency maintenance of the supply system. The 'flexible firm' model might lead us to predict that these 'core' operations would be undertaken exclusively by directly employed personnel, enjoying a relatively good package of wages and benefits. As can be seen in Table 5.1, this is not the case. Rather, Albion uses three groups of workers to carry out supply work: direct employees, direct labour organizations (DLOs) and contract labour.

Direct Labour Units

The supply function directly employs 76 non-manual workers, 179 technicians and 104 manual and craft workers. Manual employees are divided into units which serve a given geographical area. They undertake the full range of the supply function's core activities, but the bulk of their time is spent on pipe-laying and routine and emergency maintenance work. In terms of the content of jobs, there is little specialization in supply work. Almost 95% of direct manual employees are taken on as 'operatives' (the remainder being classified as 'drivers' or occasionally

Table 5.1 *Distribution of 'Core' Work among Direct Employees, Contract Labour and Direct Labour Organizations*

Type of activity	Direct labour	Contract labour	Direct labour organization
Smaller capital works	Frequent	Frequent	Frequent
Routine pipe maintenance	Frequent	Frequent	Rare
Emergency work	Frequent	Occasional	Frequent

'labourers'), which means they can be asked to perform a wide variety of tasks and so offer flexibility within the supply function. Functional flexibility is also built into the employment contracts of Albion's manual employees, which state that they can be moved between the supply and recovery functions. In practice, however, management rarely makes use of this latter form of flexibility with these direct labour unit employees.[1]

Supply work basically consists of heavy manual labour in poor conditions. Trenches are generally dug, or at least finished, manually. The machinery which is used for cutting and reinstating tarmac is deafeningly loud, and when working in open fields men are often up to their waists in mud. Training is minimal. Operatives are given a two-week course in pipe-laying skills. 'That's it, two weeks. Once you've done that you know it all, or you're supposed to anyway', as one operative commented. Clearly, a job which requires no more than two weeks' formal training cannot meaningfully be described as skilled. Yet though supply operatives are at best semi-skilled, they do gradually acquire firm-specific knowledge which is of value to Albion. For instance, they become familiar with the detailed health regulations pertaining to water supply work, and they acquire knowledge of the location of the several hundred Albion sites and depots, which saves a great deal of time.

The supply function's direct manual employees work an eight-hour day. Their pay is made up of a basic weekly rate and bonus payments (which make up approximately one-third of their pay), plus a standby payment for the weeks they are on call at night and double time for any overtime worked. This averaged out at between £170 and £190 per week in 1989. From 1983 onwards, the amount of overtime worked has been progressively reduced as the out-of-hours service offered by Albion has been cut back in response to tighter government financial control. This has also meant that standby duty, and therefore standby payments, have been reduced. Supply work is typically carried out by two-man gangs, often on small sites, each gang doing sometimes as many as five different jobs in a day, across a wide geographical area. This means that continuous direct supervision would be extraordinarily costly. Albion thus supplements direct supervision with a tightly specified bonus scheme which is effectively used as an instrument of labour control. The supply manager explains that, 'A bonus scheme is necessary, because with . . . very mobile gangs . . . you can't have a foreman supervising all the time, therefore the only way you can reward their performance is by bonus schemes.'

Although he speaks of 'rewarding' employees, clearly the key issue is controlling employees, since in order to make this bonus, operatives have to fill out time sheets and account for every moment of their day. The bonus system, described by one supervisor as a 'ludicrously complex scheme', works in the following way. Albion's work study department conducted a study of all the work undertaken by direct labour, and developed a series of pre-set times for every element of each job. So, for example, tapping in a service pipe would be given a pre-set time of two hours, which allows for the excavation of a hole of an assumed size, and the actual tapping. Every day each gang is given a job card, specifying the work to be done and the target time for that work. If they are given a job with a pre-set time of three hours and that job is completed in three hours, they will score 100% performance. For this level of performance, employees receive 30% extra pay. If they complete the job in less than three hours, their performance rating and bonus payment rises accordingly.

The bonus scheme is made more complex because it is ill suited to supply work, which cannot readily be standardized. No two jobs are exactly alike. For example, one tapping might require the excavation of a six-foot trench, while another might only require a three-foot excavation. Management argues that jobs which exceed the target time, and jobs which can be done in less than the pre-set time, cancel each other out, so that performance over a week should average out at 100%. On some occasions, gangs are prevented from meeting pre-set times by eventualities beyond their control. They can then protect their bonus by making claims on the job sheets for extra, lost or diverted time. For instance, a gang might find on arrival that a job is significantly different from that specified on their job sheet. It might transpire that a main they had been told to dig for on the left-hand side of a highway was in fact on the right-hand side. They could then claim for the time spent digging a trench across the road looking for the main, and this would be measured against the pre-set time for digging a trench across a highway. Here, then, they could still make 100% performance. Alternatively, the gang might be prevented from meeting target times by circumstances for which there are no pre-set times against which performance can be measured, for instance if access to a site is obstructed by a private vehicle. In such cases, employees must claim the 'unmeasured' rate for lost time. 'Unmeasured' hours are paid at 90% of the bonus rate.

The basic pay is low, and the bonus scheme enables employees to make their wages up to a more acceptable level. For this reason, employees welcome the scheme. Although the target times set for jobs are seen as unrealistic, most employees do fairly well out of the scheme, so well in fact that management is considering changing the system, which is now seen to contribute to wage drift. When the scheme was designed, 117% performance was believed to be the maximum performance that could be achieved without endangering either man or plant. Increasingly, however, it has proved possible for employees to score ratings well over 117, which has caused wage drift. An operative notes:

> Our boss, district manager come down and said 'Something's got to be done about the bonus scheme', because we're all earning . . .
> performances like 120, 130, and management told us themselves that 117, which is the full bonus, was supposed to be impossible to get, and we were getting well above it.

Rather than this situation reflecting either the generosity or the efficacy of the bonus scheme, however, employees argue that it merely demonstrates their own ability to 'work the system':

> The only reason everyone's earning good bonus now is because they've had the scheme for a long time and everyone's learned how to fiddle them properly . . . You can earn more with a pen than you can with a shovel. You could sit in that van all day and do nothing, so long as you know how to fill in the sheets.

'Fiddling the books' or 'working the sheets' is laborious rather than dishonest. It involves the worker claiming time for every minute detail which slows progress and prevents him meeting target times. As one operative explained:

> You see you've got to account for every minute of the day . . . they can
> give you a job for six hours, but in actual fact it might take you eight.
> That's only four hours each, but you've got to fill in that time somehow
> to get your bonus. You don't actually fiddle the books, but it's the way
> you put it down.

It becomes necessary to account for time creatively, and to note down
everything, from going to find the owner of a vehicle obstructing access,
to opening and closing a field gate. Thus, a great deal of energy is
expended on filling in sheets.

In one sense, then, the bonus scheme is seen as financially advan-
tageous to the worker, yet at the same time, because of the level of paperwork involved in the scheme, and because the scheme is used as an
instrument of control, it is also the object of great hostility. The scheme
can be worked to the employees' advantage fairly easily by detailing their
each and every move, yet this very quality which makes the scheme easy to
'fiddle' is also resented as an indignity, an insulting waste of their time:
'Everything's got to be put down, that's the stupid thing . . . The supervisor . . . can see you're doing a day's work, you should get a day's
pay for it, not have to mess about with all that.' The scheme is supposed
to provide an incentive, but operatives pointed out that it can often have
the opposite effect: 'It works against them as well as for them. You go
out, do the hours, you've covered your bonus, well that's it. Why work
more?' If gangs are allocated several 'bad' jobs where they cannot meet
the target times, they begin to 'chase bonus', which consists both of
cutting corners in terms of standards and safety procedures, and of
spending more time working the sheets.

Albion Water's direct employees are highly unionized. Supply workers
are divided between NUPE and GMBATU, and, at present, their jobs
are protected by a no-redundancy agreement between the water authorities and the water unions negotiated at national level during the 1970s.
Despite this agreement, however, perhaps the most significant change
to have taken place in Albion Water as a whole over the past ten years
is the reduction in direct manual labour levels. Supply workers have
watched their numbers gradually dwindle, and several operatives commented that 'our jobs are no safer than the next man's'. In terms of
pensions, sickness, holiday pay and so on, Albion Water remains for
these men a 'good employer'. This was particularly true for those who
had come to Albion from the private, rather than the public, sector. But
such benefits are not enough to win a sense of loyalty or identification with

Albion as a firm. One operative remarked 'We don't come to work because we love Albion, we come to earn the money', and another commented:

> A lot of the managers seem to act like the leader of a hockey team, they say . . . 'Albion this and Albion that, Albion's got a great future, it's great what we've got in store'. Not for us, not for the likes of us. There's no great joy in digging holes and that's all we do.

In terms of job content, then, operatives carry out a range of relatively unskilled supply tasks; digging trenches, connecting up pipes, cutting and reinstating tarmac and so on. They are perhaps better described as multi-tasked than as functionally flexible, since the latter carries connotations of workers undertaking a range of more skilled work. In terms of conditions of employment, the supply function's direct labour does not fit neatly with the 'flexible firm' model of 'core' workers. Whilst employment security is high and the package of pension and other benefits is good, wages are poor, training, promotion and career opportunities are minimal, and supervision through the medium of the bonus scheme is tight, allowing employees little room for autonomous decision making, problem solving or the like.

Construction Group Labour

As well as using its own direct labour, the supply function also relies on Albion's construction groups to undertake a portion of its 'core' work. These construction groups evolved from labour units employed to do capital works by the old river authorities before the 1974 Water Act brought Albion Water into being. Albion kept these units separate from the supply function's direct labour units, and continued to deploy them primarily on capital works. However, the construction groups also fulfil a 'troubleshooter' role. They are used to peak shave if the volume of maintenance and emergency work suddenly increases. Construction group workers thus spend most of their time working on specialist construction jobs, but also occasionally undertake pipe-laying and routine and emergency maintenance work. In 1982 Albion management restructured the construction groups along the lines of the government's model for local authority DLOs. In order to demonstrate their competitiveness, the construction groups were required to submit tenders for a proportion of their work. Jobs which cost under £10 000 continued to be allocated in the standard, bureaucratic way, whilst jobs which cost over £50 000 had to be won entirely by competitive tender, as had 50% of jobs costing between £10 000 and £50 000. Between 1982 and 1988, the construction groups have won from 50% to 75% of their work through competitive tendering. In 1988, Albion's original construction groups were transferred across to the National Rivers Authority, and Albion set up two new construction groups, both of which were categorized as 'enterprise initiatives'. These are independently accountable units which must not only tender for in-house work, but also attempt to generate profits by winning construction work from outside agencies.

In terms of job content, construction group work is rather more varied than that of the supply function's direct labour. Construction group employees work across both supply and recovery functions. They are used to supplement direct labour on routine and emergency maintenance, and they also undertake more specialist emergency work (such as major bursts under highways which might involve shoring up the road). The group also carries out construction work, which involves a number of skills, including bricklaying, carpentry and so on. Because of the nature of their work, they tend to work in a team rather than two-man gangs. Again, there is little specialization and the unit does not acknowledge skill demarcations. As direct employees of Albion Water, construction group workers share the supply function's direct labour force's basic pay and conditions of employment. They work an eight-hour day, and their pay comprises a basic rate, a bonus payment plus any overtime worked. They are well unionized and are covered by the same pension scheme, and are entitled to the same holiday and sickness payments as the direct labour unit's employees. However, although the construction group uses a bonus system, it differs from that used in the direct labour units. The superintendent explains, 'Once we were set up to be monitored in isolation it was agreed that the men would have their bonus based on overall profitability of the unit.'

Instead of measuring performance against pretargeted job times, performance is simply pegged at 100, and the men received a fixed bonus of 30%. The benefits of this system for Albion Water are twofold. First, it vastly reduces the paperwork associated with the bonus scheme for both the employees and the supervisors. Second, it links payment to the unit's performance and this is seen as especially important for the new independently accountable enterprise construction groups.

Like direct labour unit employees, construction group workers under-take a wide range of tasks and provide Albion with a fairly high degree of firm-specific knowledge. However, where as direct labour unit employees seldom work across functions, construction group workers commonly do so, and in general they provide both a greater range of skills and more specialist skills than direct labour unit workers. In terms of employment conditions, construction group workers are low paid but enjoy a rela-tively good package of employment benefits, and as Albion Water direct employees they have been covered by the no-redundancy agreement. The degree of employment security they now enjoy is debatable. On privatization, the existing construction groups were transferred to the National Rivers Authority and new construction groups were set up as independently accountable enterprise initiatives. Management is con-sidering further separating out the new construction groups by trans-forming them into another subsidiary firm. As will be seen in Chapter 7, the job security of direct employees in the new independent profit centres is increasingly linked to the commercial success of their unit, and this tendency to make employment continuity conditional would probably be even more pronounced if the construction groups were organized by a wholly separate subsidiary firm.

Period Contract Labour

The supply function relies on one further group of workers to undertake 'core' activities, namely labour supplied by the period main-laying con-tractor. The proportion of contract to direct labour used in the supply function appears to have increased during the 1980s (Figure 5.1), although changes in accounting practices make it difficult to measure growth in this area precisely. For the past eight years, a firm which will be called Harrup's – one of the largest contractors to the water industry in the South – has been a period main-laying contractor to Albion Water. Harrup's is a subsidiary of a substantial construction group, and has a turnover of approximately £18 million from water main-laying work alone. Harrup's internal structure is as follows: it is divided into geo-graphical regions, each region headed by an area manager. Each region is then further subdivided, each subdivision being supervised by an area agent, accountable to the area manager. The agents are responsible for all aspects of Harrup's day-to-day work, including hiring and firing gangs, supervising their work and liaising with Albion engineers and

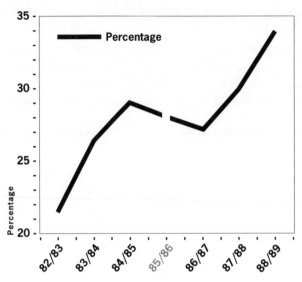

Figure 5.1 *Cost of hired and contracted services as a percentage of expenditure on all labour since 1983. Note: figures for 1985–1986 not available. Source: Albion Water Accounts 1984–1989.*

clerks of works. Contract labour undertakes virtually identical work to that carried out by Albion's direct labour. Both direct and contract labour undertake all aspects of pipe-laying work and routine maintenance as and when necessary. Contract labour is also used on emergency jobs if the volume of work is too great for direct labour to cope with. Yet whilst the tasks performed by contract and direct labour are comparable, their terms and conditions of employment are very different.

It was noted in Chapter 4 that the nature of the contract between Albion Water and Harrup's is such that even having won the PMC, Harrup's has no guaranteed, predetermined level of work. Instead the workload fluctuates, and so, therefore, does the demand for labour. A Harrup's area manager explains that these fluctuations make numerical flexibility vital to profitability. In order to achieve it, Harrup's operates a two-tier labour system. Workers are organized as gangs of two or three, headed by foremen, or 'gangers'. The gangers form Harrup's 'core' workforce, and Harrup's attempts to keep them on even during troughs. When the workload contracts, Harrup's sheds labourers rather than gangers, and will bring two or three gangers together into one gang until more work is available.

The Harrup's workforce is totally non-unionized. Clearly, this makes it easier for Harrup's to achieve the type of numerical flexibility described above. Over the past four or five years, in order to further enhance this flexibility, and in order to cut overheads, Harrup's has increasingly taken gangers on a self-employed basis, rather than as direct labour. This, the area manager argues, is a response to the increasingly 'cut-throat' environment in which contractors operate. Remaining profitable in the current economic climate is not easy for main-laying contractors. The area manager claims that pressure on prices has been so intense that Harrup's was submitting tenders for work in 1989 at the same prices offered in 1980. These price cuts cannot be achieved through investment since 'there is no new technology in this business other than a JCB'. They can only be sustained by cutting overheads and labour costs. Harrup's thus keeps overheads to a bare minimum. Where Albion has several layers of supervisory and managerial staff looking after their gangs, Harrup's has only an area agent and the area manager. The area manager has a small depot, but apart from this there are few fixed costs:

> Each main area that we're working on we get a Portakabin and a toilet and a telephone, and the agent in that area looks after all the gangs in that area from that portable sub-depot. He operates from there, he does all the booking, all the paper work, and he has to supervise the gangs as well.

The increasing use of self-employed gangers represents an attempt to reduce labour costs. To begin with, it cuts costs by removing Harrup's liability to make employer's national insurance contributions, and this saving is enhanced by the fact that self-employed gangers often employ their own labourers in a system similar to 'the lump' in the construction industry. Equally, Harrup's is not compelled to make statutory sickness and redundancy payments for self-employed gangers or their labourers. By taking gangers on as self-employed, rather than as direct labour, Harrup's is able to make cuts where it hurts profits least and to pass more risk on to the workforce, and this, the area manager argues, is how they remain viable. Increasingly in the water industry, then, risk is parcelled out down a long line of workers, with ever-decreasing continuity and security of employment. Albion passes the risk associated with fluctuating demand on to Harrup's, and, in that sense, as a Harrup's ganger remarks, 'We are the buffer between Albion's direct labour and unemployment.' Harrup's then parcels this insecurity out amongst its own workforce. For example, it will drop four labourers and bring four gangers together as two gangs when demand contracts. This means that, as one ganger acknowledged, 'The poor old labourers once again are getting the sticky end of it. They are like the buffer between the gangers and unemployment.' These trends within firms of civil engineering contractors are consonant with trends in the UK construction industry reported by Bresnen *et al.* (1985), and in the steel industry (Fevre, 1986, 1987), namely, increases in the number of self-employed workers in the industry and an increase in the proportion of work going to subcontractors, including labour-only subcontractors.

In terms of hourly rates, Harrup's gangs are better paid than Albion's direct employees. They work a nine-hour day; gangers are paid a day rate of £50, while the day rate for labourers is £40. There is no bonus system. The manager observes that Harrup's pays 'reasonable wages and we expect them to get a reasonable day's work from them'. Harrup's gangs also get even less direct supervision than Albion gangs, often as little as half an hour's supervision a day. Despite minimal supervision and no bonus scheme to act as a financial incentive, the area manager believes that Harrup's gangers work harder than Albion employees. He finds this puzzling: 'I don't know why they do. I wouldn't do it.' His agent finds the question less perplexing. Harrup's workers work harder because their livelihood depends upon it: 'The men have to work hard, because if they don't they won't stay with the contract . . . They'll just be got rid of . . . You really are there to make money, that's what it's about, and if you don't you're out.' Even though there is little direct supervision, each gang's performance is monitored, so that the agent knows immediately if someone is not working hard enough: 'I work out each gang's revenue and cost and see what they are doing. So although they're not supervised, we can tell if they're pulling their weight or not.'

The Harrup's manager argues that 'his' gangers are 'a different breed' from Albion Water's direct labour. They are predominantly Irish and are aged under 40. Most have employment histories in the construction industry, and are therefore used to a high level of job insecurity. The manager believed that despite working in 'atrocious' conditions, many of the men grow used to the lack of supervision and the outdoor work, to such a degree that 'If they do pack it in and go to work in a factory you'll often find after six months they come back, wanting a job outside. There's a freedom in the work that appeals to some people.' Some of the self-employed gangers themselves also believe that they are better off working for Harrup's on a self-employed basis than they would be as direct employees of Albion Water, both financially and in terms of the level of autonomy they experience at work. They claim that there are many advantages to their self-employed status. For example, in the words of one ganger, it allows them 'to be a bit of an entrepreneur'. The practice of employing their own labourers is seen as lucrative:

> I always have a boy working with me . . . I charge it up to Harrup's then
> take a cut. Most of us do it. Harrup's do have some of their own
> labourers, but you'd be a fool to use them . . . because they're paid
> direct by Harrup's, so of course you can't take your cut.

Harrup's pays £40 per day for a labourer. This ganger then took a cut of £40 per week out of the labourer's wages. Tax advantages are also believed to accrue from the fact that Harrup's does not supply working clothes or tools to self-employed gangers, and self-employed gangers sometimes supply their own vehicles. Larger plant or equipment can also be hired by the self-employed ganger and then charged up to Harrup's. On the whole, self-employed gangers view their position in relation to other forms of self-employment rather than in relation to direct employment, and this makes a more favourable comparison. Because they are paid on a day rate, rather than a piece rate, Harrup's does provide an element of security, however minimal. It is safer for these men to have Harrup's as an intermediary than it would be to try to win a contract from Albion directly:

> The thing is . . . if I have a good week, Harrup's do well. If I have a bad
> week, Harrup's do badly. If I was self-employed working on a price for
> Albion and I had a bad week, that would come out of my pocket. That's
> the difference between day work or on a price. It's like insurance . . .
> Harrup's take some of the risk.

Harrup's takes on a risk in terms of production time being lost or diverted during the hours a ganger works, but does not take on risk in terms of days that might be lost through ill health, holidays and so on. But by taking on this minimal level of risk, they make working for Harrup's as self-employed a more attractive option:

> The beauty of Harrup's for me is that by not being on a price I know
> exactly what I've got coming at the end of the week. If you're on a
> price, you've got to wait till the sheets have gone in, got signed, till
> they're priced up and submitted before they'll pay you . . . When I
> worked for meself I was up to three months behind on me money all the
> time. Plus the fact you're employing people, you've got things on hire.[2]

However, self-employed gangers also observe that there are disadvantages to their status. Apart from the possibility of suddenly being faced by very large tax bills, the main disadvantage of self-employment is simply that 'if you don't work, you don't get paid . . . when you're self-employed, you don't get sick'. For these men this is the definitive difference between the experience of self-employment and direct employment. Gangers also complain that Harrup's day rates have not risen for several years. This, they felt, was a consequence of the increasingly competitive environment in which civil engineering contractors now find themselves. When Harrup's cuts its prices to win contracts, it passes the cut on to its workforce. Yet despite these drawbacks, and despite their self-employed status, these gangers argue that provided you work hard, pipe-laying is not an especially insecure business to be in. They note that Albion Water will always have a need for contract labour to supplement their direct labour force, and that therefore there will always be a supply of work. One ganger commented 'I know it is insecure, and it might sound strange, but it is also secure if you see what I mean, because this work is always there to be done.' Continuity of employment is linked more to how hard working and efficient a gang is, rather than to their employment status:

> Security-wise I don't think you're any more secure being direct than you are self-employed. The tendency seems to be it's not so much on whether you're self-employed, it's more on the quality of your work . . . Harrup's aren't going to get rid of the gangs who are good.

Moreover, even though it is a highly competitive industry for the *firms* of civil engineering contractors, because such firms do not keep a large permanent labour force, *workers* in the industry can simply follow the contract from one firm to the next. As a ganger remarked, if Harrup's should lose the contract with Albion, 'We all find out more or less on the same day who's won the new contract and then we're all round there first thing in the morning.' In short, 'it don't matter who's got the contract, the work is there and so it's really a secure line of work to be in'. The economic survival of Harrup's, or whichever firm they happen to work for, is essentially irrelevant to agents, gangers and labourers, since they follow the contract rather than the fortunes of a particular firm.

In terms of the content of work, Harrup's gangers are multi-tasked. In boom periods there is rather more specialization within Harrup's; gangers carry out more skilled work, such as tappings and reinstatement, and labourers carry out the less skilled aspects of work. When the workload contracts, however, gangers carry out all facets of the work. In terms of employment conditions, Harrup's gangers are insecure, with no rights to non-statutory benefits, and not even rights to statutory benefits when they are self-employed. They receive higher hourly rates and less supervision than Albion Water employees, but work longer hours and their employment continuity is explicitly linked to high productivity. Table 5.2 summarizes the variety of employment relations entered into by Albion with the labour that undertakes its key, recurring, firm-specific activities.

Albion Water employs labour both directly and indirectly; it enters into both standard and non-standard relations. The degree of employment security associated with this work is virtually nil for Harrup's labourers, but relatively high for Albion's direct employees. Different payment systems and control strategies are employed, and the employment rights and benefits accorded to workers are polarized between the minimum imposed by the law and what is considered to be an above-average package. This variability of employment relations at the core is not a function of the content of work. The supply function does not divide its activities up into skilled and unskilled components and allocate it to different groups on that basis. Instead, all three groups of workers, to differing degrees, undertake all aspects of the supply function's recurring, staple tasks. The following section explores the rationale behind this three-pronged labour strategy.

The Rationale behind the Three-Pronged Labour Strategy

In order to understand why Albion Water adopts this three-pronged labour strategy, it is necessary to begin by examining the nature of supply work in more detail. It was noted in Chapter 4 that major capital investment schemes are irregular and require specialist plant and skills, and are therefore almost always contracted out in totality to specialist construction firms. Smaller capital investment schemes, e.g. laying new service pipes and trunk mains, on the other hand, form part of the supply function's recurring, staple activities and rely largely upon skills which are typically found within the water industry, such as pipe-laying. However, although overall the volume of such work is substantial, like all forms of supply work it fluctuates on a seasonal and even a weekly basis. To begin with, all pipe-laying and routine pipe maintenance work is cyclic, since frozen ground, bad weather and shorter days make it vastly more expensive to dig trenches during the winter. Second, Albion has to lay supply pipes to new housing, and the level of new connections varies according to level of development in the area at any given time, so that

Table 5.2 *Three Types of 'Core' Jobs and Employment*

	Direct labour	Direct labour organization	Contract labour
Job content			
Multi-tasked	Yes	Yes	Yes
Functional flexibility	No	Yes	No
Firm-specific skills	Yes	Yes	Yes
Employment			
Security	High	Changing	Low
Unionization	High	High	Low
Pensions, sick pay etc.	Relatively good package	Relatively good package	Legal minimum
Daily rate (1989)	About £33	About £33	About £50
Working day	8 hours	8 hours	9 hours

again, the volume of small capital schemes work fluctuates. Likewise, the level of work commissioned by outside agencies is unpredictable, and follows peaks and troughs in the construction industry in the area. Finally, the volume of emergency maintenance work is, by its very nature, unpredictable, although it tends to be greater during the winter when freezing temperatures can damage pipes, pumps and plant.

Clearly, the fact that supply work comes in peaks and troughs makes direct labour a costly option. If Albion directly employed enough workers to cope with the peaks, substantial numbers of them would be idle during troughs. Given Albion's no-redundancy agreement with the unions, there is little hope of simply laying off direct employees in response to contracting demand for labour. Thus, the attraction of the PMC is that it passes on the risk associated with fluctuating demand to the contractor. Moreover, contractors are exposed to market forces, which exert a downward pressure on prices. In other fields, competition between contractors might have drawbacks as well as benefits. For instance, by chopping and changing between contractors to get the cheapest price, the client may lose the advantage of working with a firm whose employees know and understand the client's specific needs and requirements. This is not the case with supply work. The fact that in the pipe-laying industry workers tend to follow the contracts, rather than staying with one particular firm means that, in the words of an Albion manager, the new contractor 'takes on the better gangs [from the contractor that lost the contract] and so we get that continuity'.

The benefits of this for Albion are considerable. Because pipe-laying workers follow contracts rather than following the fortunes of a particular firm, it is possible for Albion to use continuously the labour of good, reliable workers with a high degree of Albion-specific knowledge *without* having to give in return the package of employment rights and benefits normally associated with such a relationship. As another manager notes, 'Some of the [contractor's] gangers have been working for Albion for 10 years or more, without ever having been employed by us.' The on-the-job, firm-specific knowledge such men build up over the years is substantial, and valuable to Albion Water. Like direct employees, contract workers become familiar with health regulations, learn to identify problems and potential hazards, and build up knowledge of the area and the location of the numerous Albion sites and depots, all of which saves Albion time and expense. In these ways, then, contract labour and the numerical flexibility it affords would appear to be an attractive option for management.

However, other features of supply work make contract labour less appealing. To rely wholly on contract labour might enhance numerical flexibility, but it would also carry certain costs. This is because the supply function has to deal not only with routine maintenance but also with emergencies. If a trunk main bursts at two o'clock in the morning and begins to flood a street, Albion cannot simply leave it until normal working hours to deal with it. Moreover, emergencies can radically change Albion's priorities. A spate of burst pipes, for example, not only suddenly increases the volume of maintenance work, but also changes the level of priority attached to capital works and routine maintenance, since emergencies must be dealt with immediately. This has two main implications for the supply function: first, it needs a labour force which can provide a 24-hour service, and second, it needs to be able to rapidly redeploy labour power in response to new priorities. Both of these requirements militate against the use of contractors.

To begin with, it is extremely difficult to either draft or enforce a contract which provides a 24-hour emergency service or this crucial quality of responsiveness. Moreover, Albion managers argue that even if a contract could be designed to cover such eventualities and even if a reliable contractor could be found to undertake the work, because the level of work outside normal working hours is so high, the costs of using a contractor would be greater than that of using direct labour. Paying direct employees a standby allowance, plus overtime rates for the hours actually worked at night, is far less costly than paying a contractor to provide the same service. This is best illustrated by the fact that a Harrup's ganger will be paid almost double what an Albion Supply operative receives for night work, even before any charges Harrup's will add on, and before the administrative costs incurred by Albion are taken into consideration.

Just as there would be problems finding contractors who would provide a 24-hour service as cheaply as direct labour does, there are problems with getting contractors to respond rapidly to changing work priorities. In a direct employment relationship, the employee operates with what Williamson (1985, p. 249) terms a wide 'zone of acceptance'. Within broad limits, the employer can tell the direct employee what to do, and how, when and where to do it, on a daily, hourly, even a minute-by-minute basis. If an employer uses contract labour, it is necessary to specify all this in advance, and any changes to specifications have to be made through the framework of the contract. The employer does not directly supervise contract labour; control over contract labour is mediated through the contractor and his agents, and their priorities may differ from those of the ultimate employer. What this means in practice is that it is far more difficult to redeploy contract labour in response to shifting priorities than it is to redeploy direct employees. For example, Albion gives the contractor a work itinerary at the beginning of each week, and the contractor then arranges for his men to undertake the tasks. Changing the itinerary midweek creates problems. An Albion supervisor explains:

> Say the contractor was doing service work and I wanted to move his men off to an emergency. He will say, 'Who's going to pay me a fee to drag me off site to another site, and another fee when I come back and start doing tappings again?' Direct labour gives that much more flexibility to respond to crises. You can drag your own labour force off to do what you consider to be important, rather than have to go through the contractor to do it.

The fact that the supply function's direct labour operate within a 'wide zone of acceptance' facilitates the rapid redeployment of labour when priorities shift. Thus, direct labour not only enables Albion Water to provide a 24-hour emergency service at the lowest possible cost, but also furnishes the supply function with the ability to respond quickly and easily to shifting priorities. All this means that to rely wholly on either direct labour or contract labour would carry heavy costs, as well as benefits. By keeping a base of direct employees, a number just short of that required to cope with the supply function's workload during a trough period, and using contract labour to 'peak shave', Albion seeks to achieve both flexibility in terms of deploying labour, and numerical flexibility.

Although the period contractor provides a reserve of labour for Albion Water, there are certain circumstances in which Albion is reluctant to draw on it. The period contractor's prices for out-of-hours work are, in the words of one manager, 'exorbitant', and so contract labour is used for emergency work only when absolutely unavoidable. More significantly, Albion is unwilling to use the period contractor on high-risk jobs. Such jobs may require specialist skills and could prove time-consuming, and consequently if the period contractor was asked to price this kind of work on a schedule of rates, he would price it very high in order to cover against potential losses. It is here that the construction groups play a role.

Construction groups are organized in such a way as to be able to offer Albion a particular service more cost effectively than could either the supply function's direct labour force or outside contractors. Construction group workers are directly employed by Albion Water. The differences between construction and direct labour groups is in terms of the type of work they do, and how this is funded. Direct labour units spend approximately 60% of their time working on routine and emergency maintenance. Construction groups are numerically small, and work primarily on small capital work schemes. Because such schemes are easily delineated, defined and specified, they lend themselves far more readily to being contracted out than does maintenance work. Thus it has been possible for Albion to separate out some of the construction groups' work, and insist that it must be won through competitive tendering. Because they have to win a portion of their work through competitive tender, there is a far greater pressure for efficiency on construction groups than there is upon direct labour units, which are allocated all work in the standard, bureaucratic fashion. Although the construction group does not adhere strictly to procedures laid out in the government's Direct Labour Organization legislation, costs and efficiency have been monitored closely since 1982. Moreover, the construction groups regularly move across functional boundaries. They work for the supply and recovery functions, and until the National Rivers Authority took over responsibility for environmental functions they also worked for the environmental function. This means that overheads are spread out, and there is little likelihood of a shortfall of work leaving them idle.

The construction groups also add to Albion Water's capacity to provide an emergency service cheaply. As noted above, managers do not believe that contractors can be used cheaply or effectively in this area. However, maintaining a large enough direct labour force to cope with all potential emergency work is clearly expensive, and the construction groups play a role in reducing these costs. They are available for emergency work:

> We do repairs to bursts, mains and sewers or storm damage which can occur literally overnight. We're available literally at an hour's notice on the end of the phone, even at dead of night. Obviously to maintain a contractor on that footing would cost a lot of money.

Yet because the groups work across both the supply and recovery functions the emergency service they provide comes in cheaper than the direct labour units. The construction groups also add to the supply function's capacity to deploy labour flexibly in response to shifting priorities. The construction groups offer a supplementary source of labour which the supply function can draw upon as priorities change. The manager observes that 'It gives us another pool of skilled labour. They're skilled in most aspects of building and pipe-laying trades.' Thus, the groups provide a pool of labour which is on tap for both routine and emergency work, and this, the manager argues, gives Albion extra flexibility:

> By having them split off under a separate manager it gives more flexibility. They can be working on recovery works or supply works and we can use them for lop and peak in either function. It achieves flexibility in terms of moving people across functions.

Construction group labour is cheaper than contract labour in another respect. On awkward or dangerous jobs where risks are high, contractors build risk into their price. The close relationship between Albion and the construction groups means that the groups do not have to allow for risk in their tender, since Albion Water will protect the group should the job turn out to be vastly more expensive than expected. It is not uncommon for a contractor to quote twice the price tendered by the construction group for a high-risk job. The advantage for Albion is that if the risks fail to materialize, as is often the case, Albion has only paid for the work done, rather than having to pay an inflated price to protect a contractor from potential losses.

The employment relations and work organization in a core function described above raises a number of theoretical issues. To begin with, Albion's three-pronged labour strategy highlights the definitional problems raised by the flexible firm model's 'core–periphery' dichotomy. Pollert (1988, 1991) has argued that the core–periphery distinction employed by the flexible firm model is highly problematic. Certainly the three-prolonged labour strategy at Albion illustrates the fact that core operational activities cannot always be neatly matched with a 'core' workforce enjoying standard employment relations. Instead, employment relations at the core can vary. Also, the relative nature of the categories of 'core workers' and 'peripheral workers' is amply demonstrated by the Harrup's gangers, who are at the same time Albion's 'peripheral' workforce and Harrup's 'core' workers. Finally, the fact that Harrup's workers generally provide the same degree of firm-specific knowledge as direct employees and undertake a virtually identical range of tasks demonstrates that 'peripheral' status does not always derive from the technical content of work. Albion's three-prolonged labour strategy raises other theoretical issues which are considered below.

Skill Content, Asset Specificity and Employment Relations

It was noted in Chapter 1 that little explicit theoretical attention has been given to the variability of employment relations in contemporary capitalist economies, and that much management and industrial sociology literature works with a model of the employment relation which implicitly accords primacy to the technical content of work. Often it is the skill content of work which is assumed to determine the nature of the employment relation, which is why claims about 'enskilling' have often been accompanied by claims about a new deal for labour. Skill is, of course, a notoriously difficult concept to operationalize (the degree to which it is socially constructed and gendered, for example, has provoked much debate – see Phillips and Taylor (1980), Armstrong (1982), Cockburn

(1983), Dex (1985), Jenson (1989) and West (1990)). This may account for some of the problems experienced in matching skilled and unskilled workers to categories such as core and periphery or to secure and insecure employment. In this context, Williamson's stress on transaction costs and above all asset specificity, *firm-specific* skill or knowledge, might appear to add something new to the debate. For, as noted in the introduction, Williamson does not confine himself to considering transferable skills or formal qualifications, but also considers the effects of idiosyncratic human capital that can accrue during the course of employment on labour relations (Willamson, 1989, p. 143).

Yet Williamson's analysis is also difficult to apply to Albion Water's labour strategy. Not only is job content for contract and direct labour virtually identical, but further, because contract labour tends to follow the PMC rather than sticking with one firm of contractors, it typically offers Albion a considerable degree of firm-specific knowledge and skill. Indeed, some contract workers will have worked for Albion (albeit indirectly) for longer than some Albion direct employees. If a special governance structure, procedural safeguards and the like emerged directly as a consequence of asset specificity, as Williamson suggests, we would surely expect Albion to have as much of an interest in maintaining the continuity of employment relations with contract workers as with direct employees. Instead, we find that Albion has a casual relationship with contract workers (at least in the formal sense) precisely to avoid the costs imposed by the governance structure that has developed to safeguard direct employees' jobs. It might be objected that neither direct nor contract labour are highly skilled workers, and that the degree of firm-specific knowledge and skill they provide is not great enough to be a significant benefit to the firm. This would, of course, simply raise the question of why, if asset specificity determines the nature of employment relations, Albion should seek to maintain its relationship with unskilled, readily substitutable direct employees through an elaborate governance structure, retirement and other benefits, and so on.

Common sense tells us that there are advantages for an employer if an employee has a degree of firm-specific skill or knowledge. Productivity may be marginally enhanced simply by workers being acquainted with their co-workers, knowing the layout of the building, and so on. Yet it is not always possible to 'read off' employment relations from the degree of firm-specific skill or knowledge associated with particular jobs. For instance, the degree of employer-specific knowledge provided by the most routine assembly line worker (say, a person taking films out of envelopes and putting them on a conveyor belt to be taken to be processed) hardly seems greater than that provided by the casual farm worker cited by Williamson as an example of a worker who does not make employer-specific investments. But in Britain fruit pickers, for example, tend to be casually employed, and assembly line workers to be directly employed.

Nannies also provide an interesting example. Employers tend to value a long-term relationship with a particular nanny, and would not choose to take on a different nanny each day from a pool of casual labour. The nanny herself makes employer-specific 'investments' in terms of getting to know the child, the layout of the house, the family routine, and so on. Yet no elaborate governance structure has been developed to protect the relationship between employer and employee here (indeed, such workers are not even covered by the most basic employment legislation and can be arbitrarily dismissed on the whim of the employer). Nor do nannies 'insist' on protecting themselves against these risks with high wages. It is impossible to understand either the employer's desire for a long-standing, stable relationship or the nanny's inability to protect her 'investment' without considering a whole range of social and ideological factors.

Meanwhile, in Britain over the past decade much work that had formerly been associated with permanent contracts, pension rights and so on now often offers two quite separate tiers of employment. Teachers, nurses and research workers, for instance, all of whom might be thought to make substantial employer-specific investments, are now often taken on on a casual or temporary basis. Many employers have been attempting to dismantle elaborate, protective governance structures, yet they still rely on exactly the same degree of firm-specific skill or knowledge from their workers. Further evidence that firms can and do obtain firm-specific skill and knowledge without providing 'standard' direct employment comes from Fevre's (1986) study of British Steel. The company made large numbers of direct employees redundant, whilst simultaneously extending its use of subcontractors. These firms of subcontractors then employed British Steel's ex-employees, who often undertook exactly the same jobs they had formerly carried out, only under far worse conditions of employment. Likewise, Cousins' (1990) study of contracting out in the NHS shows that ancillary workers in the NHS who, although execrably paid, had previously enjoyed a high degree of job security and other fringe benefits, now undertake the same tasks (and more of them) for contractors who provide no reward at all for their organization-specific 'investments'.

The idea that firms will seek to maintain a relationship with workers who have acquired a high degree of firm-specific skill needs to be qualified on at least three counts. First, very substantial degrees of firm-specific skill or knowledge may be required before it makes much difference to employment relations. Second, employers are not compelled to sustain such a relationship with every single employee who 'invests' in firm-specific skills and knowledge. Employees are not *automatically* rewarded for making the 'investment'; some will be losers. Finally, it is important to see that there is no ahistorical, automatic link between asset specificity and governance structures. Governance structures can be modified, even transformed, without any change at all to the degree of employer-specific skill or knowledge supplied by the worker. This leads to the final set of issues: can the employer's choice between different types of employment relation be understood independently of the historical context in which the decision is made?

Transaction Costs and the Wider Political and Institutional Context

The choice between direct and contract labour appears to have parallels with make or buy decisions, and so to be accessible to transaction cost analysis. In practice, however, the attempt to apply such an analysis to Albion's labour strategy again draws attention to the key weakness in the new institutional economics literature; namely its lack of focus on the relationship between power relations and forms of economic organization.

The variability of employment relations in the supply function arises from the need to minimize the labour costs associated with undertaking a complex range of activities; an 'authority relation' with direct employees is intended to reduce the costs associated with redeployment and prioritizing labour, whilst the use of contract labour is intended to reduce the costs associated with a fluctuating workload. The rationale for using direct labour is clearly compatible with Williamson's argument that employment contracts, which are more responsive and flexible, allow firms to 'adapt more effectively than can inter-firm trading to changing market and technological circumstances' (Williamson, 1985, p. 249). The use of contract labour could be said to minimize the transaction costs associated with terminating an employment contract with direct labour when the volume of work contracts.

Williamson has explained the demise of the putting out and inside contracting systems, which rely on extensive and continuous contracting, by exploring the contractual problems they raise. He argues that where production is organized across markets, as in the putting out and internal contracting systems, problems of *ex ante* contractual specification and haggling over the interpretation or adjustment of contracts can lead to high transaction costs (Williamson, 1985, pp. 206–39). Clearly the transaction between Albion Water and its period main-laying contractors carries precisely these kinds of costs. And yet Albion not only persists with the relationship, but has increased the amount of work it puts out to contractors in recent years. Firms of contractors, meanwhile, have continued to make asset-specific investments to serve a firm which has not constructed an elaborate governance structure to protect the transaction (if anything, Albion has done the reverse). These facts can only be understood in relation to the wider economic, institutional and political climate in which the transaction takes place.

To begin with, if Albion's direct labour force was not well unionized, and protected by a no-redundancy agreement, it too could be taken on and dropped in response to changing volumes of work. The attractions of contract labour would then be diminished. The strength of the unions and their ability to protect this agreement is not a given, but is related to wider political and economic trends. Similarly, the attractions of contract labour will vary according to such trends. If competition amongst contractors is intense, and if there is high unemployment or a slump in the construction industry, contract labour is going to be cheaper than during boom periods. In the South East in the mid-1980s, for example, when construction workers could earn up to £500 per week on Channel Tunnel work, contract workers were difficult to recruit or keep, and this encouraged water authorities in the South to use more direct labour. By the same token, firms of civil engineering contractors make their decision to sublet labour in a particular historical context. They presumably would not see the transaction as worthwhile if they were not able to pass the risks on to their own workforce – for instance, if construction industry workers were highly unionized, or if labour legislation insisted that all workers were eligible for the same good package of pension and sickness benefits that Albion workers have struggled for and won through their unions.

The point is that Albion is prepared to carry the costs of haggling with contractors, because despite the time and nuisance of so doing, contract labour is still cheaper than direct labour, which is entitled to pension rights, holiday and sickness pay, and which cannot be easily

disposed of when the workload contracts. In other words, it is not inefficient to haggle *per se*, it is only inefficient to haggle if the costs of haggling
become equal to or greater than the costs of entering into a direct employment relation. Since the costs of a direct employment relation are not
a given, but are contingent upon the strength of labour, government
legislation, union density, labour market conditions and so on, it would
seem impossible to dissociate transaction costs from issues of social power,
as Williamson seeks to do.

It was argued in Chapter 4 that the efficient boundaries of the firm
and appropriate governance structures cannot be 'read off' from the
properties of the transaction alone. The properties of the transaction
may be important, but cannot be analysed independently of the wider
political economy in which it is located. In the same way, the properties
of the 'transaction' between employer and worker alone are not enough
to explain the nature and form of the employment relation. The equation
between direct and contract labour is not unchanging, since the costs and
benefits associated with each are continually modified by circumstances
external to any one firm itself.

Notes

1. Before the formation of the regional water authorities in 1974,
workers in the three different water functions (water supply, recovery
and environmental functions) were all employed by different bodies
and so had different terms and conditions of employment. The newly
created water authorities abandoned these varied sets of conditions and
established one, blanket set of conditions for manual workers – the
Green Book. This included a flexibility agreement known as the Water
Authorities Broad Banding Task Schedule. Rather than workers being
tied to any one function, they were banded, and could be asked to
carry out a 'broad band' of activities cutting across all three functions.
There has been the potential for functional flexibility since 1974, then,
but Albion Water management only ever made use of this during the
strike of 1982, when supply operatives were deployed in the recovery
function.

2. This is, of course, precisely why only substantial companies can
afford to take on the period contract (see Chapter 4). Small firms
cannot carry the same level of risk.

6

THE PURSUIT OF FLEXIBILITY?: REDUCING LABOUR POROSITY IN THE RECOVERY FUNCTION

The previous chapter examined the factors which constrain Albion Water's choice between direct and contract labour. It showed how decisions between direct and indirect employment relations are not necessarily a function of the technical content of work, but are inseparable from the particular political, economic and institutional framework in which they are made. This chapter, and the chapters which follow, move on to explore the changing nature of direct employment in Albion Water. For though the formal employment relation saw little change in the run-up to privatization (Albion's direct employees are still entitled to the same sickness, holiday and pension benefits, and are still covered by the nationally negotiated no-redundancy deal), the organization of work and tacit agreements over the wage–effort bargain have been substantially altered.

This chapter focuses on recovery work. Recovery is Albion's largest function both in terms of turnover and profit and in terms of direct labour levels (employing almost 60% of Albion's manual workforce). Management has recently instituted changes to payment and work allocation systems for these manual workers (it intends to introduce similar changes in the supply function in the future) and claims that this restructuring is being effected in pursuit of greater 'flexibility'. This term has proved to be the leitmotiv of change throughout the 1980s, so much so that, as Pollert (1991, p. 1) observes, 'it has acquired the presence of a fetish'. All that is changed, indeed all that employers do, whether it be deskilling and casualizing work or 'upskilling' jobs and initiating integrationist labour policies, melts into 'flexibility' (Sivanandan, 1990). The concept is capable of embracing:

> developments as diverse as the growth of part time employment;
> changes in relations between manufacturers and suppliers; changing
> industrial relations practices regarding contracts and pay determination;
> the application of new technologies; the removal of statutory regulations
> governing the labour market; the use of legislation to reduce trade union
> powers; the changing structure of large organizations; and the
> development of new forms of regional economic organization. (Blyton
> and Morris, 1991, p. 1)

In general, however, the term is counterpoised against the 'rigidities' of Taylorist and/or Fordist methods of work organization, so that anything which is seen to break with the principles underlying these traditional forms is described as promoting 'flexibility'. As Wood (1989a, p. 12) notes, recent flexibility theorists take mass production as 'the benchmark of the past', and the starting point for their analysis of change is the extreme Taylorist division of labour. So far as recovery work at Albion is concerned, Taylorism is part of its very recent history. It was not until Albion was created in 1974 that there was any systematic attempt to rationalize this work. In the space of only 14 years, Albion management attempted to: gather together the traditional knowledge of recovery operatives; break it down into a series of closely specified subtasks; and take control over allocating and pacing those tasks. Having done so, management became aware of the limitations of such a system of work organization and sought to modify it. In other words, processes which took place over many years in other industries have been compressed in Albion, and perhaps because of this, it is easy to see that much the same principles and objectives underpin both the initial Taylorist-type rationalizations and the current rationalizations in pursuit of greater 'flexibility'.

Systematic Management: Payment and Work Allocation Systems for Recovery Workers from 1974

At its inception in 1974, Albion Water took over responsibility for the operation of around 350 sewage treatment works and over 1000 sewage pumping stations. Responsibility for sewerage and sewage treatment had previously been dispersed across a patchwork of over 80 small sewerage and sewage disposal authorities, which taken together had employed around 450 manual workers. The various forms of work organization adopted by these authorities were inherited by Albion along with these workers. In the words of one manager, the working practices and work organization bequeathed to Albion by its predecessors were 'pretty rudimentary and completely uncoordinated'. At the smaller works and pumping stations, the manual worker's role was effectively that of caretaker. Indeed, it was not unknown for workers to park caravans at the site and live there. A manager comments:

> There would be one man at each site, no matter how small. He would decide how to fill his day. He might have spent half a day looking after the works, and the rest maybe cutting grass, or whatever he felt like, any incidental thing he thought needed doing.

At larger works, a number of men would work under a supervisor, but again, no systematic method of working had been established. It was, as a manager put it, 'a question of every man doing what he thought fit in a very haphazard sort of way'. Standard working practices and work organization could not be immediately imposed from above for two reasons. First, there was no standard work environment since the treatment works and pumping stations had been built at different times, by different agencies. Second, Albion management simply did not know what tasks were involved in operating this array of differently designed works. The idiosyncrasies of the smaller pumping stations, for example, were often known only to the individual worker who ran them.

Albion Water set about rationalizing this situation in the late 1970s by applying essentially Taylorist principles of work organization. A recovery manager explains that 'The only way to advance from that basically chaotic situation was through standardization, making everything very regimented, systematizing the work and working practices.' The first step was to gather the knowledge which had previously been the almost exclusive property of manual workers. The Productivity Services function was heavily involved in this process. Recovery work was studied in detail. The work of operating a pumping station or treatment works was broken down into its constituent parts (keeping pumping stations and treatment works running involves the cleaning and unblocking of filters, screens and pumps, monitoring the flow of sewage through the various stages of the treatment process, and generally undertaking routine maintenance work). These activities were studied in order to draw up a series of closely specified tasks. Those tasks which were undertaken on a regular basis were subjected to extensive time and motion studies and allocated a standard minute value. The next step was to turn this information into the backbone of a work allocation and incentive system. As with the supply operatives described in the preceding chapter, a measured bonus scheme for manual workers was introduced, and this scheme also served as a method of allocating work and controlling the operatives in a context where continuous direct supervision would be costly.

The scheme worked as follows. Every day, the supervisor would hand out a job sheet to each operative. This sheet was a 'tick list' of the standard, routine tasks that the supervisor wanted the operative to undertake that day. Activities such as travelling between sites, gaining access to a site and walking around the site were also allocated a standard minute value, and on the rear of the sheet there was space for the operatives to note down any task they performed that did not appear on the sheet. Like the supply operatives' bonus scheme, the sheets required the operative to account for every minute of his working day. At the end of the day, he would tick off those tasks he had undertaken, note down distances travelled, provide any supplementary information about his activities, and then submit the sheet to the supervisor. Performance ratings were worked out on the basis of the standard times, and if operatives scored a rating of 100, they received a one-third bonus payment. Bonus payments then increased in line with the performance rating, and Productivity Services estimated that the maximum performance rating possible, without injuring man or plant, was 117.

In this way, then, Albion Water management took control over the specification, allocation and pacing of recovery tasks. Change was probably more dramatic for manual workers on the smaller pumping stations. They had previously had only the loosest of job descriptions (simply to do whatever was necessary to keep the station going), and had exercised a high degree of discretion, planning and pacing their own work, with visits from a supervisor being rare. Under the new system, though direct supervision was still minimal, the supervisor had taken over their planning role, and they were issued with minutely detailed instructions as to how to undertake their work. They were also required to account for every moment of the working day in order to qualify for bonus payments. Though workers on larger treatment works and pumping stations had never enjoyed the same degree of autonomy, being in far closer proximity to their supervisor, the new system of closely specified tasks and pretargeted job times also undermined the degree of discretion they could exercise at work. In the past, supervisors might have directed them to undertake certain tasks, but armed with Productivity Service's standard minute values supervisors were able to make far more extensive demands. Moreover, supervisors themselves were now under far greater pressure to ensure that productivity matched the demands made by management.

The rationalization of recovery work effectively meant that management exercised far greater control over the planning and pacing of work. This was seen as the key to increasing the productivity of labour. If management controlled the work more closely, it could ensure that waste and idle time were minimized. As a recovery manager commented:

> The problem with the old system was that, sure, some of these guys out on the smaller works did work hard, but we didn't have any way of making sure they did . . . We couldn't measure what they were doing, so we didn't really have any idea how hard people were working. We certainly knew there were productivity gains to be made . . . If you tell people they must do x, y and z, then they've no excuse to sit around reading the paper or whatever.

Thus, initially management greeted the scheme as a great success and it continued to operate until 1989.[1] As time went on, however, four key problems with it emerged. First, it led to wage creep. The same recovery manager explains:

> The bonus scheme wasn't properly maintained, and as working methods changed the scheme got slack, and bonus just kept creeping up and up . . . Gradually operatives were able to earn up to 50% on top of the standard rate, instead of the one-third maximum they should have got if they did all they were asked to do.

Second, administering the scheme absorbed a great deal of both the operatives' and their supervisor's time. A supervisor comments that 'It was a lot of unnecessary paperwork . . . About an hour a day was spent by each man filling in his time sheet, and then the supervisor would have to spend all of Thursday morning just sorting out the men's bonus.' Third, the scheme was seen to concentrate control over recovery operations in the hands of Productivity Services Officers, rather than in the hands of recovery managers. A manager observes:

> The thing I didn't like in that system was the sort of abdication of managers at a first line level, because their men were working to a

system designed elsewhere. They were really just handing out the
sheets, and the people who were really running the units were the
Productivity Services Officers.

Whilst the scheme exercised a form of bureaucratic control over the
operatives, it made it very difficult for supervisors and recovery managers
to exercise direct control. The manager continues: 'The role of the first
line manager was stripped bare of its man-management aspects. It was
an unhealthy situation.' This point is closely related to the final reason
why the measured bonus scheme was seen as problematic, namely that it
impeded 'flexibility'. Because the operatives' work was closely specified
in advance on the tick sheets, and because asking operatives to undertake
work that was not specified generated so much administrative work, the
scheme engendered a rigid pattern of working, whereby routine work
could be easily allocated, but non-routine work could not. A supervisor
explains that:

> This bonus scheme was the type what was used on piece work in
> factories twenty years ago. The type of work we do doesn't lend itself to
> target times and things like that. There is so many unforeseen factors
> affecting the job. It's not like manufacturing where you know in advance
> all the materials you'll use and all the tasks you'll have to do. Here
> there's factors like health and safety . . . There's all sorts of things that
> can go wrong, like blocked pumps, things you can't put a time on sorting
> out.

If supervisors diverted operatives away from the routine work allocated
on their job sheet in order to sort out an emergency, the operative would
have to clock off the task he was currently working on, and clock on to
the unmeasured rate paid for unspecified work. As well as losing time on
the paperwork, the operative would lose money as the unmeasured rate
was less than the bonus rate. It also meant that the supervisor would be
saddled with more paperwork. Another supervisor comments, 'As a
supervisor you'd avoid swapping men about whenever you could, because
of the work involved. There was so much hassle involved in going outside
the normal routine, so much paperwork, you would avoid it like the
plague.' Moreover, management feared that the close specification on the
job sheets prevented operatives from undertaking anything other than
the limited range of tasks they had been allocated. 'They'd do exactly what
was on their sheets and nothing more', as one manager remarked. In

short, the scheme imposed rigidities on how labour power could be utilized. It 'emasculated front line managers', so they could not directly control workers, and it enabled workers to limit themselves to undertaking a narrow range of predefined tasks. The 'flexibility' management sought in redesigning the work allocation and payment system was the 'flexibility' to get around these problems.

'Flexibility': Payment and Work Allocation Systems from 1989

In 1989 the system of allocating work through closely specified daily tick sheets was replaced by far more loosely defined weekly 'job plans'. All the routine tasks for the week at one works, or in one area, are divided into two or three job plans. This means that at a works with two operatives, for example, Plan A might include all possible tasks associated with the routine maintenance of one-half of a treatment works, and Plan B would cover all the rest. The tasks on the plan are not 'cast in tablets of stone'; the supervisor can substitute other tasks if priorities change. Moreover, time is allowed for non-routine activities, so that the supervisor can ask the operative to do any work he considers necessary, and at the end of the week, all the operative has to do is tick that he has completed his job plan.

This has the immediate effect of cutting out all the hours spent on administering the old, complex bonus scheme. The time previously spent by supervisors and operatives on this unproductive activity is freed up, and can be used to better purpose. More importantly, the system gives management greater control over the deployment of labour power. The tasks on each job plan can be varied by the supervisor, without incurring any paperwork, and labour power can thus be matched to the most urgent tasks. An area manager explains:

> Although the operatives do still have targeted daily jobs, there is a great deal more flexibility now because the supervisors can switch and change them around according to what he thinks is required, on to the tasks he thinks are most important.

Because the operatives' work is no longer rigidly predefined, their labour power has become a more fluid and malleable resource for management. This cuts out porosity in the working day. As a supervisor notes:

> With the old scheme, they knew exactly what was on the sheet, and they'd do that and no more . . . whereas now, they just carry on working. They can't rush to finish and then sit around chatting because they don't ever finish as such.

The operatives cannot finish because they are now required not only to undertake a pre-set routine, but also to carry out any tasks allocated to them by the supervisor. The supervisor's job has thus been transformed; first line managers have recovered their 'man-management' role and exercise direct control over the workforce:

> Whereas the old bonus scheme was self-supervising, you got all the jobs on your sheet and that was what you did . . . now the emphasis is more on supervision, making sure it is done properly. Now I can look at what is going on, and if I want anything different doing, or something done in a different way, I can say so. And nine times out of ten, if I do divert men onto another job, that job gets done plus what was on the original job plan, so Albion is doing very well out of it. The men are working to more than a third performance, but Albion only has to pay a third bonus.

Fox (1974) argues that looser job specification implies a more 'high-trust' relationship between employer and employee, and much of the literature on 'flexibility' has similarly suggested that new forms of work organization are accompanied by greater autonomy for workers. At Albion Water, however, disposing of tight task specification has had the reverse effect. A recovery manager notes that wider and more flexible weekly job plans 'have to be more effectively policed' than the old tick sheets, because 'obviously if the guys don't do their jobs properly, if they just tick "Yes, I've done Plan A" and they haven't really, the whole thing collapses'. Because the new scheme is simpler to administer, supervisors can now spend more time directly supervising the operatives, and Albion has also introduced a new tier of supervision in the form of charge hands. Under this new, more 'flexible' system of work allocation, then, operatives are more intensively supervised.

It is not just the method of work allocation which has been altered, however. The bonus scheme has also been transformed (Table 6.1). The bulk of the one-third bonus payment from the old scheme has been consolidated into the standard weekly wage, and only 5% of it hinges on the operative completing his week's job plan. This is known as the 'step stabilized scheme'. As well as the step stabilized scheme, a 'bolt-on' bonus

Table 6.1 *Old and New Bonus Schemes in the Recovery Function*

	Old scheme	New scheme
Basic wage	70%	95%
Bonus tied to individual	30% (intended)	5% (intended)
	50% (actual)	5% (actual)
Bonus tied to area effluents quality	0%	4%
Bonus tied to area sites standards	0%	1%
Total possible payments	120%	105%

payment of 5% has been added, 4% of which is payable at the end of each quarter, and 1% of which is paid annually. This 5% bonus is conditional upon the performance not of the individual operative, but of the area he works in as a whole. The effluents quality of all sites in a given geographical area is measured, and those areas meeting the target standards set by management receive up to 4% bonus. Site maintenance in the area as a whole is also given a rating, and those areas which, on average, meet the target standard receive a further 1% bonus payment.

Given that 'wage creep' under the old system had meant that operatives were generally earning a 50% bonus payment, the new scheme has considerable financial advantages for Albion. Now, with the consolidated bonus, the step stabilized bonus payment and the bolt-on 'effectiveness' bonus payment, operatives receive 15% less than they were generally able to under the old scheme. As the manager involved notes:

> We agreed to consolidate, but we reduced the opportunity to earn 50% and pulled it back to standard. This extra 5% effectiveness payment is not really an extra bonus, it's what they would have earned under the old system, but it's no longer a reward for work done, it's a reward for standards achieved.

In summary, the step stabilized scheme itself has two main advantages for management. On the one hand, as a payment system it brings wages down and is intended to prevent further wage drift. On the other hand, as a system of work allocation the step stabilized scheme cuts out time previously wasted on filling out tick sheets, ensures that operatives are faced by a continuous, rather than a finite, workload, and allows management to target labour power on those tasks which it considers to be top priorities, thereby reducing the need for overtime working since emergencies can be dealt with in normal working hours. The pursuit of 'flexibility' has thus meant finding ways of squeezing more labour power out of fewer working hours. According to a recovery manager, 'The scheme has improved productivity. In real terms, Albion is getting more value for money out of a smaller workforce.'

Meanwhile, the bolt-on 'effectiveness payment' makes 5% of the operatives' bonus conditional upon the area as a whole's performance. The sums of money involved for each operative are fairly small, between £60 and £80 per quarter, and the impact any individual operative can make upon the area's 'effectiveness' is minimal, as even managers will acknowledge. Effluents quality is determined in large part by management decisions, such as the level of investment in treatment works and staffing levels in the maintenance function on which the recovery function depends. It is also affected by extraneous factors, such as population density in a given area, heavy rainfall, and even criminal activity such as the illegal dumping of waste. Management rhetoric about the 'effectiveness payment' stresses its role in providing incentives and increasing accountability for the individual operative. However, its arbitrary nature makes it tempting to conclude that the bolt-on scheme is attractive to management for precisely the reverse reason. It fixes the bonus to something over which workers have no control, and this ensures that the operatives cannot 'learn to work the system', and so guards against 'wage creep'.

'Flexible' Forms of Work Organization: Collaboration or Compulsion?

Although Albion managers state that recovery work is now organized more flexibly, reorganization has not actually entailed changes to the technical content of work, nor has it involved any retraining. Operatives are now provided with far looser task specifications but this has served to increase their daily workload, rather than to 'upskill' their jobs. Whilst managers claim that these changes have benefits for employees (saying that they enable workers 'to take pride in their work' and that looser job specifications allow them to exercise greater discretion) and that the reorganization has improved effluents standards, recovery operatives paint a very different picture of the restructuring of their work, stating that it amounts to nothing more than making them do more for less pay.

Through the 'natural wastage' policy, direct labour levels have fallen dramatically in the function. Management claimed that these cuts were supported by the increasing level of automation in treatment works, but as one operative comments:

> They cut the workers on the back of this automation, but they were assuming it would work, whereas at least a quarter of the time it doesn't. And that's when you need the back-up.

The workload of the remaining operatives has thus increased. As another operative remarks:

> Since privatization we've been cut down to the bone. As soon as you get someone sick, or someone out on holiday, you're left with a few men trying to do everything. It just isn't possible. And then you get the equipment breaking down all the time, sometimes you're waiting months and months for parts, and we're left to do it manually where we can, so again that's adding to the work.

These operatives argue that the new system of work allocation has more to do with intensifying labour than it has to do with flexibility. They argue that recovery operatives have always provided a high degree of flexibility in terms of the range of tasks they undertake. The difference is that under the new scheme, management does not limit the number of tasks it can require them to undertake in advance. By allocating more loosely defined work schedules it ensures that these workers' labour power is continuously available:

> Flexibility came in years ago with the broad banding as they call it. They've had flexibility for years . . . We share all the jobs, we always have done. One of us doesn't stick to one particular job. We're all classed as operators, we all do everything . . . We never just stuck to one thing . . . The only change is now they want us to do more of it.

Though these operatives are now working more intensely, they receive no extra financial rewards. In fact, they have lost money. The effects of the new bonus scheme are to increase the number of tasks which have to be carried out and to decrease the payment made for them. As an operative puts it:

> If they want better performance, the machinery has to work 100% all the time. The job cards they bring out, you get one machine goes wrong and the whole situation changes. It might take two of us an hour and half just to sort it out, so how can we stick to the programme? The old bonus scheme, you would write down what extra you'd done, but this new scheme, you have your set week's work and you have to fit that in another day if you haven't done it today because something's gone wrong. Now everything has to be done or your bonus is gone.

As well as this, management has devised other ways of reducing labour costs. Another operative explains:

> We've always been low paid, but they're always finding ways to take things away. Like we used to be on shifts, then they stopped the nights, and made us do two shifts. So we lost our night work payment. Then they cut out all the overtime. So they keep finding new ways to pay you less.

In short, then, the pursuit of 'flexibility' in the recovery function has above all meant the intensification of labour, and it is therefore interesting to consider whether this can, in any real sense, be considered as a break with the principles that informed Albion's first round of Taylorist-type rationalizations.

Systematic Management and 'Flexibility'

It was noted in the introduction that new 'flexible' forms of work organization are often presented as marking a fundamental break with both the principles and practice of Taylorist and Fordist methods of production organization. Indeed, one unifying theme behind the flexible firm and flexible specialization literature is the idea that we have witnessed (or are witnessing) Fordism's *götterdämmerung*. It is argued that Fordist and Taylorist production techniques were founded upon stable demand for large numbers of standard products, and that, paradoxically, its success destroyed the very conditions upon which it was founded (Piore and Sabel, 1984; Sabel, 1982). 'Post-Fordist' product markets demand 'post-

Fordist' production techniques, which in turn are predicated upon closer collaboration between capital and labour.

It is difficult to apply arguments about product markets to a public utility which is a monopoly supplier of an essential service,[2] and, of course, this research deals with only one case. Moreover, although it has been stated that Albion Water adopted Taylorist principles in its initial restructuring of recovery work, in that it subdivided recovery work into a number of closely specified tasks, Albion never transformed each individual operative into a detailed labourer. Thus, the fact that 'it is not economical to employ a specialised, detailed worker for each operation' unless there are mass markets (Littler and Salaman, 1984, p. 74) is not an issue here. But despite these caveats, in general Albion management faces similar problems to those faced by managers in other industries. For instance, Littler and Salaman (1984, p. 79) note that 'Taylorism and Fordism carry co-ordination and control costs. As the division of labour is extended, co-ordination measures must accompany such extension: for example, production planning, supervision and monitoring, and inspection procedures,' and this was certainly one of the main limitations of Taylorism from Albion's point of view.

Detailed job specifications also made it difficult for management to match labour power closely to the ebbs and flows of productive activity. Can it be argued, then, that the introduction of looser job specifications and a more flexible system of work allocation marks a fundamental break with past forms of work organization? The rationalization of recovery work along Taylorist lines was designed to increase management's control over the planning and pacing of work. It was only after extensive time and motion studies that management acquired detailed knowledge about the work process itself, and thereby also the capacity to define 'a fair day's work'. The detailed specification of tasks on job sheets represented a means of increasing the intensity of working, since operatives could no longer plan and pace their own work but had to undertake specified tasks at a specified rate.

The most recent rationalization could be said to be informed by the same basic objective. It not only cuts out unproductive time spent on filling in tick sheets and administering the system, but also, allocating recovery workers a continuous rather than a finite workload and enlarging their jobs to cover all aspects of the work process eliminates pauses and breaks in their working day, and so squeezes more labour power out in a given period. Indeed, the recovery manager himself sees these two sets of rationalizations as stages of the same basic process, and sums up as follows:

> [Systematic management] was a necessary stage of development. I firmly believe that you could not have gone from a completely uncoordinated distribution of work as we had originally . . . with every man doing whatever he felt was necessary, to this kind of flexibility. I think the only way you can advance is to go through this standardization, to make everything very regimented, systematize the work and working practices . . . This gives you your building blocks. Once you've got them, you can do what you like, you can construct something far more flexible.

Chapter 2 argued that in the run-up to privatization Albion was under pressure to keep labour costs down, and that this pressure has continued post-privatization. The pursuit of 'flexibility' in Albion Water is best understood in relation to this imperative. The factors that underpinned Albion's need to increase profits and operate with a smaller direct labour force during the 1980s were, of course, particular to public sector organizations being first squeezed and then privatized by successive Thatcher governments. However, Albion's response does not seem to be dissimilar to that of firms in other sectors during the 1980s, which have been seeking to increase their rate of profit for other reasons. Changes to work organization in Albion are consonant with the more general trends described by Elger (1990, 1991), who argues that over the past decade

> there has been some bias, more evident in the moves towards 'flexibility' than in technical change per se, towards the horizontal enlargement rather than the multi-skilling of jobs and towards some intensification of labour. The latter seems especially to have involved a reduction in the 'porosity' of work routines, through the paring down of pauses, resting and waiting time and thus a 'closer filling up of the pores of the working day'. (Elger, 1990, p. 69)

The pursuit of 'flexibility' in the recovery function has above all been the pursuit of a denser working day. But the experience of recovery operatives is not an isolated example of labour intensification in Albion Water. Management plans to institute virtually identical changes for supply operatives, and, as will be seen in the two following chapters, a denser working day has already been effectively imposed on other groups of manual workers. This chapter has shown (and the point is reiterated in Chapters 7 and 8) that achieving this end is not reducible to technical issues. Labour can also be intensified by manipulating the social organization of work, without making any changes at all to its technical content.

However, such changes are only possible in a particular historical context. Throughout the 1980s, employers' attempts to increase 'flexibility' and to intensify labour have been bolstered by legal assaults on trade unions, by the dismantling of national negotiating procedures and key employment legislation, and by cuts to wages and social security benefits (Hyman, 1988). Developments at Albion show that even relatively advantaged 'core' workers are not always sheltered from the impact of these broader political and legal changes. In the recovery function, well-unionized, directly employed, male workers are pessimistic about their capacity to resist job enlargement or work intensification. As one operative put it, 'All they want is the flexibility to pay us less for doing more work . . . but since the miners' strike and all these laws about ballots and picketing, there isn't much the unions can do about it.'

Notes

1. During this time, the manual workforce in the recovery function has been cut by more than half. This is partly a consequence of tighter government financial control, and partly because of the increasing level of automation in the function, with many larger treatment works now being almost fully automated. Only around 200 manual workers are currently employed in the recovery function.

2. It could, however, be argued that Albion Water chose to rationalize recovery work because, unlike the smaller authorities that had previously been responsible for sewerage, it was catering to a large as well as stable market. It could also be argued that the higher standards demanded by EC legislation are experienced by water companies in much the same way as other companies experience consumer demand for higher-quality goods.

7 ORGANIZATIONAL CHANGE AND THE COMMERCIALIZATION OF EMPLOYMENT RELATIONS

Until the early 1980s, Albion Water provided but two types of employment. On the one hand, it provided what might be termed 'standard' direct employment, i.e. full-time, permanent employment, with all direct employees from groundsman to engineer enjoying a high degree of job security and a good package of fringe benefits. On the other, it made substantial use of contract labour. This bifurcated pattern is now changing as Albion Water begins not only to enter into a variety of non-standard contracts with labour, but also to transform the nature of direct employment for certain groups of employees. The previous chapter explored how changes to payment and work allocation systems in the recovery function have impacted upon tacit agreements over the wage–effort bargain, and led to work intensification, thus changing the nature of direct employment. This chapter is concerned with new forms of employment relations within Albion Water. It examines how and why workers are brought into the new 'enterprise initiative' areas on new, non-standard terms, then moves on to a case study of the changing fortunes of Albion's building maintenance workers. By commercializing its relationship with these employees, Albion has won various concessions from them in terms of new working practices, reduced manning levels and decreased job security, concessions which once again have served to intensify labour.

Employment in Ancillary Functions and New Initiative Areas

Albion Water's 'core' activities of supply and recovery are supported both directly and indirectly by a range of functions and services. Traditionally

Albion has used a mix of contract and direct labour to undertake both core and support functions. Chapters 4 and 5 showed how 'core' work is contracted out, and while historically the vast majority of support functions and services (such as payrolling, vehicle maintenance, personnel services, scientific services, grounds maintenance) have been undertaken in house by direct employees, a few ancillary functions, such as the maintenance of central heating and air conditioning systems, and window cleaning, have always been contracted out to specialist firms. Thus, in itself, the use of contract labour and the putting out of certain activities to external firms are nothing new in Albion Water. However, in response to tighter financial controls imposed by government upon the water industry throughout the 1980s, Albion has attempted to cut costs by contracting out certain ancillary activities which were previously undertaken by direct labour. Vehicle maintenance, which used to be carried out by an in-house unit, is now undertaken by an independent firm. Grass cutting and grounds maintenance (a fairly substantial volume of work, since Albion owns a great deal of land and several hundred buildings, works and installations) used to be the responsibility of direct labour. It is now contracted out to small firms and self-employed individuals. However, perhaps more important than the *amount* of work which has been contracted to outside agencies is the way this strategy has been used against Albion's direct labour force. The *threat* of bringing in outside contractors to replace direct labour has been used to push through changes in direct labour's working conditions and practices. A senior manager comments:

> I have used contractors, or the threat of them, to drive down my own costs. If you take sludge for example, our sludge boat. We said to them 'We've been out and got tenders. That's what they can do it for, we've got to do it for less than that.' The same with the canteen services . . . we said 'That's what we can get it done for by someone down the road. We've got to aim to match those prices.'

In this way, the putting out of a small number of ancillary functions to outside contractors has served a dual function. Not only did Albion cut costs by getting some services more cheaply from outside firms, but it also made other groups of direct labour feel more exposed and vulnerable, and so more ready to acquiesce to cuts in manning levels and other cost-cutting 'work rationalizations'. In the words of another senior manager, subcontractors provide

a bit of a stick to beat direct labour, saying that 'If you don't pull your
weight and they can prove they can do it better in corporate terms, we'll
use more of them and less of you.' But that isn't the way it's been said,
obviously.

Managers may not have said precisely this, but employees are aware that
this is what they mean.

Whilst the contracting out of certain functions may not be new to
Albion, the use of outside contractors as an instrument of labour discipline
is. As such, it cannot be understood except in relation to broader economic
trends. The threat of contractors becomes far more real during periods
of economic recession and high unemployment when direct employees
know with certainty that there are many small firms and self-employed
individuals ready to compete for such contracts. Contractors are thus
being used in new areas and for new reasons. Moreover, the development
of two organizational strands – 'core business' and 'enterprise activities'
– in response to the government's plans for the post-privatization financial
regulation of the industry provided the impetus for introducing new forms
of non-standard employment. From 1987 on, Albion began to devote time
and resources to developing 'enterprise activities'. Many existing core
activities offer the potential for commercial activity and profitable diversification. This is especially true of maintenance activities, since many
of the skills, tools and equipment involved in building maintenance and
mechanical and electrical maintenance are transferable, rather than firm-
specific. Albion has also started to branch into new fields such as plumbing, septic tank emptying, and disposing of industrial waste.

These commercial initiatives are notionally autonomous and separately
accountable units, and their performance is measured against short-term
profitability. Their managers are thus provided with strong incentives to
cut costs, and since maintenance work is highly labour intensive, labour
costs are a prime target for cost cutting in maintenance function profit
centres. It is primarily in these new and commercial initiative areas that
new forms of non-standard employment relations are being introduced.
For instance, Albion Water's new plumbing service relies entirely upon
self-employed workers. The manager involved in setting up the service
argues that this is because:

Despite it being under the umbrella of Albion Water, it's still a risk
business, and we feel that initially the unit should be staffed by
subcontract, self-employed plumbers . . . so that should the risk prove

too great and the thing should fold, the only people that will fold are not directly employed people.

It is further envisaged that some existing direct employees may wish to retrain and move over to the new plumbing service, entering into a different form of employment relation with Albion Water. The manager comments 'If the service grows and really takes off then we will offer existing staff the opportunity to come over into enterprise areas . . . existing employees if they want to come into it would have to become self-employed.' He also notes that 'If we train our own men up we'd certainly put a claw-back clause into the training cost, so that if they do leave within, say, two years, they pay a proportion of their training costs back.' This further illustrates management's new commercial orientation. In the past, training was supplied unconditionally as part of the job, just as tools, transport and anything else necessary to undertake the work would be provided by the employer. Here, it is treated as a commodity with a value above and beyond the ongoing relationship between employee and employer. Again, rather than the employer having obligations towards employees, a notion of commercial exchange is being introduced – Albion Water will not supply this 'commodity' to workers without being guaranteed reimbursement in one form or another. Commercial initiative areas are also increasing the proportion of subcontract to direct labour. A senior manager explains the criteria on which decisions about employment relations are based:

> The way we'll staff those [deregulated enterprise areas] I'd suggest will depend purely on the bottom line, that we're in it to make a profit . . . if subcontract labour in the enterprise area is the way forward in terms of profit, then that's probably the way we'll go . . . certainly it's more flexible in terms of putting people on and off.

He argues that the use of non-standard labour is particularly attractive in these areas because what standard, direct employment has meant traditionally in the water industry is an employment relation which is 'inappropriate to a new fledgling commercial concern' and continues:

> Over the years the unions have negotiated on a national basis . . . terms and conditions of employment . . . overtime is paid at time and a half on Saturdays and double time on Sundays and after midnight, call-out allowances are paid . . . standby allowances . . . all these things

effectively fight against us in the market place so that we'd be totally uncompetitive.

Obviously, these benefits are not accorded to self-employed or subcontract labour, and also Albion Water is not responsible for other labour overheads, such as holidays, sickness and national insurance, when it uses such labour. Here, then, new forms of non-standard, indirect labour are employed. This adds another dimension to the overall pattern of employment relations within Albion Water (Table 7.1). Moreover, it represents a new labour strategy. In the past, contractors have been used in areas which demand specialist skills and equipment because the volume of work is insufficient to warrant investment, and for 'lop and peak' because the volume of work fluctuates. Now, ancillary functions have been put out in totality in order to cut costs, and in PlumbCare and other new initiatives contract labour and the self-employed are used explicitly to shoulder risk.

Table 7.1 *Old and New Patterns of Employment Relations*

	Traditional	**New**
Direct employees	X	X
DLO employees	O	X
Contract labour	X	X
Self-employed	O	X

$X = present, \; O = absent$

It has been seen that even quite small increases in the extent to which ancillary work is put out to contractors impacts upon all other direct labour units which provide ancillary services, by making the threat of contractors far more real to them. Equally, the introduction of new forms of non-standard employment has an impact upon the rest of the direct labour force. Several direct employees saw the manning strategies in the new initiative areas as 'the thin end of the wedge'. As one commented, 'This is what it's all about, going private. Once it's private, profit is all that matters and you can forget about security or pensions or all what we've fought for.' Labour is thus being brought in on new terms and conditions. But as well as this, existing groups of direct labour are now being used in non-standard ways in the commercial initiative areas. The following section examines what becoming a 'commercial initiative unit' has meant for one group of employees, the building maintenance workers.

The Building Maintenance Unit

Like other water authorities, Albion Water operates over a large geographical area. It supplies water services to a population spread over several thousand square kilometres. This, combined with the nature of its operations, means that it owns many hundreds of buildings of varying sizes and descriptions, ranging from large office blocks in major cities, through smaller satellite depots and treatment works in outlying towns and villages to very small pumping stations obscurely located in the depths of the countryside. It must maintain, renovate and repair these buildings and this involves the provision of both routine and emergency maintenance. Albion has traditionally used direct labour to provide this service. However, since 1979 Building Maintenance Services has undergone successive 'rationalizations'. Perhaps the starkest indicator of the extent of change is the size of the direct labour force – in 1979 35 men were employed in Building Maintenance Services, but by 1989 only eight remained.

Prior to 1985, Building Maintenance Services was allocated an annual budget with which it provided a routine and emergency maintenance service. It both responded to requests for work, and initiated work as and when necessary. It thus enjoyed a fairly unambiguous relationship with Albion Water. It was a department of Albion Water in its own right, with its own budget, its function being to maintain Albion's buildings as best as possible within the constraints of that budget. Building Maintenance Services employed both unskilled labourers and skilled tradesmen. Fairly rigid skill demarcations were observed, and work was broken down into components of carpentry, plumbing, painting, bricklaying and so on. Tradesmen each had their own mate with whom they worked. Where a job required specific skills that they could not provide, subcontractors would be used, but this was rarely necessary.

From 1980 onwards, Albion Water committed itself to reducing manning levels by 2% per annum, and the number of Building Maintenance Services employees gradually dwindled as those who left were not replaced. By 1985 only 14 employees remained. Throughout this period, the use of subcontractors increased. In 1985, management decided to restructure Building Maintenance Services along the lines of the compulsory competitive tendering model imposed upon local authority Direct Labour Organizations (DLOs) by the 1980 Local Government Planning and Land Act. Building Maintenance Services became the Building Maintenance Unit (BMU) and rather than allocating an operational budget to this unit, Albion distributed the maintenance budget amongst the various departments which used building maintenance services. The departmental managers responsible for buildings and plants no longer automatically requisitioned jobs from the BMU, but were obliged to put all maintenance work out to tender. They were required to consider at least three quotes, and to give the job to whoever submitted the lowest estimate.

This meant that the BMU now had to submit competitive tenders for Albion jobs, and in order to ensure that the BMU priced jobs realistically it was obliged to give fixed price quotes, and was required to show a return of 5% on capital employed. Thus, the unit was obliged to 'win' its operating costs from other departments. The unit was given a probationary period of one year, after which time, if it failed to meet this nominal profit target and demonstrate its competitiveness, it would be closed down and all maintenance work put out to contract. Only two months earlier, the vehicle maintenance unit had been closed down and vehicle maintenance put out to a private firm, and this fact meant that BMU employees perceived the threat of closure as very real.

In pursuit of the profit target, a range of new working practices were adopted which qualitatively changed the tradesmen's jobs. Skill demarcations were no longer acknowledged, each tradesman being expected to perform all elements of a job. Where tradesmen had previously worked with a mate, they now worked alone. Tradesmen took on new responsibilities, e.g. the ordering of some materials rather than relying wholly upon the supervisor to do so. Instead of reporting to the nearest depot at 8 a.m. each morning, on-site reporting was introduced. This meant that tradesmen were working longer hours. Where previously they travelled to and from jobs in Albion time, they now travelled in their own time. They had to report on site at 8 a.m., and rather than returning to the depot for 5 p.m. they now had to stay on site until that time. This increased the average time actually working on site by up to two hours per day, and so lengthened the tradesmen's working day, yet their basic pay remained the same apart from the addition of a small travelling allowance.

During the first year the introduction of these new working practices was successful, inasmuch as the unit exceeded its notional profit target. However, central government demands to further cut revenue expenditure led Albion Water again to cut its overall maintenance budget, and it was decided to further reduce manpower in the BMU, which was asked to shed six more men. Since 1986 the BMU has operated with a direct labour force of only eight men, topping up manpower with subcontractors. In April 1988, further changes were instigated as part of Albion Water's pre-privatization reorganizations. The BMU was designated as one of Albion Water's 'commercial initiative' areas. As such it is expected to seek commercial work from third parties as well as 'winning' in-house work through competitive tendering. It is now wholly accountable as a separate unit, and must be profitable in its own right. The unit still comprises eight directly employed tradesmen, but since April 1988 its workload has greatly increased. This is in part because it has been successful in winning commercial work, and in part because Albion instigated a refurbishing programme, repairing, redecorating and refurbishing many of its properties prior to privatization. Resort to subcontractors has greatly increased in order to cope with this volume of work. The main changes to the organization of building maintenance work are summarized in Table 7.2.

Simulating Market Forces: The Relationship between the BMU and Albion Water

The new relationship between the BMU and Albion Water is designed to simulate market relations *within* the authority. The idea is that Albion Water, like any other buyer in the marketplace, is now free to choose between the BMU and other small firms, pursuing its own self-interest by buying the best service at the lowest price. The BMU, like any other seller, is supposedly free to pursue its self-interest, choosing only to enter into profitable transactions. Thus the manager responsible for new initiatives presents the relationship between Albion Water and the BMU as one governed by market laws. They are buyers and sellers with an essentially commercial relationship: 'The unit . . . can actually go out and seek work elsewhere. In theory if we can do it up the road for more money than we can get doing Albion work, we'll stop working for Albion.'

The unit is also subject to the disciplines of the market; its survival is conditional on its continued profitability. The manager characterizes these changes in terms of increased freedom for the unit: 'The unit will always have a relationship with Albion, it's just now it's going to be freer to make a profit.' However, such notions of 'freedom' and 'markets' are illusory. Because the unit is part of Albion Water and is not a small firm, its

Table 7.2 *Changes to the Organization of Building Maintenance Work*

	Old system	New system
Resource allocation	Bureaucratic	Internal and external market
Division of labour	More craft-specific	More craft-diffuse
Continuity of employment	Tacitly guaranteed	Tacitly conditional
Formal Labour relation	Standard (full time, permanent)	Standard (full time, permanent)
Use of subcontract	Minimal	Increasing

freedom to pursue profit is ultimately constrained by factors over which it has no control. The manager speaks of greater freedom to pursue profitability, and argues that the unit must demonstrate its commercial viability or else be closed down. But he also acknowledges that the allocation of central overheads by Albion will largely dictate whether or not the unit can be economically viable. This manager believes it would be 'fair' for him to pay on a commercial basis for the central services he uses, such as payroll, pensions and administration, in other words for those overheads directly attributable to initiative areas. However, he argues that it would be 'unfair' for BMU employees to carry the overheads associated with, for example, Albion Water's overall billing centre, which processes water rates for the whole region (estimated at approximately £2000 per employee), when none of the BMU's income is processed by that centre. He argues that in order to run the initiative areas successfully, he needs the authority to control the level of overheads.

His anxiety about the allocation of central overheads mirrors the ambivalent response of other Albion Water managers to the profit centre model (see Chapter 3). They welcome profit centre management because they believe it will increase their own autonomy, yet also fear that the board might conspire against their particular profit centre in such a way as to make it impossible to manage profitably. The key question for this manager must be whether in reality Albion Water would allow him the freedom to seek out alternative, cheaper offices, payrolling, accountancy, financial services and so on. In practice, he thinks not: 'I mean you can't go totally along the small centre road, saying what's right for me is right for everyone. Yet, that's a big problem and that's why we've got a corporate strategist now, to piece things together.' The level of overheads carried by the BMU will then finally be a decision of the corporate strategist, along with finance and accountancy personnel, whose prime objective when allocating overheads will be the maximization of corporate goals, rather than being 'fair' to individual profit centres. Thus the manager's view of the relationship between Albion Water and the BMU embodies a contradiction, since he believes in the idea of a free play of market forces between Albion and the BMU, and yet at the same time recognizes that the economic viability of the BMU is largely determined by decisions made by senior managers, and not by market laws.

It is the unit's supervisor, who effectively controls the day-to-day running of the BMU, who experiences this contradiction most sharply. His brief is to manage the unit in such a way as to achieve the profit targets set. To do so, he must compete with other small and medium-sized building firms. However, the supervisor argues that the unit is forced to enter this competition with an insurmountable handicap in the form of various rules and procedures laid down by the authority. For instance, there are established procedures for taking on subcontractors, designed to ensure that all workers are on the cards. There are various bureaucratic procedures which regulate the ordering and purchasing of materials. There are regulations which prevent employees from taking company vans home at night, thereby making on-site reporting an impossibility. The supervisor comments that 'Albion is quite a big company and they've got to have red tape to make sure that no one's fiddling, but when you try and run a unit of eight men, you can't afford all that red tape.'

Where possible the supervisor simply ignores the rules, but there are limits to the extent to which he can do so. For example, he argues that high labour costs reduce the unit's competitiveness, but he has no control in this area. He is also forced to 'buy' services such as payrolling and transport from Albion Water, at rates which the unit cannot, in his view, afford. Furthermore, although the supervisor is required to operate a profit and loss account, in fact it is Albion's finance office that deals with payments for materials. The office does not show him the invoices or inform him of any bulk discounts negotiated, so he never actually knows the precise costs involved. Even in terms of in-house work, the supervisor feels that the unit is disadvantaged through a lack of real autonomy. In reality, it is not free to choose only the most profitable jobs and leave Albion Water to try to contract out difficult or loss-making jobs. Albion management will even sometimes use BMU employees to compensate for labour shortages in other departments. For example, management instructed the unit to take on a job cleaning sluice gates, which should have been undertaken by employees of another department, even though the supervisor explicitly said he did not want the work. The BMU lost £1700 on that job over the year.

The supervisor characterizes the relationship between Albion Water and the BMU as 'ludicrous'. He does not believe the unit can operate profitably within the constraints imposed by Albion. The unit cannot afford to buy services from Albion, the regulations that Albion imposes reduce the unit's competitiveness, and Albion Water gives no preferential treatment in terms of supplying work for the unit. Indeed, the supervisor claims that Albion is more exacting and difficult than other private customers. Given the very evident tensions which arise from this form of relationship, it is interesting to explore why Albion has not simply put all building maintenance work out to contractors. The work itself is what might conventionally be regarded as a 'peripheral' or ancillary function, and there are plenty of small firms of building contractors around. The question is, then, why should Albion attempt to simulate a market relationship with direct labour when it could have the real thing with a firm of contractors?

Direct Labour versus Contractors

In order to answer this question, it is necessary to consider the particular requirements Albion Water has of building maintenance. As noted above, Albion owns literally hundreds of buildings dotted over the several thousand square kilometres it serves. The logistical problems of coordinating and supplying an efficient maintenance service to these widely dispersed buildings is further compounded by the fact that many small pumping stations are obscurely located, making local and Albion-specific knowledge an important factor in efficiency.

Albion has several requirements of a building maintenance service. It wants the cheapest service possible, and one way of achieving this is to cut labour costs. It also requires a labour force with local knowledge (to locate sites quickly), that is trustworthy and reliable (since the geographical dispersal of sites makes direct supervision costly), and that is flexible in the sense of being easy to redeploy in response to emergencies. Neither direct labour nor contractors are seen as being able to fulfil all these requirements. The manager believes that a normal direct labour maintenance service is more expensive than outside contractors for two reasons. First, direct labour is insulated from market pressures. Because they do not compete for work, they are not forced to find ways of cutting costs or driven to seek the most efficient working practices and manning strategies. Second, as Albion Water employees, they are unionized and are covered by the wages and conditions negotiated in other, core, areas. The manager argues that:

> It is a symptom of local government in general that they are heavily unionized areas, and the unions have built up quite substantial pay and working conditions, whereby jobs will be double manned for this, and people will have to have a health and safety team with them for something else.

In his view, all this may mean that direct labour receives a higher hourly rate than subcontract tradesmen would, and certainly means that Albion is paying more in terms of pension, holiday and sickness benefits than it would if it used contractors. However, to rely solely upon contractors raises another, different set of problems. First, there are problems of contract. The nature of the maintenance work is essentially open ended; it varies from year to year and cannot be wholly predicted in advance. It would be easy enough to draw up a contract at the beginning of the year for painting the exterior of 20 particular buildings, for example, but impossible to do so for the myriad unpredictable jobs – mending locks, replacing broken toilet cisterns, repairing damage by vandals, and so on.

To obtain maximum benefits in terms of competitive pressures, someone within Albion Water would have to continually identify and specify necessary work, put each and every job out to tender, process quotes, and negotiate contracts with the various contractors. Clearly, all this would be time-consuming and bureaucratic, and the costs of *ex ante* contractual specification and administration might well prove greater than the savings gained through competitive pressures driving costs down. The only form of contract which could cover all possibilities and allow negotiation to take place in advance would be a 'period contract', such as that described in Chapter 4. Although this would save Albion having to draw up innumerable contracts, there would still be high administrative costs in terms of contract specification. Also, there are other problems associated with this type of contract which have already been discussed; not least, in this case, would be the question of whether a firm could be found which would be willing to enter into such a precarious and risky contract for what might amount to fairly insubstantial returns.

The second main problem with the use of contractors rather than direct labour involves the costs arising from a loss of local and firm-specific knowledge and from the need for increased supervision. The fact that many sites are obscurely located would mean that Albion personnel would have to physically show the contractor many of the sites. Neither would contract labour provide the same degree of firm-specific knowledge that is provided by direct labour, e.g. familiarity with Albion health regulations pertaining to movement between supply and sewerage sites. Over time a contractor may come to acquire local and firm-specific knowledge and so reduce the need for detailed guidance from Albion personnel, but to gain such knowledge would require a long-term relationship, and the contractor's prices might eventually rise to take account of the specialized knowledge and service it would then offer.[1]

Likewise, there is the problem of reliability. It would be expensive for Albion personnel to have to travel to all the many disparate sites in order to verify the contractor's claims, and check the standard of work. Again, if Albion entered into a long-term relationship with one firm of contractors, it might be able to take more on trust, but again, entering into a long-term relationship would involve sacrificing the pressure on price which comes from competition. As well as the costs associated with the drawing up and executing of contracts, and the supervision of contract labour, there is also a cost associated with loss of control. As a customer rather than an employer, Albion Water surrenders the power to directly control and organize labour. If Albion is only one of several customers a contractor serves, he may be unable to respond as immediately to its requests. The contractor's prime commitment is to the continued viability of his own firm, which may not on every occasion amount to the same thing as providing the fastest and most reliable service to Albion. In pursuit of low labour costs, Albion would have to sacrifice a degree of control over prioritizing and organizing the workload.

Direct labour provides flexibility in terms of having labour on tap which can be deployed as management sees fit. By using direct labour, Albion retains the power to prioritize work, to call men off one job and send them to another:

> One advantage of having your own labour force is they are very flexible. They can be quite busy doing a job and something crops up, and if management decide that's higher priority they can tell the men to drop that job and go to the other one.

The aim of using a small, DLO-style unit, topped up by subcontract labour, is to achieve the best of both worlds. A small direct labour unit provides the local knowledge, flexibility and responsiveness required by Albion, whilst subcontractors furnish Albion with numerical flexibility. However, Albion Water is no longer prepared to 'buy' this control with the traditional package of wages, conditions and job security. It now makes the BMU compete for work, which is supposed to ensure that its internal organization is rational and cost efficient, whilst the explicit linking of employment security to the economic viability of the unit serves to discipline the direct labour force. The manager notes: 'I don't think to a limited degree a bit of uncertainty is a bad thing, that they're not entirely sure that they are secure, so that they work harder to make sure the company goes.' Again, topping up with subcontract labour yields the twin benefits of cutting costs and reminding direct labour that they are expendable.

BMU employees are all unionized, yet because the unit has been restructured without any formal change to the employees' employment contract there have been no negotiations, formal or informal, between Albion and the tradesmen's unions. This is in part because the eight BMU employees are divided amongst three unions: GMBATU, UCATT and EETPU. Not only is this group of workers divided amongst three different unions, but the unions themselves have problems of organization and coordination within Albion which were outlined in Chapter 3. The main difficulty is that because their members work in numerous, small satellite depots, unless a shop steward is present in each depot the union is unlikely to be informed of changes. For example, a UCATT regional official was confident that no changes had been made to his members' working conditions as a result of restructuring in the BMU, as the UCATT shop steward would have informed him if there had been. This was perhaps doubly optimistic since the shop steward concerned said he had 'given up' being a steward, apparently without notifying the regional office. Likewise the EETPU has only a handful of members in Albion Water, and the regional official for water did not even know that he had members in building maintenance.

If the unions had been informed of the changes talking place in the BMU, it is doubtful that they would have offered much resistance to the proposed restructuring. Another GMBATU official explained the impasse in which unions find themselves when employers use the threat of contractors to force through rationalizations. If they resolutely oppose change, management may simply go ahead and contract the work out, and their members may suffer the same fate as that of steel workers described by Fevre (1986). The official notes:

> They [could] end up with contractors, doing the same job, under worse conditions and worse pay than they would have had with Albion . . . We're jumping into bed with people we'd rather not be in bed with, but if we don't, our members will just turn round and say, 'You've done nothing for us. You've protected your own end, of course, you can say with your hand on your heart that you've done no deals, you've not traded, you're pure. Thanks. You're OK, chum, you've retained your purity, but I'm the guy who's out there with the contractor, doing all the horrible things that you said we shouldn't do.'

The unit has, then, been restructured without any negotiation with the employees' trade unions, or any change to BMU employees' formal employment contracts. Moreover, the work itself has not been redesigned in any sense, and the actual content of BMU employees' jobs remains much the same. What has changed in practice is the *informal* understanding of what can be expected by the employer of the employee and vice versa. Employees are still directly employed on permanent contracts. However, in exchange for the same pay, Albion Water now expects BMU employees to work harder and more flexibly. Furthermore, although Albion employs them on a permanent basis, it offers them no guarantee of work. Whilst all employees' job security could be said ultimately to rest on the commercial success of their employer, the difference here is that Albion has explicitly dissociated itself from the fortunes of the BMU, and so has distanced itself from the direct labour force. These men are direct employees of Albion Water, but they work within a unit which must compete with outside firms for in-house work. Their job security does not rest on the commercial viability of Albion as an organization, but on the capacity of their supervisor to win work from Albion and other outside agencies. Albion is attempting to set itself up as both their employer and their customer. It pays them as direct employees, but does not commit itself to providing a continuous workload. They have a job, but that job is always 'on the line'.

These employees see the relationship between the BMU and Albion as it stands as untenable and they are sceptical about how enduring it will be. As one tradesman remarked, 'Really they can't do this half and half, we've either got to stay with Albion, or else we've got to make a clean break.' Whether or not the arrangement can last remains to be seen.

For the moment, however, simulating market forces has proved a powerful tool for Albion. Very real concessions have been won from these employees. They now work longer hours and more intensely for the same basic pay, are more likely to be required by the supervisor to provide a range of skills rather than sticking mainly to one craft specialism, and work alone instead of with a mate. One summed up the new conditions of work: 'Time is of the essence all the time . . . When you work on your own you sort of take more chances, the safety aspect goes out of the window . . . It's constant pressure.'

The shift to profit centre and DLO style management is described by one senior manager as no more than a change in accounting practices. This is disingenuous. Simulating market forces by turning different groups of direct labour into separately accountable units makes cuts, redundancies, intensification of work, deteriorating working conditions and so on appear as objective necessities imposed by Darwinian laws of survival, and therefore harder to resist. Accountants may only interpret the world; the point, however, is that the way in which they do so can make it more difficult for others to change it.

On Control and Flexibility

This chapter illustrates the point that job content is not the sole or even necessarily the primary determinant of the employment relation. The changing relationship between Albion Water and certain groups of existing employees demonstrates that the tacit bargain struck between employer and employee over a range of issues, such as intensity of work, working practices and employment security, can be transformed without any substantial change to the technical content of work. The commercialization of employment relations effectively degrades employment without deskilling, fragmenting or standardizing the work itself.

The case study of the BMU workers also raises questions about management strategies. Wood (1989a) notes that flexible specialization theorists have tended to measure change against an oversimplified and highly generalized model of mass production. This has meant that an extreme form of Taylorist control has been counterpoised against an equally extreme vision of craft autonomy and flexible production, whereas in practice 'control and flexibility are not two ends of a single unidimensional continuum' (Wood, 1989a, p. 28). The point is that no matter how production is organized, whether along Taylorist, Fordist or 'post-Fordist' lines, management always and necessarily wishes to maximize both control and flexibility. This point needs to be made in relation to the IMS model, which implies that internal flexibility (the 'ability to adjust and deploy the skills of its employees to match the tasks required by its changing workload, production methods and/or technology' (NEDO, 1986, p. 4) and numerical flexibility (the ability to adjust labour levels to fluctuations in the volume of work) can be conceptually separated and differentially pursued. No matter how functionally flexible and highly skilled the workforce, management would not volunteer to sacrifice its control over its size. Thus, even large Japanese firms, renowned for using the *nenko* system of lifetime employment, will use redundancy measures during long periods of recession (Kioke, 1990).

By the same token, employers would not actively choose a totally disposable workforce which offered no internal flexibility at all. Ideally, firms wish to match all employees to the tasks required by changing workloads, production methods and technology, not just 'core' workers. As Hyman (1987, p. 43) observes, 'Employers require workers to be both dependable and disposable. Once again, contradictory pressures within capitalism help explain the restless but fruitless search for managerial panaceas.' It may be strategically a more important priority to achieve numerical flexibility with certain groups of workers and internal flexibility with others, but this should not obscure the fact that in an employer's nirvana, workers would provide both internal and numerical flexibility. As it is, the degree of flexibility which employees provide is the object of struggle (Pollert, 1988, p. 70). This theme is developed in the following chapter, which looks at how Albion Water has commercialized its relationship with another group of workers in pursuit of both greater internal and numerical flexibility.

Notes

1. Although Williamson's (1985) stress on the properties of transactions is pertinent to understanding these contractual problems, it should also be borne in mind that the limitations of 'market solutions' are also a function of factors external to the transaction itself. There is no absolute sense in which the costs of contractual specification and administration are too great to make contracting out worthwhile. If the labour of contract workers was far cheaper than that of direct employees, for example, the savings to be made from

contracting out could outweigh the costs of contract. Since the price of labour varies according to labour market conditions, union density, state legislation and so on, it can be argued that while the properties of the transaction have a significant influence on the firm's choice between market and hierarchical solutions, they are not the sole or even necessarily the primary determinant. Likewise, in certain circumstances, it is possible for firms to acquire firm-specific knowledge and skill from contract workers, as the example of Harrup's workers demonstrates.

8 COMMERCIALIZATION, RATIONALIZATION AND CONTROL

This chapter examines changes to work organization and employment relations for the group of Albion Water employees who undertake mechanical and electrical maintenance (M&E). Once again, the function has undergone substantial restructuring which management argues was necessary to enhance flexibility. This restructuring has affected M&E workers' jobs in a number of ways, none of which can be readily matched to 'post-Fordist' visions of a shift towards more integrationist employment relations as a consequence of more flexible forms of work organization.

Mechanical and Electrical Maintenance until 1988

Both the supply and recovery functions rely crucially upon a range of pumps, motors and engines which are in continual need of service and repair. A maintenance service for mechanical and electrical plant and equipment is therefore vital to the authority's operation. Although this service is indispensable, the question of who best to provide it and how is problematic for management. There are three possibilities: the service could be provided by an in-house unit of mechanics and electricians, or by outside firms, or by a combination of the two. Until recently, the last option was adopted by Albion Water. Responsibility for the maintenance of pumps and equipment in a number of pumping stations and treatment works was contracted out in totality, often to local authorities. The remainder was carried out by direct employees with contract labour occasionally being used for 'lop and peak', or for specialist repair work such as motor rewind.

The position of M&E in Albion Water's organizational structure changed twice during the 1980s. Until 1982, each of Albion's three operational divisions included a separate M&E function, headed by an M&E engineer beneath whom was a layer of M&E supervisors and craftsmen. However, this arrangement was found increasingly unsatisfactory. The operations function served by M&E constantly complained that the quality of service was poor, that M&E was not accountable for the work it did or did not do, and that the M&E service as it was would be incapable of responding to the rapid technological change, especially the introduction of telemetry systems, which was taking place within the operations function.

In 1982, a decision was taken to integrate maintenance, both mechanical and electrical (M&E) and instrumentation, control and automation (ICA), into the operations function. Thus, the responsibilities of the divisional M&E engineer were placed upon operational managers, who now took overall responsibility for the maintenance of pumps, plant and telemetry as well as for their operation. Integrated into the operations functions, the coordination and planning of the M&E service was spread between a number of divisional operations managers, and then further subdivided amongst a number of maintenance engineers and operational area controllers. In effect, this meant that there were several pockets of M&E direct labour dispersed among each division, all functioning independently of each other. Each pocket of craftsmen or technicians worked from a different depot, headed by an operational (rather than an M&E) supervisor, and each was linked to the divisional manager through separate, long chains of command (Figure 8.1). This dispersal of labour was replicated in the other two divisions.

Between 1982 and 1988, the budget for M&E work was allocated to the operations function as part of the overall operational budget. All work undertaken by operational employees was recorded on job cards, which were coded in such a way as to show the nature of each job, where it was done, and for which function (i.e. environmental function, water supply or recovery). In theory, then, the operations manager was able to keep track of expenditure on M&E and all other operational work, since expenditure could be broken down and analysed. Spending on each operational activity, such as M&E, was supposed to balance with the amount allocated to that activity in the overall budget.

M&E and ICA work consists of both routine maintenance, installations and repair of mechanical and electrical plant and equipment and telemetry. Under this system responsibility for the allocation of work was widely dispersed. Although work was primarily allocated by the operational supervisors to whom M&E craftsmen reported, routine

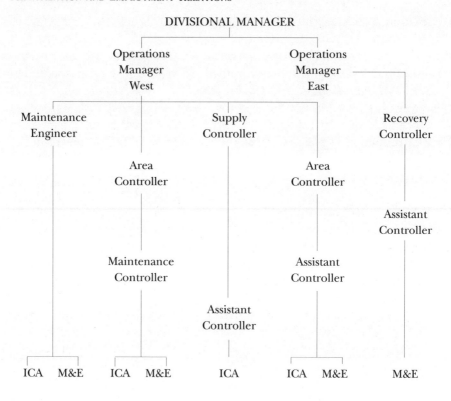

DIVISIONAL MANAGER

Figure 8.1 *Pockets of M&E and ICA labour in the pre-1988 structure. Note: ICA, technicians and apprentices; M&E, craftsmen and apprentices.*

maintenance was planned by M&E engineers and, furthermore, virtually anyone could request work directly from the craftsmen. For example, if a craftsman went out to repair a pump at a pumping station, the station's operational controller or even a site operative might ask the craftsman to have a look at another piece of plant which was malfunctioning while he was there. The craftsmen themselves would also initiate work. If they were sent to a site to do one job, and noticed other problems, they would simply get on and deal with them.

Just as M&E direct labour was dispersed under this system and accountable through separate chains of command, so planning and information about maintenance was in pockets, rather than centralized. There was no formal procedure for making decisions about maintenance on a 'macro' level, i.e. general decisions about direct labour levels, resourcing maintenance, ordering stocks of spare parts, new pumps, vehicles and so on. Responsibility for this type of planning was dispersed amongst area controllers, operational supervisors and the divisional M&E engineer.

The operational supervisors were based in depots and responsible for all aspects of operations in their particular geographical area. One of their many duties, then, was to plan, coordinate and supervise M&E work and craftsmen in their area. M&E craftsmen and technicians reported to their depot, where the supervisor would allocate jobs to them. When they finished a job, they would either radio in or report back to the depot, and the supervisor would tell them where to go next. He had to plan for routine maintenance, but if emergencies cropped up, to redeploy men as necessary.

Maintenance workers were employed as mechanics, electricians or technicians. Their pay comprised the basic rate plus a bonus payment. This could be topped up occasionally with standby payments and overtime. On average, the craftsmen's weekly wage was around £180 per week, including bonus. The bonus scheme at this time worked on a 'slot' or post-targeting system. According to an electrical engineer, this system was designed 'because the unions said they wanted everyone on a bonus scheme, Albion agreed but M&E didn't fit into any scheme'. The extraordinary nature of the slot scheme bears testament to this. The scheme consisted of a series of time slots – A was 12 minutes, B was 24 minutes, C was 36 minutes and so on. Craftsmen would note how long a job took and at the end of each week the supervisor would go through the time sheets and fit each job and each travel period into the nearest slot. The slot times for the week were then added up, and on the basis of this total a performance rating was awarded. If craftsmen scored a performance rating of 100% or over, they were entitled to a 33% bonus payment. Almost invariably the craftsmen received their one-third bonus payment, because there was a tacit agreement between management and unions that supervisors should fill out the slots in such a way as to ensure that they would. The electrical engineer comments, 'The blokes were told ''You will earn a third'' and the supervisors were told ''You will slot in at a third''.'

Skill demarcations were acknowledged to a degree (depending on the size of plant and complexity of the job), and certain jobs were broken down into skill components. For instance, if a pump was to be removed and sent for an overhaul, usually an electrician would disconnect the pump electrically, and then a fitter would disconnect and take it out mechanically. However, electricians would occasionally do mechanical work and mechanics electrical work, if they felt qualified to do so. Again, this decision was left to the craftsman's discretion. On the whole, craftsmen worked alone, but if they were working on a particularly large piece of plant, they would be assisted by a fellow craftsman.

The craftsmen reported to their depot to receive job sheets from their supervisor. Some craftsmen would collect a number of job sheets at the beginning of the week and rarely report back to the depot, while others would report back frequently. Having collected their job sheets, the craftsmen tended not only to do the job specified on the sheet, but also to carry out any work at that site which they deemed necessary or which was requested by the site's controller when they arrived. In short, there was a large element of discretion in their daily work. Craftsmen were tacitly encouraged to use their initiative in identifying and dealing with any further problems on sites to which they had been sent, and they were not usually under pressure to move on to the next job providing that they were usefully employed on the site where they were.

Problems with the Pre-1988 Structure

The way that M&E and ICA maintenance was organized between 1982 and 1988 generated many difficulties for management, built inefficiencies into the maintenance system and caused dissatisfaction amongst those who relied upon the service. One of the main problems to beset management was low productivity. This was basically caused by a lack of effective planning, resulting from the dilution of responsibility for M&E work amongst numerous area controllers and operational supervisors, and from poor communications between links in the chain of command. Those making decisions had information only about the craftsmen directly under them, and only about the demand for maintenance or repair work in their given 'patch', rather than about the maintenance needs of the division as a whole, which meant that labour was used inefficiently. For instance, two supervisors in different areas might send two craftsmen 30 miles to two sites virtually next door to each other, rather than one craftsman attending to both jobs consecutively. Such problems lowered both productivity and the standard of service. The dispersal of labour under several separate chains of command also built rigidity into the system, and this lack of flexibility and responsiveness was seen by management to be another key problem with the pre-1988 structure. A divisional M&E engineer explains that before the 1988 restructuring, 'You had lots of little pockets of manpower just working in one set area . . . If another area was under pressure, you couldn't really move the men across . . . people just tended to stay in their own patch.' It was therefore hard to respond rapidly to peaks in emergency work in one area, even when craftsmen in another area were engaged solely in non-essential or routine work.

Another problem with this structure was that it led to high overheads, in part because there were so many supervisory layers built into it. Assistant controllers and supervisors in different patches within a division were often duplicating each other's work, and no economies of scale in terms of supervisory and planning costs were realized. Poor communication and the dispersal of responsibility also led to waste and high costs. Because each controller only had information about the plant and equipment in his given 'patch' it was impossible to monitor or evaluate the performance of items of plant. A supervisor cited an example of a pumping station on a small housing estate where:

> The Division spent in a year about ten times more than it was getting in water rates for it, because different people would go in and do repairs and nobody had taken into account the overall picture . . . There was actually a fault where people weren't cleaning the site properly, but one person would go in, repair it, put a new component in, it would last a couple of months then go wrong again and someone else would go in and repair it and so it would go on, with nobody identifying the cause of the problem.

Within a 'patch' there was no systematic collection of data on plant and equipment, and no real communication between the various layers of personnel. Whilst a craftsman might know he had been called out to repair the same piece of plant five times in a year, the controller, who had responsibility for replacing plant, often did not. Equally, because the maintenance system was broken up into small patches, costs for the whole division's M&E and ICA maintenance were not monitored systematically, so that inefficiency and waste was effectively obscured from view.

The system of depot-based supervision and the lack of information about plant further meant that a great deal of a craftsman's working day was spent travelling, and this in itself increased costs. The problem was compounded by the system of bonus payments. Travelling time had been negotiated in such a way as to allow 2.78 miles per minute. This meant, for example, that craftsmen were allowed a one-hour slot to travel 23 miles. A supervisor explained 'If you sent someone 20 miles, they'd get 100% bonus before they even did the job, just on the travelling.' For this reason, craftsmen had a maxim, 'miles means money'. The bonus scheme created other anomalies. For instance, if a job was completed in 15 minutes, the nearest slot was an A (that is, 12 minutes) and so the crafts-man overshot the target time by three minutes. If, instead of completing in 15 minutes, he strung the job out and took 20 minutes, the nearest slot was a B (that is, 24 minutes) and on paper his performance was improved, since he had come in four minutes under the target time. There were thus no incentives built into the scheme, except an incentive to book in times that fell just short of a benchmark.

Another problem for management which arose from this system was the lack of effective control over craftsmen. Because the supervisors' plan-ning and co-coordinating role effectively tied them to their depot, there was little possibility for supervisors actually to oversee or check crafts-men's work. The divisional M&E engineer comments 'What happened in reality was that if a supervisor was at his base, he had contact with his men from time to time, but essentially he wasn't supervising his men, they were supervising themselves.' Being largely self-supervising, the craftsmen enjoyed a degree of autonomy in their work. For example, as noted above, once on a site they would carry out any jobs they felt needed doing, rather than only that work allocated by the supervisor. Clearly, this diminished supervisory and managerial control in terms of planning labour power, since a job that the supervisor had allowed, say, two hours for could turn into three jobs and take all day. Moreover, because the discretionary element of their work was so high, it was virtually impossible for supervisors to monitor individual craftsmen's performance and produc-tivity. They simply had to take it on trust that a craftsman had spent longer on a site because he was replacing dead lightbulbs or oiling machinery or whatever. Communications between craftsmen and supervisors was so informal and so limited, and procedures for monitoring craftsmen's where-abouts so haphazard, that supervisors could easily lose track of craftsmen altogether. Some craftsmen would report back after virtually every job. Others would work virtually independently of the supervisor, only picking up job sheets once or twice a week. One electrician commented:

> I've been in situations where a supervisor's said to me, 'Sorry I haven't been able to see you this week, I've been a bit busy', and I've turned to him and said, 'I was on holiday all week'. They didn't even know . . .
> You could be dead at the bottom of a tank for a week before they even missed you.

Finally, the way in which maintenance was organized meant that there was a high level of dissatisfaction with the service that was provided amongst those who depended upon it. Poor planning meant that large backlogs of work built up over time, inadequate communication and inefficient organization made the response to emergencies sluggish, and lack of systematic data on plant and equipment delayed jobs requiring new parts and components. For the reasons outlined above, costs for M&E and ICA maintenance were high, and because a great deal of work was initiated by the craftsmen themselves, or otherwise bypassed supervisors and so were never recorded, the service appeared on paper as even more inefficient and costly than it actually was. Moreover, because M&E personnel reported to operational supervisors, and because the operations function had suffered a drop in direct labour levels, M&E craftsmen would often be given operational work, such as unblocking pumps, instead of M&E work. In this way, the M&E budget was covertly used to supplement the operations budget, so that operations appeared to be functioning efficiently whilst a vast backlog of M&E work built up. Taking all these problems together, it is clear that from management's point of view there was an urgent need to tighten managerial control of M&E in order to provide a more rational and efficient service.

The New Mechanical and Electrical Maintenance System

The new M&E system brings together all the M&E and ICA staff under the management of one M&E engineer, who has responsibility for all M&E maintenance (Figure 8.2). M&E's position in Albion Water's organizational structure has changed. Rather than being integrated into the operations functions it is now a separate unit. At the same time as it was separated from the operations function, it was also transformed into an independently accountable profit centre which must 'buy' and 'sell' services from and to the core business of supply and recovery. Alongside these changes went a major restructuring of M&E work. This involved the introduction of new technology, which facilitated more systematic planning and the introduction of new forms of work allocation and supervision.

Albion Water began computerizing its operations in 1978. Gradually the 4000 maps of its assets and responsibilities (rivers, sewers, mains, and so on) have been turned into digital data which can be instantly summoned on to screens in central control rooms. The controller can immediately access information about where pipes are, when they were laid, what they are made from, their size, where the valves are and so on. Alongside this

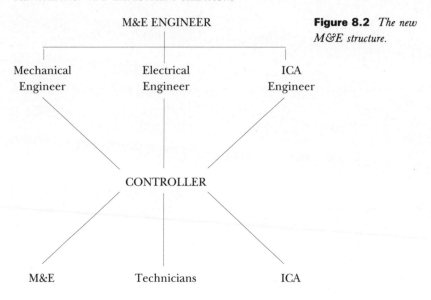

Figure 8.2 *The new M&E structure.*

digital mapping system, a computer-based telemetry system has been introduced. This monitors information about water levels, flows and pressures in the region, as well as information about how effectively plant and equipment is functioning. The introduction of telemetry has meant that rather than relying primarily upon staff and customers for information about malfunctions, Albions now receives such information automatically. Likewise, many routine adjustments to flow and pressure within the system are now effected automatically, rather than manually. The M&E engineer argues that as computerized telemetry transformed the way that plant and equipment was monitored and increasingly centralized control over core operations, the old system for providing maintenance gradually became inappropriate.

Previously, Albion's supply and recovery operations were fragmented into a patchwork of locally controlled areas, and the old M&E structure catered to this pattern. The numerous operational supervisors knew their own little patches, and wanted an M&E service which provided them with their own 'pet fitters' and 'pet electricians' to maintain those patches. The introduction of new technology to the operations function displaced local control. As information about breakdowns and malfunctions became centralized a less fragmented M&E system began to look more economic. The new M&E system is computerized, using specially designed software. All the division's M&E work is now centrally coordinated by one controller, who sits in front of a bank of computers which store information about the unit's workload, about the craftsmen, and about plant and equipment. All the craftsmen carry radio message pagers; the controller can send messages out on these at any point, and thus remain in constant communication with the men.

The introduction of new technology has facilitated the introduction of new methods of work allocation. All requests for work are now channelled through the central controller. Operational superintendents contact him, and specify the nature of the job and the priority attached to it. A sliding scale of priorities is used. Class A jobs are urgent and must be attended to within two hours. Class B jobs must be attended to within the day. Class C jobs must be carried out on a specific day, or by a given date. Making requests for work directly to craftsmen on site is now discouraged. If such requests are made, however, the craftsman concerned must contact the controller and clear the job with him before undertaking it. The controller then logs this request on the computer. This method of allocating work through one central controller is designed to provide a system which records all work carried out by M&E craftsmen, monitors their performance in terms of response times and allows the 'customer' to prioritize the work being requested.

The main aim of the new system is to improve productivity through more effective planning. It is therefore characterized by extensive collection and monitoring of information, and by rigorous coordination and planning techniques. Clearly, simply by bringing all M&E and ICA staff together under the management of one M&E specialist, the job of planning at a 'macro' level was made into an easier and more rational process. Moreover, the new system centralizes all relevant M&E information. Plant histories (IDs) are being compiled and computerized which allow detailed information about the type and size of plant and equipment at every site, its serial number, the type of components used, the component suppliers and so on to be retrieved at the stroke of a key. Again, this dramatically increases the efficiency of planning. Not only does the system facilitate more efficient planning in terms of spare parts and components, but it also makes it easier to focus capital investment where it is most needed. If the performance of each item of plant is monitored:

> It will enable us to be in a better position to say to the people who run the capital side, 'This is why we want to replace it.' We can actually show them the costs involved in repairs and maintenance. It's very important because before capital investment was very ad hoc, it was very often at the whim of whoever happened to be about.

Decisions about manning levels and the use of contract labour will likewise be better informed. The system makes it possible to monitor the costs of direct labour per unit of work more effectively, and to gauge what percentage of M&E work is subcontracted. Data are collected in such a way as to show up where there are shortages or excesses of labour – for example, it might be that there are too many mechanics and not enough ICA technicians. In the past, area or assistant controllers might have realized there were problems in their particular patch, but on the whole, the supervisor comments, 'It was very isolated and you couldn't see the overall picture of what the situation was.' The centralization of information thus makes for more efficient planning of manning levels. Rather than the day-to-day planning of work and labour power being carried out by a number of disparate supervisors, all such planning is now carried out by the central controller.

The controller has information about all work outstanding and about the whereabouts of each craftsman at his fingertips, and as requests for work come in, he enters them into the system. If they are class A jobs, he can immediately contact a craftsman in the vicinity of that job, find out how soon he could get there, and allocate the job if appropriate. If they are class B jobs, he can review each craftsman's workload for the day and, again, allocate the job appropriately. The aim of this new method was to rid the service of the rigidities which came from dispersed, local planning, and create a system capable of responding rapidly to requests for emergency work. But as well as making the service more responsive, the system is also designed to cut costs. The central controller attempts to plan in such a way as to reduce the amount of time each craftsman spends travelling. In part this has been achieved through the introduction of on-site reporting. Craftsmen are no longer based at a depot; they go straight from home to the first job, and straight home after the last job of the day. The central controller can pinpoint all the jobs that have been requested on a digital map at the end of each day, and allocate each craftsman a job for the following morning that is near his home. Improved communications with a central controller remove the need for craftsmen to report back to a supervisor during the day to pick up new job sheets or spares. Throughout the day, the controller can call up the locations of each craftsman on the screen, and give him follow-on jobs in his vicinity. The controller also tries to ensure that craftsmen carry an appropriate level of spares to minimize the number of journeys to and from depots.

Under the old system, operational supervisors had three functions:

supervision, planning and provision of back-up in terms of ordering spares, tools and equipment. Now, in the words of the divisional M&E engineer:

> The supervisory layer has essentially been removed. The need to visit a supervisor to pick up work has been eliminated . . . What we've done is to circumvent the supervisor's role as a planning source, because what we found was our supervisors were not inclined on a systematic and commercial basis to plan work . . . The supervisors were very often under so much pressure they'd say they hadn't got time to plan.

This problem could have been partially ameliorated by the introduction of on-site reporting and by developing a communication network which improved contact between the craftsmen and their supervisor. However, it was clear that if investment was to be made in improved communications, economies of scale could be realized by reducing the number of supervisors: 'One good planner, or controller, can keep a lot more men going than two or three supervisors can.' Not only does the new system eliminate the supervisors' planning role, but it also supplants their supervisory role. Under the old system, the supervisors had very little real control over the craftsmen. They were often supposed to be supervising as many as ten men, each working on perhaps five different jobs a day, on sites spread across a large geographical area. It was not possible for a supervisor to supervise directly. On the whole, they had to simply take on trust the fact that the men were working productively. The M&E manager likes to present this stripping out of the supervisory layer as a form of job enrichment for the craftsmen:

> The craftsmen are skilled, trained, qualified personnel, intelligent men . . . and really they don't need the level of supervision that has hitherto been thought necessary, because the reality is that they worked on their own anyway. So we're saying we're going to give you a lot more freedom . . . a lot more responsibility. You are no longer going to be closely supervised so you've got to be self-motivating . . . You're going to be responsible for your movements and the work you're going to be doing.

This vision of highly trusted, autonomous workers is quickly dispelled as the manager continues:

> On the other hand, we're going to have far closer control over what's happening because everyone's job is going to be planned. They'll be told

> to go to that job, when they've finished that job they'll be reporting in
> and they'll be told the next job and so on. Everyone's day is going to be
> very closely charted . . . We'll know all the productivity, we'll have all
> the management information, movements, productivity, the whole lot will
> be fed into the system . . . It's closer supervision because everyone will
> be accountable for their time, far more accountable than they have been
> because the supervisor hasn't been able to keep this level of control.

Thus rather than stripping out the supervisory layer because the craftsmen 'really don't need the level of supervision that has hitherto been thought necessary', the supervisors have been dropped because a more effective method of control has been found to replace them.

The new M&E system has one further key feature. In 1988 M&E was identified as an activity with 'commercial potential', and as part of Albion Water's broader restructuring in preparation for privatization the unit was reorganized as a profit centre. Where previously M&E maintenance was included in the operations budget, now the unit is allocated its own annual budget, controlled by the M&E engineer. However, as a separate profit centre, the unit must 'win' its operating costs, and thus this budget is effectively an advance on the services they will 'sell' to in-house customers. In other words, the sum they are allocated is calculated to cover the unit's labour costs and overheads, but the unit then has to charge its in-house 'customers' for each item of work carried out, and must generate enough 'income' from these sales to cover the budget they have been allowed.

Though formally 'independent', the M&E unit does not have the authority to set its own prices. Instead, Albion Water's finance department decides what hourly rate the unit can charge its 'customers'. Finance has designed a sliding scale of hourly rates, whereby class A jobs are the most expensive, and this rudimentary price system is intended to serve as a rationing device which will inhibit the making of excessive or unnecessary demands on the service by 'customers'. The setting of these hourly rates was a complex procedure. It involved arriving at a figure which was supposed to represent a realistic assessment of the unit's annual labour costs and overheads, based upon historical performance and projected productivity improvements, then dividing this figure by the projected number of man-hours the unit could, potentially, sell. Various incentives and penalties have been built into the system, which are intended to encourage the unit to function efficiently.

The shift to profit centre status has not only affected accounting practices, but has also impacted upon labour policy. Under the old system, a portion of Albion's M&E maintenance work was carried out by direct labour and a portion was contracted out. Now this pattern is changing as old and new elements are brought together in a new configuration. When M&E was vertically integrated into the overall operations function, M&E employees saw themselves as part of the operations 'team'. Now that M&E has been stripped out from this structure and horizontally linked to the operations function, M&E employees, like the BMU employees, are distanced from their employer. The tie between M&E and Albion Water is now presented as a commercial one, and the M&E manager exhorts the craftsmen to consider the operations function as 'our customer'. As a separately accountable unit, M&E occupies a more exposed position than it did as an integral part of the operations function. Its costs, performance and productivity are open to far closer scrutiny and it is now under pressure to demonstrate that it offers a service as competitive, or more so, than outside firms of contractors. This pressure is the force behind the drive both to win back work that has previously been contracted out, and to contract out work previously undertaken by direct employees.

Pilot tests of the new system of centralized control indicated that it would yield very large productivity gains. The M&E manager comments that the unit had to make these gains 'count', either by increasing turnover or by reducing its direct labour levels. To cut direct labour to a level which would make the unit appear efficient would have been impossible in the short term, given Albion's no-redundancy agreement with the unions. Thus M&E was forced to try to expand its workload by winning back work previously contracted out to local authorities and private bodies, and by securing work on a commercial basis from third parties. For, as a profit centre and commercial initiative area, the M&E unit is now required to generate profits from external work, as well as serving the needs of in-house 'customers'.

Athough the M&E manager speaks of expanding the unit's workload as a 'positive' approach which will soak up direct labour's productivity improvements, in practice increasing M&E's workload by bringing Albion work back in house and tendering for commercial jobs does not denote a preference for the use of direct labour *per se*. The unit will still subcontract the sort of repair work for which there is a low and irregular demand, and will still use contract labour for lop and peak. This means, then, that as the unit's workload expands, so too will the amount of work it contracts out. The new system means that the M&E manager can now make decisions concerning manning levels and contract labour, and use contract labour to mop up peaks instead of subcontracting whole units of work to outside agencies. Thus he is able to exercise greater control in this area, and can choose to use contract labour where it will be most cost effective. Another engineer explains various ways in which contract labour can now be used to cut costs and facilitate planning:

> If I'm taking on outside work charging our hourly rate, and if the contractor is charging us lower than our hourly rate, so we can make money on it, then it will be contracted out . . . Even with in-house work, if someone says to me 'I want a cable running from there to there and a starter put on it', what I do is say, 'Are we effective at running that cable?' If not, we can get a contractor to run that cable and we'll just do the connections at the end . . . Also, planning is about saying 'We aren't going to be able to cover all that, I'll get a contractor in', and that leaves us a bit of slack to cover emergencies.

In summary, then, this new organization of M&E work represents an attempt to cut costs and raise productivity through the centralization of planning, allocation and managerial control. The new system has rationalized the maintenance service provided to Albion Water's core operations. Centralized control of M&E maintenance mirrors and complements the operational control system; centralized planning and coordination replaces what was an essentially haphazard process of resource allocation. Planning and performance monitoring means that, in effect, Albion can extract more labour from M&E craftsmen for the same wage. Meanwhile, elements such as in-house maintenance work, work contracted out to external agencies, direct labour, contract labour and commercial ventures have been rearranged to form a pattern more suited to the unit's new, profit centre status. However, although this new system has addressed many of the problems associated with the pre-1988 structure, it is not without contradictions of its own.

Contradictions in the New System

As with the BMU, the relationship between M&E and Albion Water is ambiguous. As a profit centre, M&E is notionally independent. It is supposed to be competitive with outside firms of contractors, and it is encouraged to seek commercial work outside Albion. Most significant of all, it is told that Albion is a 'customer' rather than an employer, that the relationship between them is conditioned by market forces and that therefore the unit's continued viability rests on its capacity to both generate profits and keep the 'customer' satisfied. However, like the BMU, M&E is not a truly independent unit, and those running it on a day-to-day basis (the electrical engineer mentioned earlier and the central controller) have little real say over many issues which crucially affect the unit's capacity to generate profits and keep the 'customer' satisfied. It is they who experience the contradictions of the relationship between Albion and M&E most sharply.

It was noted above that although the M&E unit is supposed to act as a small firm, its rates are set by accountants in the finance department who attempt to build various incentives and penalties into the pricing system. One such penalty concerns overtime. The rate it is allowed to charge its 'customers' is £12.50 per man hour. This is calculated to cover overheads and labour costs. The amount allowed for labour costs is fractionally over the actual labour costs for normal daywork, so that when M&E charges £12.50 an hour for work done in normal working hours it makes a few pence on it. However, the electrical engineer explains that 'If we do work at night we lose on it because we can only charge that standard rate, regardless of whether we're actually paying overtime.' Moreover, if the unit exceeds what is seen by the finance department as an 'acceptable' level of overtime, it will be penalized the following year by having its on-costs raised, so that, in effect, the hourly rate it can charge falls, whilst the 'income' it must generate rises. The electrical engineer comments:

> It's a real grot system. I would prefer that we stand by our merit . . . If
> people want to use us, say on capital works, and it's cost effective for us
> to do that on overtime then we should be able to charge back properly.
> But management theory as I understand it is that overtime is a penalty
> for the department, it looks better for them so there's a permanent effort
> to reduce it.

The M&E unit has been instructed that, like a small firm, it should go out and actively seek commercial work. So far, it has been successful not only in winning back in-house work from local authorities, but also in winning a variety of contracts outside. Some of these contracts are for work very similar to Albion Water work, e.g. the maintenance of pumps and plant in private sewage pumping stations. Others are very different ventures; for instance, the unit won a contract from the Home Office to design and maintain high-security electrical doors in a prison. Meanwhile, the unit has still to cope with a huge backlog of M&E work for Albion itself. This causes problems for those who run the unit, for it is hard to balance the competing claims on their resources from in-house and private work. If they do not attend promptly to private clients they will not win more commercial work, and so cannot generate profits. If they do not attend promptly to in-house work they will be unable to fulfil their brief to satisfy in-house 'customers'.

This problem is compounded by the fact that those who actually run M&E cannot make decisions about direct labour levels. They are unable simply to recruit more craftsmen as a small firm might do in these circumstances. Instead, all they can do is attempt to meet the shortfall with subcontract labour, over which they have less control, and which they do not believe is suited to all types of work. On top of this, as with the BMU, those involved in the day-to-day running of the unit and who are responsible for winning outside work are not in control of the unit's accounts. Instead it is Albion's finance department which bills private customers. The finance department does not accord the same urgency to this task that a small firm would. Indeed, it even omitted to bill a number of private customers altogether, and it was some months before the electrical engineer noticed and drew the matter to their attention.

The electrical engineer and the controller are at the sharp end of these contradictions. Like the BMU supervisor who encouraged his workers to meet notional profit targets in order to save their jobs only to find that when they had done so, management went ahead and cut the workforce by half, the M&E electrical engineer and controller have been placed in an invidious position by management:

> I'm really caught in the middle . . . To my mind if we increase productivity then we ought to be able to pay for that, but if our productivity goes through the roof all that will happen is they'll ask me to trim the figures back so they don't have to pay for the new productivity. They'll want me to make sure the men's bonus works out the same as it was before . . . When the men's bonus went up, [a senior manager] was on the phone right away: 'What the bloody hell do you think you're doing?' We said, 'The new scheme's working, productivity's gone up.' The attitude was that we were totally inefficient before so now they should be getting a third bonus, but that was what they were on before.

The craftsmen want rewards for productivity increases, and when these fail to materialize they direct much of their anger towards the electrical engineer and the controller, who are powerless to do anything about it. Both the controller and the electrical engineer played key roles in designing the new system. It is now proving to have qualities reminiscent of Frankenstein's monster. They believed that by increasing the unit's efficiency, the system would protect their fellow workers from the threat of contractors, and by improving the unit's productivity, the system would enhance the craftsmen's take-home pay. In practice, it is undermining M&E workers' job security and pay:

> We designed the system and there were a lot of promises from management. We didn't expect it would be used like this, there's definitely been a lot of backtracking . . . They haven't exactly played fair.

The larger point is that, as with the BMU, the simulation of market forces within the firm generates a series of contradictions, since the economic viability of the M&E unit is determined by Albion Water's senior managers and not by commercial principles and consumer choices. Yet it was not necessary to turn M&E into a profit centre in order to rationalize the unit; control of M&E work could have been centralized without at the same time commercializing the relationship between Albion and the unit. This raises two questions. First, why were these two sets of changes (rationalization and the shift to profit centre status) introduced in tandem? The second is that raised by the restructuring of the BMU, namely, why simulate market forces when it is possible to have the real thing with an outside firm of contractors?

Market Mechanisms and the Threat of Contractors

In order to understand why the two changes were introduced simultaneously, it is helpful to consider briefly the way in which M&E employees were introduced to the new system. The M&E engineer, who now manages all Albion Water's M&E work, anticipated a certain amount of resistance to the new system from the craftsmen. In part this was because he believed that people are innately conservative and will always resist change, yet he also acknowledged that opposition to the new system would not be entirely irrational. He could see that changing the system of travel payments, for example, would reduce the craftsmen's take-home pay, and he also acknowledged that under the new system, because more of the working day would be spent actually 'on the job', the men would effectively have to work harder and longer. However, he argued that without a fairly dramatic increase in productivity the craftsmen would be gradually winnowed out as more and more M&E work would be contracted out, and that therefore, in the final analysis, it was in their long-term interests to accept change. This manager believed that he should take positive action to secure the men's cooperation. He therefore set up a training week, requiring all 60 craftsmen to attend a two-day course at a conference centre in the country. This was intended to be a social and 'morale-boosting', as much as a training, exercise.

For two days, the craftsmen were treated to the kind of perks normally reserved for management. They stayed overnight at a seventeenth-century manor house converted into a conference centre, and were provided with lunches and a three-course dinner. A social outing to play skittles at the local pub was also included in the programme. The general aim was to develop an *esprit de corps* amongst the craftsmen, encouraging them to identify with their new position as a separate unit within the Albion Water structure.

The training schedule included items such as a Tom Peters training video entitled 'A Passion for Customers'. The video opens with Peters vigorously explaining to an audience how poor customer service is at the root of economic decline in the advanced industrial nations. It goes on to exhort managers and workers alike to pool all their resources, initiative and skills and concentrate them on satisfying the wants of their customers. Peters does not expect firms to do this out of benevolence, but argues that it is profitable to focus on service and quality. He illustrates this point with case studies of five companies that have profited through their 'passion for customers'. This set the mood of the training exercise, which was essentially an attempt to make the craftsmen accept their new, commercial relationship with Albion Water. The M&E engineer explained to the men that M&E personnel must now learn to see the operations function as their customer, rather than as their employer, and become passionately devoted to answering their 'customer's' needs. He argued that many of the practices adopted by Peters' five exemplary firms should likewise be adopted by the new M&E unit; for instance, increased communication between producer and 'customer'; increased mechanization of routine tasks; increased 'team spirit' and total eradication of demarcations of skill or responsibility; increased worker interest in the firm's (or unit's) success through profit-sharing schemes and share ownership.

The craftsmen's response to the Peters video was less than enthusiastic. Several said that they did not feel it was relevant to them but only to managers, since at the end of the day all workers, even those in Peters' exemplary firms, simply do what they are told: 'You can only use your initiative if the boss tells you to.' Just as no one seemed to believe that a 'team' approach signified any genuine redistribution of power or control over the work itself, so all seemed sceptical about the idea that profit-sharing schemes give workers a bigger share in the fruits of their work. There was a sense that, as with piece rates or bonus schemes, profit sharing would be used only to bring wages up to a certain, predetermined level and never beyond that:

> Tom Peters says about them steel workers, that profit sharing makes up 40% of their wage. Well to me, all that says is that their basic wage can't be so great. It's like our bonus. If you say it makes up 30% of our wage it sounds like a lot, but it's not, and we only get it because our basic rate isn't that good anyway.

Craftsmen also expressed concern about the idea of considering Albion Water as their customer and about the new emphasis on profitability. One craftsman remarked that the operations functions 'won't be very happy if we try to make a profit out of the service we provide them', while another commented:

> He [Peters] gauged success by how much money people make. Are we going to have to do that? At the end of the day it's the taxpayer or the consumer who pays if we make a profit, so therefore if we make a profit it's because we're charging too much.

During the day, the new system of centralized planning and control was described to the craftsmen, as were the predicted productivity gains. Craftsmen were urged not only to view their employer as 'customer', but to actively contribute to the unit's profitability by volunteering for retraining in order to provide multiple skills, and by seeking commercial work for the unit. Over and over again, these changes were presented as the only means of saving the craftsmen's jobs from contractors. The M&E engineer pointed out that large portions of M&E work were being put out to contract, and argued that with reduced direct labour levels and the huge increase in M&E plant, the direct labour force was struggling. The need to offer a service at a competitive price was a recurring theme throughout the two days. The centralization of control under the new system was presented as a means of protecting the craftsmen's jobs. The M&E engineer argued that by centralizing control and monitoring both performance and requests for work, it would be possible to collect evidence that would demonstrate the value of direct labour. As the M&E manager put it, 'What we've got to do is prove that we're competitive with contractors.'

Details of how the system would affect pay and working conditions were continually interwoven with references to the threat of contractors. These threats were articulated most explicitly when craftsmen raised objections to the new system. For instance, craftsmen pointed out that plans to introduce on-site reporting and slash travel time could add at least an hour to their working day, that they would now effectively be doing more work for the same, or less, money, and one summed up general feelings by saying, 'You've shown the new system's got a lot of advantages, they're all to Albion though, there's nothing in it for us.' This was met with an angry rejoinder from the M&E engineer to the effect that their interests and Albion Water's interests were one and the same. Undeterred, the craftsman continued, 'You've said you want to produce a bonus scheme that pays the same as now, only with more jobs done. How is that to our advantage?' The answer, of course, was that the prime objective behind the restructuring of M&E was to make the craftsmen competitive with outside contractors, and as such was an attempt to ensure continued job security in the post-privatization era. As with the BMU, simulating market forces within the organization and invoking the spectra of contractors served an ideological function, making change appear to be the inevitable consequence of immutable laws rather than an instance of 'macho management'. Again, as with the BMU, these tactics proved an effective instrument in winning very real concessions from direct labour, for as will be seen in the following section, the restructuring of M&E work led to substantial changes to the employment relation.

A Changing Employment Relation

Until these reorganizations, M&E craftsmen stood in what can be termed a standard or traditional employment relation with Albion Water. Their employment and work was funded bureaucratically through internal budgets; they carried out only in-house work; control over them was exercised through supervision; skill demarcations were acknowledged

Table 8.1 *Organization of Work and Employment under Old and New M&E Systems*

	Old system	New system
Formal labour relation	Standard (full time, permanent)	Standard (full time, permanent)
Employment security	Tacitly guaranteed	Tacitly conditional
Division of labour	Craft specialization	Multi-skilled
Resource allocation	Bureaucratic	Internal and external market
Means of control	Direct supervision and post-target bonus scheme	Performance monitoring and incentive payments
Degree of worker discretion	High	Low
Level of firm-specific knowledge	High	High

and they were tacitly guaranteed continuity of employment. Under the new system M&E craftsmen remain direct employees of Albion. They are entitled to all the same fringe benefits and for the time being their jobs are protected by the no-redundancy agreement. Thus, in a formal sense, the employment contract between Albion and these men remains unchanged. However, as with BMU employees, the way that contract is interpreted informally (i.e. the tacit bargains struck around wages and effort, discretion and control, job security, flexibility, and many other issues) has changed. In other words, what is expected of the employee by the employer, and vice versa, what the employer is 'buying' with a wage, what it means to be directly employed, have all been transformed by the new system. The key changes are summarized in Table 8.1, and are discussed more fully below.

Working Hours and Work Intensity
Depot-based working has been replaced by on-site reporting and craftsmen must arrive at the allotted site at 8 a.m. each day. Rather than reporting back to their depot after the completion of a job, they receive instructions on the message pager about where to go next. These new

arrangements affect the length of the working day, since the sites they report to and finish at may be further away from their home than the old depot was. Thus, on-site reporting can increase the time between leaving home in the morning and arriving home at night. On-site reporting combined with the travel time rationalizations has lengthened the amount of the day actually spent on site, working. In this sense, then, productivity gains are a straightforward consequence of intensified labour.

Basic Pay and Bonus Payments

The craftsmen's basic pay remains the same under the new system. Thus, despite working more intensely, the craftsmen's pay packet remains at around £180 per week. Some believe this is because they are not being paid for the time spent travelling to and from work: 'It is eroding our money . . . we're not being paid for travelling' and 'It means the working day's a lot longer'. This is a major bone of contention. As one mechanic put it, 'They're expecting us to do more work for the same money. People don't work harder for the love of it.' Furthermore, a new bonus scheme has been designed to replace the old 'slot' or post-targeting system. For a ten-week period the craftsmen's performance on each different M&E activity was monitored and timed. The average time for each activity was then used to design a complete set of pretarget times for all M&E jobs. These pretarget times were then built into the central controller's computer system, so that each time he allocates a job, a target time for its completion is automatically given with it.

Initially under the new system the craftsmen were paid their one-third bonus if they met, or improved on, these target times. After some negotiation with union representatives and Productivity Services it was agreed that a three-banded system could be put in place, whereby craftsmen would receive only a 28% bonus payment if they do not, on average, reach target times; the one-third bonus payment if they reach target times; and up to a 38% bonus payment if they improve on target times. This means that under the new system it is possible for craftsmen to earn 5% more than they could have done under the previous system. However, in order to earn their one-third bonus, they now have to do more work.

Discretionary Content of Work

Centralized planning of work effectively removes the discretionary element which used to be present in the craftsmen's work and greatly increases managerial control over the men. Under the old system, craftsmen exercised a high degree of discretion over the pace, planning and content of their work. The new system has changed this, and instituted in its place two new forms of control. First, centralized control means that craftsmen can no longer plan, pace or allocate their own work. Second, the length of time spent by each craftsman on each job is recorded and monitored, so that the central controller has detailed information on each individual's performance and productivity. Craftsmen are now monitored far more closely than ever before. Several of the craftsmen refer to the central controller as 'Big Brother', and in general these new forms of control are seen as one of the worst features of the new system. One mechanic commented:

> Whereas before we used to be able to plan our week, we knew what we was going to have to do ahead of time, now we don't know in advance. They just tell you. So it has taken away our freedom. We used to be left to our own resources, you worked alone and we liked that.

Multi-tasking and Job Enlargement

In the past the division of labour within M&E was, broadly speaking, characterized by craft specialization, with mechanics, electricians and ICA technicians being employed to undertake a different, and clearly demarcated, range of tasks. M&E craftsmen did not always stick rigidly to these skill demarcations, however, and would on occasion undertake those aspects of each other's work which they felt qualified to do. As noted earlier, this was another aspect of their work which was left very much to their discretion. What is different about the new system is that it aims to introduce multi-skilling on a formal and systematic basis. It is ultimately intended to operate on a one-job one-man basis, eradicating skill demarcations completely and building up, in the words of an M&E manager, a 'wholly flexible and multi-functional team of employees'. This would entail training all craftsmen in at least two new areas of skill so that each worker would become a qualified mechanic, electrician and ICA technician. None of the craftsmen interviewed opposed this idea in principle, provided there is adequate training and that they are financially rewarded for their newly acquired skills and increased efforts.

Social Organization of Work

The introduction of on-site reporting and travel time rationalizations mean that craftsmen no longer enjoy the same degree of contact with their co-workers. The electrical engineer comments that on-site reporting has the dual advantage of reducing the amount of the working day spent travelling, and preventing craftsmen from 'wasting time having a good old chin wag in the depot first thing in the morning'. This means that each craftsman works in virtual isolation, only seeing fellow maintenance workers on large jobs and once monthly at team briefings.

From Quality and Service to Speed of Throughput

Working practices and conditions have also changed because of M&E's new profit centre status, and concomitant emphasis on cost cutting. The craftsmen argued that pressure to cut costs means that they can no longer pride themselves on the quality of their work to the same degree, since their performance is measured against costs and productivity rather than quality:

> They say they want us to satisfy the customer, but they're also giving us these pretarget times and if we don't do the work in the time, we won't make our bonus. They're not going to give us our bonus because we done a good job if it took longer.

Employment Security

Finally, the restructuring of M&E as a separately accountable profit centre has changed M&E employees' subjective perceptions of employment security. As with the BMU employees, Albion Water has made their continuity of employment conditional upon the success of their unit in 'winning' work. As an independent profit centre, M&E workers feel more exposed. Organizationally separated from the operations function, the unit's performance and profitability is now far more visible. Yet most M&E employees realize that the commercial 'success' of the unit depends as much upon the accounting procedures employed to assess it as upon their individual efforts.

Furthermore, the craftsmen have witnessed the gradual depletion of M&E direct labour levels over the past ten years, whilst the volume of M&E work has increased during that same period. They have observed a growth in the use of contract labour for M&E work. This, combined with observations of more general economic trends, has led to a general sense that as an isolated unit M&E is increasingly vulnerable to replacement by contractors. A shop steward describes how the new accounting practices make the threat of contractors appear very real:

> It amounts to . . . working out what the costs of each unit are to see whether it's viable or not. Of course, how you measure viability is

another matter, least said the better. But within Albion now, everybody is hived off into separate little entities and the profitability of all those departments is being scrutinized and if they find one of the departments is an expensive luxury that they can't afford then that's it, out they go.

Yet, as with the BMU, how genuine a threat contractors pose is open to debate. For M&E work, even more than building maintenance, requires local and firm-specific knowledge, firm-specific skills and the commitment and capacity to respond quickly in emergencies. To a far greater degree than with building maintenance, M&E work involves idiosyncratic exchange, and, here again, problems of contract specification, supervision and control make it unlikely that Albion Water would choose to contract out M&E work in totality. As one electrician comments, 'It's all a question of whether you can specify the work easily, this sort of thing you can't and that's why I think they want to keep an in-house maintenance and electrical structure.' The question is more one of how large an in-house unit and at what price. A shop steward's comments illustrate the tension between the idea that direct labour is expendable and therefore must compete with contractors, and the idea that direct labour provides Albion with firm-specific knowledge and skills that cannot readily or cheaply be bought from contractors:

> We want to work effectively, because it's inevitable that if we stopped tomorrow Albion can bring in an outside firm and replace us. It might take 12 months before that firm had the inside knowledge we have, but they could learn with time, it's not impossible. One of the biggest problems here is finding the pumping stations and so on, it can take months or years to learn where things are, they can give you maps but that doesn't help, but in the end these things can be learned, though not overnight. So whereas you think, 'Yes, anybody could do my job', that's true, but they couldn't do it as easily as I could because I know all the ground and so on. An outside firm would have to be led by the hand and shown where it is.

However, another shop steward argues that at the end of the day management will fail to appreciate such complexities, and its short-termism is what really puts jobs at risk: 'There won't be a conflict, money will always win . . . They might pay more in the long run but it's the short term that counts.' The real point is that, just as with the BMU employees, concessions in terms of work intensity, working practices and working hours have been extracted from M&E craftsmen without any formal change to their employment contracts. The simulation of market forces within the firm and the constant reiteration of the threat of contractors have both proved effective ideological weapons. However, the power of these tactics cannot be abstracted from the specific context in which they are being used. Two points in particular must be borne in mind. First, throughout the early 1980s, M&E craftsmen witnessed falling manning levels, even while the volume of M&E work increased in line with the increase in plant used by Albion (in one area alone the amount of plant increased by 33% between 1984 and 1988). As a consequence, more and more M&E maintenance and installation work went to outside contractors. In the southern area of Albion Water, for example, 45% of M&E work now goes to outside contractors. Thus, Albion does not merely invoke the spectra of contractors for ideological purposes.

Second, wider political and economic forces must be considered. These changes are being instituted in a period when organized labour is weak, and in an organization which has the explicit backing of a right-wing government. All the M&E craftsmen and technicians are union members, being divided amongst the EETPU and GMBATU. Amongst those interviewed, only the shop stewards claimed to be active members. However, no one, including the shop stewards themselves, believed that the unions could do anything to resist the changes in working practices and conditions within Albion Water as a whole, or M&E in particular. The shop stewards argued that the unions have been effectively castrated by the Thatcher government: 'There's nothing they can do now with legislation as it is . . . There's no choice you see, you can't fight it.' They point out that the men still turn to union representatives when they feel that changes threaten their working conditions: 'People still come to us and say they're unhappy, but there's not a lot we can do . . . We haven't anything to bargain with.' The stewards feel that Albion management, inviolate in the mantle of government's blessing, is so confident about restructuring that winning the union's consent or approval is a matter of supreme indifference to them: 'In the last 18 months the unions here have been completely ignored. The attitude is like it or lump it.' In short, by simulating market forces within the organization and by holding the threat of contractors over an exposed group of employees, very real concessions have been won by Albion Water in terms of work intensity, working practices and working conditions. In a different political and economic climate, such a strategy might not prove so effective.

Flexibility, Labour Porosity and Employment Relations

The changes to the bargain struck between employer and employee described above have not hinged on deskilling or degrading the technical content of work, but have been effected through the transformation of its social organization. Both the BMU employees and the M&E craftsmen have been subjected to something rather like the processes described by Burawoy (1985, p. 150), when he argues that increased capital mobility has enabled large firms to use the threat of relocation to force through rationalization, technological change and intensification of work, so that:

> Where labour used to be *granted* concessions on the basis of expansion of profits, it now *makes* concessions on the basis of the relative profitability of one capitalist vis-a-vis another . . . the fear of being fired is replaced by fear of capital flight, plant closure, transfer of operations and plant disinvestment.

Albion Water, of course, is hardly in a position to relocate, but comparisons of the relative profitability of direct and contract labour is likewise being used by management to extract concessions from direct employees. 'Post-Fordist' commentators have argued that the pursuit of flexibility will force employers to seek more cooperative relationships with labour (Murray, 1988; Sabel, 1982; Piore and Sabel, 1984; Katz and Sabel, 1985). All that M&E craftsmen have been offered in exchange for providing greater internal flexibility and working more intensively is a two-day stay in a converted manor house, a game of skittles with their managers, and the opportunity to watch a very expensive pop management video. Albion has not found it necessary to woo them with material concessions in terms of improved wages, conditions or job security. If anything, the reverse is true. Once again, this raises the whole question of what is meant by 'flexibility'. To the extent that craft specialization and job demarcations are being eradicated, with M&E workers now being asked to provide multiple skills, and work on a one-job one-man basis, we can say that the new form of work organization fits with the trends described by 'post-Fordist' commentators. Yet such analyses suggest that flexible forms of work organization are a response to the limitations inherent in Taylorist and Fordist methods of work organization. How strange, then, that this flexibility should be coupled with a new control system which is effectively a micro-electronic application of Taylorist techniques.

The only way to make sense of the apparently disparate trends within

M&E (internal flexibility combined with rationalization and greater managerial control, bringing work back in house whilst simultaneously contracting more work out, devolving responsibility down to the level of the unit whilst simultaneously strengthening centralized control over budgets, overheads and so on) is to focus on their impact upon labour. Changes to the organization of M&E work, like the other forms of restructuring in Albion which have been described in previous chapters, have one unifying theme; all aim to reduce the porosity of labour. Indeed, Tomaney's description of recent restructuring in manufacturing precisely captures the nature of change in M&E:

> What is striking about current attempts to restructure the relations of production in new ways is the presence of strong continuities with the past . . . The focus on new forms of labour control through electronic surveillance, forms of neo-Taylorism . . . represent new developments of existing tendencies. The re-integration of some tasks or the introduction of controlled group working can be seen as efforts to reduce the 'porosity' of the working day. Moreover, the existence of relatively inexpensive micro-electronic systems means that the work system and productive process can be subject to a higher degree of management regulation. Invariably at the heart of the changes is an intensification of the work process. (Tomaney, 1990, p. 52)

Much of the work reorganization at Albion Water reduces labour porosity by compressing more labour power into a given period of time. Allocating recovery workers a continuous rather than a finite workload and enlarging their jobs to cover all aspects of the work process eliminates pauses and breaks in their working day, and so squeezes more labour power out in a given period. Introducing on-site reporting for M&E craftsmen and building maintenance tradesmen cuts out the 'idle time' spent on social interaction with their co-workers, and on waiting for their co-worker to finish one element of a job before they can start on the next, so that, again, more labour power is squeezed out of a given period.

However, restructuring has also improved the productivity of labour by preventing labour power from being unproductively consumed, e.g. in unnecessary travel time or in filling out job sheets. Whilst this time was unproductive from Albion's point of view, from the worker's point of view it was still time which was spent actively working for Albion, rather than resting, relaxing, or socially interacting with co-workers. It could be argued, then, that in these cases the craftsmen's labour has not been *intensified* as such, but diverted into more productive activity. (In practice, the craftsmen themselves tend not to see driving as work; it is 'time out' and 'a bit of a breather' and they therefore see themselves as working harder as a consequence of the travel time rationalizations.) Managers at Albion certainly like to present change as inconsequential for labour, especially in negotiations over possible financial concessions in exchange for new working practices. As one manager commented, 'We're not actually asking them to do any more than they used to do, we're not asking them to work harder, we're just asking them to work more effectively.' This of course ignores the fact that rest periods and waiting time have been pared down so that the craftsmen are actually working more continuously, and so more intensely.

At a more general level, it is worth noting that technical advances in coordinating and planning work which cut out non-productive labour for one group of workers can intensify labour in the firm as a whole, even if that particular group of workers is not forced to work harder or longer, but simply more 'effectively'. This is because, as Marx observed, labour is almost invariably interdependent *social* labour; the fact that separate elements of the work process take place simultaneously means that each worker feeds the next with his or her work: 'the result of the labour of one is the starting point for the labour of the other' (Marx, 1976, p. 464). Indeed, this simultaneity of the separate processes in manufacture, Marx argues, is of enormous benefit to capital since:

> the direct mutual interdependence of the different pieces of work, and therefore of the workers, compels each one of them to spend on his work no more than the necessary time. This creates a continuity, a uniformity, a regularity, an order and even intensity of labour, quite different from that found in an independent handicraft or even in simple co-operation. (Marx, 1976, p. 464)

Thus, even if improvements in the productivity of one group of workers could be secured without any increase in their efforts, these improvements may well entail work being passed on to another group of workers at a faster pace; a momentum for speeding up and intensifying labour may be set in motion by eliminating the non-productive activities of one group. Marx observed that it was necessary to consider the workshop as a whole, and not just one single element of the labour process, in order to understand the benefits of a detailed division of labour for capital. It may be that attention should be focused upon the consumption of labour power in the organization as a whole, rather than in one productive subunit, in order to fully understand how 'flexibility' intensifies labour.

Change at Albion has not been characterized primarily by technical innovations in working methods. Instead, the most conspicuous and distinctive feature of change is that it involves the introduction of new methods for coordinating, organizing and controlling labour power, and attempts to match labour power more closely to the organization's productive activity. Work organization and employment practices are designed to make continuous and more productive use of the labour power which has been purchased, and this is true of moves both towards 'internal' and towards 'numerical' flexibility. In much the same way as Tomaney (1990) argues that 'Japanese methods of work organization can be seen *primarily* as a means of work intensification based upon the elimination of wasted time in production', Albion's primary objective is to make labour power (rather than labour or the labour process itself) more flexible, to turn it into a more malleable commodity that can be consumed and digested whole, without waste. The pursuit of 'flexibility' for both 'core' and 'peripheral' workers in Albion is above all the pursuit of a denser working day.

9 THE CAPITALIST EMPLOYMENT RELATION

This book has shown how tighter financial control over water services through the 1980s and their subsequent privatization impacted on employment relations in one water company. Government policies thrust Albion Water into a more commercially orientated world, wherein the organization was under pressure first to show, and then to continually expand, a return on capital employed. This transformed the pattern and nature of employment relations within the organization. Until the mid-1980s, the pattern of employment relations in Albion Water was basically a simple dichotomy. On the one hand, Albion relied predominantly upon full-time, well-unionized, direct employees, all of whom (regardless of whether engaged in ancillary functions such as building maintenance and catering, or in the core business of supply or recovery) enjoyed stable and secure employment and a relatively good package of fringe benefits. On the other hand, Albion made significant use of workers employed by firms of sub-contractors in both the supply and recovery functions. Now this pattern has changed. To begin with, the ratio of direct to subcontract labour has altered. But more importantly, perhaps, the pattern is now more complex, weaving together a number of quite different forms of employment. As well as 'standard' direct employment, many groups of direct employees are now organized along the lines of Direct Labour Organizations. Albion has started to make use of self-employed workers, as well as to contract out work previously undertaken in house to self-employed individuals and small firms.

In the run-up to privatization Albion began to redefine its boundaries, contracting out work previously undertaken in house by direct employees and bringing work back in house that had previously been contracted out. But these changes represent more than a simple quantitative shift away from 'standard' employment relations. They also facilitated qualitative changes to the nature of direct employment and enabled management to force concessions from labour in terms of working hours, working practices and work intensity. This was because Albion's direct employees recognized that the boundaries of the firm are elastic and not determined solely by the technical exigencies of production. The threat of subcontractors therefore proved an effective instrument of labour discipline in a period when organized labour was weak and unemployment high.

Management states that changes have been instituted in order to make Albion a more 'flexible' organization[1] and though the pursuit of numerical flexibility is hardly likely to augur well for labour, both the flexible firm and flexible specialization literature might lead us to predict that management's desire for internal flexibility would lead to improvements to the employment package for at least some groups of employees. However, the experience of Albion workers suggests that the link between internal flexibility and a better deal for labour is not an automatic or necessary one. Albion Water secured greater internal flexibility from several groups of workers without ceding any benefits in terms of pay or conditions in return. Indeed, often the reverse has been the case.

The pursuit of flexibility appears, above all, to have led to a reduction in the porosity of the working day, both through eliminating unproductive activities and 'idle' or 'wasted' time, and by ensuring that each worker is provided with a continuous flow of work. Albion's prime objective in restructuring employment relations has been to make labour power (rather than necessarily the work process itself) more flexible. For example, by directly employing a number of workers that falls just short of that required to meet demand during troughs, and buying any extra labour power necessary through the medium of period main-laying contractors, Albion Water ensures that it can consume every last drop of labour power purchased. Direct employees will not be underemployed even during troughs in the workload, and contract workers' labour power will only be purchased as and when necessary.

Similarly, changes to the organization of recovery, BMU and M&E work are all intended to prevent labour power from being squandered on unnecessary activities such as filling in time sheets, travelling, set-up time between jobs, social interaction between co-workers, resting or relaxation between tasks. At the same time, management has sought the 'flexibility' to move workers cheaply and quickly to where their labour power can be most profitably consumed, so that, again, less of this commodity will be wasted. In sum, the effects of these changes to employment relations have been to wring more value out of the labour power purchased. This changing pattern of employment relations has certain implications for theoretical analyses of the determinants of the capitalist employment relation, and the source of its variability. This chapter attempts to briefly develop them.

Dualism, Diversity and Job Content

It was argued in Chapter 1 that recession and protest in the advanced industrial nations in the late 1960s and 1970s constituted a powerful empirical challenge to liberal theories of industrial society, and that the need to explain the diversity of capitalist employment relations and industrial structures (particularly the persistence of 'peripheral' jobs and workers) encouraged many authors to talk in terms of dualisms. Primary and secondary sectors and jobs have been identified; workers within single firms, as well as in the economy as a whole, have been classified as 'core' or 'peripheral'. Whilst recognizing the variability of capitalist employment relations, labour market economists, institutional economic theory and flexibility theorists have, however, tended to explore it in relation to the technical content of work or the particular skills and competences of the worker. This has created a tendency for employment relations to be conceptualized along one single continuum, with closely specified, low-discretion work accompanied by minimal and Taylorist employment relations at one pole, and loosely specified, high-discretion work coupled with more favourable employment relations at the opposite pole. This same basic model has also been employed by some radical and labour process theorists who have sought to explain the range of control strategies adopted by capital. One of the recurrent themes of this book has been that the link between the technical content of work and employment relations is not as strong or as direct as much of this literature on work implies, and it therefore highlights the limitations of existing models of the employment relation.

To begin with, a unidimensional model suggests that employers can choose between strategies that increase their control over labour and strategies which harness labour's active cooperation. Yet, as Cressey and MacInnes (1980) note, relationships at the point of production are necessarily contradictory, since capital wishes *both* to control labour as a commodity and to unleash its power as a human, subjective force. Even the most closely specified, fragmented and deskilled work entails a degree of cooperation, and, in liberal democracies at least, no employer will seek a purely coercive relationship with employees. Indeed, Henry

Ford (1922, p. 126) commented that the introduction of the five-dollar day and the reduction of working hours in 1914 was necessary because 'Good will is one of the few really important assets of life.' Alfred Sloan observed that General Motors' 1948 employment contract stated: 'A continuing improvement in the standard of living of employees depends upon technological progess, better tools, methods, processes and equipment, and a co-operative attitude on the part of all parties in such progress' (Sloan, 1986, p. 398). Finally, Taylor himself talked about the 'mental revolution' which should accompany his schemes, and claimed that scientific management would lead to 'close, intimate cooperation, [and] constant personal contact between the two sides' which 'more than all other causes' would tend to diminish the conflict between management and labour and improve productivity (Taylor, 1947, p. 19).

Thus employers can simultaneously seek increased job fragmentation and automation and increased cooperation. Moreover, there is no automatic relationship between the technical organization of work and particular control strategies or employment relations. Drucker's (1946) examples of wartime production techniques provide an interesting illustration of this point. Drucker contends that the wartime experience demonstrated 'the flexibility of the concept of modern mass production'. Mass production techniques can be used to speed up and cheapen production without necessarily turning workers into detail labourers. A key problem for wartime production was that skilled labour was in very short supply, and consequently, unskilled workers had to undertake the work of highly skilled mechanics. To make this possible, Drucker claims that task fragmentation was used to simplify the work process but not to extend the division of labour, and assembly lines were used to control the flow of materials to workers, rather than to move the product from worker to worker to perform successive operations:

> The skilled job was reconstructed as a series of unskilled operations to be performed in sequence *by the same worker* . . . the new technique which replaced the assembly-line-in-space by an assembly-line-in-concept, and which thus enabled one man to turn out a finished product all by himself, was as efficient technically as the old methods. (Drucker, 1946, p. 186) (emphasis added)

Where traditional mass production techniques were used to organize production, various strategies to increase the worker's active participation and cooperation 'to establish a relation between the war-worker and his product' were sometimes adopted, and these strategies often differed from those which are generally associated with Taylorism. For example:

One of the smaller divisions of General Motors in northern Michigan converted from the production of steering gears to army carbines . . . The management worked out a plan under which a special department of skilled men was entrusted with the training of new employees . . . a man from the special department took [the new worker] out to the target range, showed him a carbine, took it to pieces, explained how it works, and showed the part on which he himself worked . . . After this the representative of the special department and the worker sat down together and worked out the most efficient production methods based on time–motion studies of the job and on the individual's rhythm . . . Most important, it was the worker himself who worked out the procedure and set the schedule . . . The worker knew not only what he did at every step but also why.

Drucker's account is doubtless a romanticized one, but it does suggest that the *degree* to which task fragmentation and flow line production techniques diminish worker autonomy and control can vary, and that there is no direct or mechanical correspondence between a particular form of work organization and particular managerial tactics.

The tendentious nature of the link between job content and employment relations is also evidenced by a consideration of the gendered nature of work. Although it would be misleading to suggest that definitions of skilled and unskilled work are wholly socially constructed and have no material basis whatsoever (West, 1990), it would also be difficult to explain patterns of sexual inequality in employment relations solely through reference to variations in job content. As West observes, the range of viable employment relations open to employers has to be understood 'in the wider political context of government economic and social policy', and thus the growing phenomenon of women's part-time employment, for example, 'depends on the vulnerability of women in the labour market' (West, 1990, pp. 263–65).

Employment relations cannot be mapped out along one continuum with low-discretion work and coercive managerial tactics at one pole and high-discretion work and integrationist policies at the other extreme. As has been seen at Albion Water, job content is not the sole determinant of employment relations. Contract workers and Albion's direct labour undertake identical 'core' tasks, and provide the same degree of firm-specific skill and knowledge, under very different terms and conditions of employment. The tacit bargains struck with certain groups of direct employees over pace and intensity of working have been transformed without any changes to the technical content of their work being effected. Direct employees have been forced to provide greater internal flexibility and to work more intensely without any new benefits being ceded in exchange. Indeed, often such changes have been accompanied by reductions in bonus payments and possibilities for overtime working. Any model of the employment relation which accords primacy to the technical content of work is therefore of limited utility in accounting for the changing pattern of employment relations at Albion Water.

Since labour process analyses have focused on the degradation of work through deskilling, it might be claimed that this approach is open to similar criticisms. However, it is argued below that whilst such analyses have not always embraced the variability of employment relations, the insights that the approach offers into the capitalist labour process still remain the most useful starting point for a theory of the capitalist employment relation.

The Variability of Labour Power

Throughout the 1970s, Marxist writers made important contributions to the analysis of direct employment relations. In particular, they drew attention to the fact that for most workers in the advanced industrial nations, direct employment was far from 'self-actualizing'. Instead, it typically involved undertaking routine, mindless operations in a closely controlled, alienating environment. Many of the early analyses were not concerned with the variability of capitalist employment relations, then, but sought to identify the dynamic which led to employment relations being concentrated at the left-hand pole of the continuum described in Chapter 1. At the heart of these analyses is Marx's argument that the labour power purchased by the capitalist is a commodity of indeterminate value. Capital invested in its purchase is variable capital, since the amount of use value that can be squeezed from the commodity varies. This means that when the decision is taken to employ labour directly, management is faced by one overarching problem: how to realize the full potential of the commodity purchased. For Braverman, ultimately there is but one solution to this problem. Accumulation rests on capital acquiring greater control over the labour process by deskilling labour in a specifically Taylorist fashion, and Braverman does establish very clearly how capital can benefit from Taylorism. What is not established is why the process is uneven across industrial sectors, or why alternative modes of employment and work organization persist or are developed (Brighton Labour Process Group, 1977; Littler, 1982, 1990; Elger, 1979, 1982).

Unless Braverman's thesis is modified in some way, all instances of work organization involving anything other than direct, Taylorist employment relations have to be treated either as an anachronism or an anomaly. In practice this means the experience of vast numbers of workers has to be explained as transitional or exceptional, while the experience of those workers who have recently found themselves cast from direct employment into indirect employment relations with their former employers (see Fevre's (1986) account of steel workers, for example) is perhaps even more inexplicable. Within those large firms which have traditionally been organized along Taylorist lines, any change in control structures or work organization poses similar theoretical difficulties. Though some reports of 'polyvalence' through job recomposition, the introduction of functional flexibility or multi-tasking should be taken with a pinch of salt (Nichols, 1986, pp. 201–4), the fact that changes do occur is difficult to account for if Taylorism is taken as the final, pure articulation of a deskilling dynamic, and the ideal of capitalist work organization.

Many writers who adopt a broadly Marxist perspective have challenged Braverman's emphasis on Taylorism as the most pure expression of capitalist control, noting that in reality a variety of control structures have been and are adopted by capital. It is often argued that Braverman's focus on labour solely as an object of capital leads to a distorted view of the capitalist labour process, and awareness of the fact that labour remains a subjective force at the point of production regardless of how deskilled the work it undertakes has provoked a plethora of modifications to, and criticisms of, Braverman's work. Some have emphasized the importance of subjectivity by arguing that employers are forced to adjust their control strategies in response to worker resistance (e.g. Edwards, 1979; Friedman, 1977a, b; Clawson, 1980). Others have stressed the fact that since the subjectivity of workers cannot be totally eliminated by Taylorist work organization, employers must seek cooperation from workers, as well as control over them. Burawoy (1979, 1985), Cressey and MacInnes (1980) and Littler and Salaman (1984), for example, all take issue with the idea that because the objective interests of capital and labour are diametrically opposed, it follows that relationships at the point of production are subjectively antagonistic and capital's overriding concern must always be to subjugate an intractable workforce. Littler and Salaman (1984, p. 57) explain the source of the employer's need for cooperation, as well as control, as follows:

> All forms of control contain, in different degree, two dimensions of control: the specification of levels of performance (and this may vary from highly specified to highly autonomous) and some effort to develop some level of consent, or acceptance of the legitimacy of the employment relationship. Both these dimensions are necessary for any work relationship. The utility of the specification of levels of performance depends absolutely on some minimal level of compliance.

The employment relation embodies a contradiction for both capital and labour; capital wishes to control labour in the same way that it controls other commodities, yet at the same time wishes to harness its active, human cooperation. Because specifications always require interpretation, even the most detailed Taylorist job descriptions cannot eradicate the employer's need for active consent. Labour is controlled and exploited by capital, but since it is dependent upon wages for subsistence, it also has an interest in the success of its exploiter.

Analyses which attempt to accommodate the idea of labour as both an object of capital and as a subjective force in the labour process do not always surmount the analytical obstacles which have been reviewed thus far. They can reproduce the control cooperation continuum outlined in Chapter 1, which takes job content to be the primary determinant of employment relations (e.g. Friedman, 1977a, b), or re-create a linear model of history, linking phases of capital's development to particular control strategies (e.g. Edwards, 1979). Despite these problems, however, it is argued below that the insights of labour process theory still provide the most useful starting point for analysing the diversity of capitalist employment relations.

Labour process theory stresses that the labour power purchased by the capitalist is a commodity of indeterminate value – the amount of use value that can be squeezed from it varies. The critical problem for management, so far as directly employed labour goes, is how to realize the full potential of the commodity purchased. Realizing this potential is, as Braverman (1974, p. 57) puts it, 'limited by the subjective state of the workers, by their previous history, by the general social conditions under which they work as well as the particular conditions of the enterprise, and by the technical setting of their labor'. It is worth analysing this statement in more detail, for it suggests that, in practical terms, the variability of labour power has two main sources.

On the one hand, how much value can be squeezed from labour power depends on the technical and social organization of production within a given firm. Marx observes that the capitalist can only consume his purchase (of labour power) by recombining the three elements of the labour process (purposeful activity, the object on which that work is performed, and the instruments of that work). The capitalist labour process is, in this sense, 'the process by which the capitalist consumes labour power' (Marx, 1976, p. 291). Clearly, this process of consumption can be effected in a more or less efficient fashion. If a direct employee is set to work using hand tools, his or her labour is less productive than if he or she works with machines; the direct employee's labour may be made more productive by setting him or her to work at deskilled tasks on an assembly line in a factory instead of at skilled tasks in a workshop. In other words, the amount of value that can be wrung from the labour power purchased varies according to how capital organizes its process of consumption.

On the other hand, the variability of labour power stems from the fact that workers are human beings, not automatons, and that they exist and work in a particular historical context. Because direct employees are conscious, purposive actors, they can, for example, put more or less effort into their work. If they design or plan their own work, they can undertake these tasks in a manner which coincides more or less closely with the employer's interests. If their work is closely specified, they can stick to the letter of their job specifications or they can interpret them in a fashion helpful to the employer. Workers can submit passively to the employer's commands and wishes, or they can organize against the employer. Likewise, the fact that workers are human beings makes them capable of learning, of acquiring knowledge and skills that can enhance the productivity of their labour power. The amount of value that can be squeezed from labour power is also affected by the fact that direct employees are not insulated from history, but live in a particular political, economic and social context. Fear (e.g. of unemployment, of prosecution, of poverty) can make workers drive themselves, or submit to being driven, harder. The level of education and health care provided by the state can also affect the amount of value which can be wrung from labour power.

There has been a tendency amongst some Marxist commentators to suggest that capital's need to control the first source of variability (that which stems from the efficiency of the technical and social organization of production) is necessarily subordinate to capital's need to control the latter source of variability (that which stems from the subjectivity of human labour). For example, radical analyses such as those provided by Marglin (1976) and Stone (1973) imply that the development of capitalist work organization represented no real technical advances in terms of *creating*, rather than just securing, surplus value (Brighton Labour Process Group, 1977, p. 8). Marglin suggests that the early factory system did not squeeze more value out of labour power because it organized production in a more technically efficient fashion, but because it gave capital greater control over effort levels by limiting the degree of choice that workers, as subjective beings, exercised over the pace and intensity of working. Productivity gains 'had nothing to do with efficiency, at least as this term is used by economists. Disciplining the workforce meant a larger output in return for a greater input of labour, not more output for the same input' (Marglin, 1986, p. 36).

Such views are contradicted by Marx's discussion of the social productivity of labour, in which he shows that the bringing together of large numbers of workers *does* enhance the productivity of labour. By bringing workers together under the same roof 'the socially productive power of labour develops as a free gift to capital' (Marx, 1976, p. 451). Because these powers are not developed until workers are brought together by capital, it appears as though they actually derive from capital, whereas in reality they derive from cooperation itself. The specialized division of labour developed in the period of manufacture involved a particular form of cooperation, and Marx (1976, p. 458) notes that many of its advantages spring from the nature of cooperation in general, rather than this specific mode of it. However, this division of labour also lays the foundations for the development of machinery and forms of work organization which do, in themselves, increase the productive powers of labour:

> The manufacturing period simplifies, improves and multiplies the implements of labour by adapting them to the exclusive and special functions of each kind of worker. It thus creates at the same time one of the material conditions for the existence of machinery, which consists of a combination of simple instruments. (Marx, 1976, p. 461)

Marx clearly did see increased direct control of labour as a precondition for, and a consequence of, the transition from handicraft to manufacture.

Yet Marx also shows how the specialized division of labour had material advantages over handicraft production which did *not* derive simply from increased direct control or supervision of labour it afforded. Because this form of the division of labour means that the independent operations of the labour process are performed simultaneously, workers are effectively called upon to continually feed each other with work:

> It is clear that the direct mutual interdependence of the different pieces of work, and therefore of the workers, compels each one of them to spend on his work no more than the necessary time. This creates a continuity, a uniformity, a regularity, an order, even an intensity of labour, quite different from that found in an independent handicraft or even in simple co-operation . . . In manufacture . . . the provision of a given quantity of the product in a given period of labour is a technical law of the process of production itself. (Marx, 1976, p. 465)

The productivity of labour increases not *just* because a capitalist, or foreman, is personally preventing workers from taking rests or embezzling or otherwise exercising subjective control over work, but because the way in which production is organized forces workers, in an impersonal way, to work at a different pace, rhythm and intensity. This division of labour also provides other benefits for capital by cutting the costs of production e.g. by making more effective use of capital. Marx gives the example of glass bottle manufacture, noting that because the specialized division of labour here enabled several operations to occur simultaneously, one of the means of production, namely the furnace, could be in continual use, thus causing it 'to be consumed more economically' (Marx, 1976, p. 467).

The point is that Marx recognized that from capital's point of view, the specialized division of labour did constitute an advance in terms of coordinating and managing the labour process itself. Capital developed increasingly efficient techniques for *consuming* labour power, and in this way managed to extract more value from the commodity than had previously been the case. Marglin is without doubt correct that increased direct supervision and control of workers did, in themselves, lead to a greater output in return for a greater input of labour. But this should not obscure the fact that this greater input of labour produced more than it would have done under handicraft production. The factory system did enhance the productivity of labour and in this sense it was a more efficient mode of exploitation. It simultaneously addressed both sources of the variability of labour power. The same point needs to be made in relation to Stone's discussion of Taylorism. Whilst Taylor was explicitly concerned to increase the employer's direct control over the workforce in order to reduce the degree of subjective control workers could exercise over effort levels and pace of work, this should not obscure the fact that Taylorism also raised the technical productivity of both labour and machinery (Kelly, 1982; Nyland, 1987). The systematic nature of scientific management did improve the coordination of the production process as a whole. Furthermore, it led to labour-saving product innovations and production techniques. Nyland (1987, p. 59) observes that:

> Taylor, for example, made significant contributions to the systemisation of the production process in the areas of stores accounting, stores management purchase, standardization and plant design and layout. He also developed a number of important new products the most significant of which was high-speed steel.

Again, Taylorism addressed *both* sources of the variability of labour power. It not only sought to limit the degree to which the worker's subjective state could restrain the employer from consuming his purchase, but also sought to wring more value out of the commodity by improving the technical conditions for consuming it, through rationalizing organization, administration and distribution systems.

Braverman does not fall into the trap of suggesting that capital's need to consume labour power efficiently and create surplus value is subordinate to its need to control the subjective elements of variability. He sees deskilling as necessary for both the creation and expropriation of surplus value. This is because, as his discussion of machinery illustrates, relationships at the point of production, like all social relations in capitalist economies, are fetishized. For Marx, fetishism necessarily involves both mystification and domination. Domination is concealed in a set of apparently objective economic relations, but mystification is not an end in itself; it cannot be separated from those economic relations. Domination is not simply political control, then. Capitalists are not the dominant class because they exercise direct control over workers but because the capitalist class alone has access to the means of production. Workers are dominated not simply because they lack authority and control in the workplace, but because dead labour in the form of capital rises up, vampire-like, to suck their living labour; because the instruments of labour employ the worker, rather than vice versa (Geras, 1971, p. 72).

Like Marx, Braverman argues that machinery under capitalist social relations is dead labour which dominates living labour, and is used to squeeze surplus value from workers. It is fetishized because it appears to make particular demands of workers on the basis of technical or objective exigencies, whereas in reality it is the exigencies of capital accumulation which determine the demands on labour. But for Braverman, this notion of fetishized production relations is inextricably linked to an overarching imperative to deskill and extend the division of labour in a specifically Taylorist fashion. The promise of machinery to allow workers true control over production 'is frustrated by the capitalist effort to reconstitute and even deepen the division of labor in all of its worst aspects, despite the fact that this division of labor becomes more archaic with every passing day' (Braverman, 1974, p. 230), and 'If the machine is fetishized, the division of labor in its present form is the subject of a veritable religion' (Braverman, 1974, p. 232).

For Braverman, both mystification and domination are at work. Workers appear to be meeting the technical needs of machinery and production, but in reality they are meeting the requirements of capital, namely increasing productivity so that capital can wrest more surplus value from their labour. The more that workers produce, the more their labour is objectified and the more living labour is subjugated to dead labour. This is not an ideological or purely subjective process. It is not simply that workers *feel* more alienated when they are driven by machines – they *are* increasingly alienated. The greater their productivity, the more capital comes to dominate them materially.

But is this alienation, this material domination, really directly linked to 'the present form of the division of labour', by which Braverman means a Taylorite division of labour? Many recent examples of manufacturers abandoning the type of specialized division of labour epitomized by Taylorism precisely in order to increase their profitability show that the material domination of living labour by dead labour can be increased without 'deepening the division of labour' along Taylorist lines. It can be argued that Braverman only makes this link because his work is informed by an idealist philosophy of history. Such a philosophy explains determinate phenomena 'by reference to the essences which they are thought to express' (Hindess and Hirst, 1975, p. 8). Braverman begins with a general theory of labour which holds that labour comprises two elements – conception and execution – from which he deduces two ideal forms – unity and divorce of the two elements. Handicraft production is then explained as the expression of the former, whilst Taylorism expresses the latter. Some critics have argued that Braverman's entire thesis is invalidated by this 'simple philosophical anthropology' (Cutler, 1978, p. 76). Without 'the romance of labour', Cutler argues, no essential features of the capitalist mode of production or broad dynamics can be generalized to deduce or predict the internal structure of any industrial sector. However, a consideration of the development of Marx's own writings on alienation suggests that it may still be possible to identify general features of capitalist employment relations even if the contrast of alienated capitalist labour with an ideal of unalienated labour is abandoned.

In the *Economic and Philosophical Manuscripts* of 1844, Marx also contrasts an ideal, unalienated society, a 'natural' human state or 'essence', against capitalist society (Marx, 1977, pp. 65–6, 90; Perlman, 1972, p. xxi). However, as his work progressed, the concept of alienation as man's alienation from his 'essence' was transformed, and, as Rubin (1972) argues, was ultimately developed in *Capital* as the theory of commodity fetishism. The theory of alienated human relations became a theory of reified social relations. As noted above, fetishism involves both mystification and domination. Although these 'two aspects are intimately related, inasmuch as men are in no position to control, rather than submit to, social relations which they do not correctly understand' (Geras, 1971, p. 72), domination cannot and should not be ignored as a feature of commodity fetishism. It is only through a consideration of the historically specific forms of domination exercised in capitalist economies that we can move beyond 'a concept of alienation founded on an essentialist anthropology' (Geras, 1971, p. 73).

If we abandon Braverman's general theory of labour, it is possible to see the transformation of the labour process that he describes not as the unfolding of an abstract historical tendency which reaches its zenith in Taylorism, but as a particular strategy adopted by particular units of capital in particular historical circumstances in order to secure capital accumulation through increasing the extraction of relative surplus value. Braverman's discussion of the degradation of work does not ultimately rest on 'the anthropology of humanism' as Cutler implies. To reject the idea that natural, harmonious conditions of labour existed in pre-capitalist societies does not prevent one from appreciating that the kind of unskilled, closely specified, closely supervised work Braverman describes is degrading. To reject the proposition that working conditions under capitalist production are at variance with 'natural' working conditions does not prevent one from arguing that capitalist working conditions are at variance with the objective interests of workers. To reject the notion that the capitalist labour process must take a single, universal form involving the separation of execution and conception as characterized by Taylorism does not prevent one from seeing that under certain circumstances, the capitalist labour process will take this form.

The core propositions of labour process theory (that because the capitalist labour process is also an accumulation process, capital is forced constantly to revolutionize the production process; that this, combined with the fact that labour power is a commodity of indeterminate value, produces an imperative for control; that the social relation between capital and labour is antagonistic – see Thompson (1990, pp. 99–102) can be sustained without in themselves logically implying progression towards a Taylorite division of labour or, indeed, any one, ideal form of work organization or employment relation that could be determined independently of a number of other factors. In order to effect such an analysis, it is necessary to begin by reiterating that the degree of value which can be wrung from labour power depends on two things; on the subjective state of the worker, and also on how efficiently his or her labour power is consumed. In practical terms, it is not always easy to separate out the employer's attempts to deal with these two sources of variability. Though the introduction of employee share schemes, for example, can be seen as primarily an attempt to deal with subjective elements of variability (such schemes are often intended to create feelings of loyalty and identification with the firm which in turn are supposed to make the employee work more intensely and reliably, paying more attention to quality and so on), other tactics address both problems simultaneously. For instance, assembly lines not only seek to improve the productivity of labour by cutting out unproductive time spent moving between work stations and so on, but also squeeze more labour out of employees by denying them opportunities to exercise discretion over the pace of work, so forcing them to work more intensively. Scientific management principles likewise tackle both elements of the variability of labour, sometimes individually (e.g. attempting to increase effort levels through financial sanctions and incentives, attempting to speed up throughput by rationalizing work organization), sometimes simultaneously (an increasingly specialized division of labour not only improves the productivity of labour for the reasons identified by Adam Smith, but also limits the worker's subjective control over the pace and intensity of working).

The problem of management cannot be reduced to a question of dealing with one source of variability alone. Neither the labour process nor the employment relation are designed solely in pursuit of technically efficient consumption, as the work of Williamson (1985), for example, suggests. Equally, neither is designed with the sole aim of restraining labour as a subjective force. The problem of management is to continually try to control both elements of the variability of labour power. Fragmenting work into routine unskilled tasks and ensuring that the throughput of work is efficiently organized so that each detail worker is presented with a new task every 10 seconds throughout the day does not solve the problem of the variability of human labour power, because unless there is some degree of consent (which may be secured through dull economic compulsion, 'bought' through various incentives, encouraged by certain ideological constructs, or some combination of these things), the labour process will grind to a halt. By the same token, motivating employees through financial incentives and integrationist labour policies, for instance, will not secure the full potential of human labour power unless these tactics are adopted in conjunction with work organization that minimizes unproductive labour time and fills in the pores of the working day, with technologies that maximize productivity, with rational systems for planning and distibuting work, and so on.

It is without doubt misleading to suggest that Taylorist methods amount to the elimination of the subjective element of variability. No form of work organization can effectively separate labour from its motive force.[2] But Taylorism has been effectively used to reduce the limits that workers can impose on how much of their labour power is consumed, and it has also been used to improve the efficiency with which it is extracted and consumed. However, Taylorism was not the last word in efficiency. Indeed, as has often been observed, Taylorist forms of work organization not only carry high coordination and control costs, but also can come to impose limits on how much value is squeezed out of labour power (Littler and Salaman, 1984; Littler, 1985). Unless there is a steady and high volume of work, assigning fragmented tasks to detail workers will enlarge rather than close up pores in the working day. If clerical work, for example, is rigidly demarcated into filing, typing, sorting mail and so on, and these tasks are assigned to detail workers, it will only be an efficient way of consuming labour power so long as there is sufficient work to keep each person working steadily throughout the day. If the work comes in peaks and troughs, each detail worker will be underemployed for a portion of the day or week, unless that person can be moved from one task to the next, and matched to the flow of work.

In other words, though Taylorism can be an effective way of controlling both sources of the variability of labour power, it is not the only, nor always the best, way. As has been seen at Albion Water, in particular historical and political climates employers can achieve these ends through other means. Take employment relations in Albion's supply function, for example. The technical setting of both direct employees and PMC labour is virtually identical, yet different tactics are adopted to control the subjective elements which make their labour power of indeterminate value. Albion seeks to extract as much effort and value from direct employees' labour power through a bureaucratically administered bonus system and a range of incentives in the form of benefits that are intended to make workers want to stay with the firm. Harrup's workers' efforts are controlled more crudely. On the one hand, Harrup's uses the threat of unemployment to try to squeeze more value out of the commodity it purchases. On the other, Harrup's attempts to pass the problem of controlling variability on to the workers themselves; its self-employed workers exploit themselves on Harrup's behalf. Meanwhile, the three-pronged labour strategy in itself makes for more efficient consumption of labour power, and thereby increases the amount of value that can be extracted from the commodity.

Furthermore, Albion has recently adjusted its methods of controlling the variability of labour power. Because privatization forces Albion to make and continually enlarge a return on capital, it is now far more concerned to extract the full usefulness of the labour power it purchases. The changes to work organization, payment systems and employment relations for recovery, M&E and BMU workers represent attempts to tackle both sources of the variability of labour power. There have been attempts to create a social and technical setting in which labour power can be consumed more efficiently (by cutting out unproductive labour time, presenting workers with continuous workloads, rationalizing work organization and so on). There have been attempts to reduce the extent to which workers can control how much labour is squeezed out of them. Firm job demarcations once imposed limits upon how much of their labour power could be consumed and where, and these demarcations are now being removed. Central, computerized planning of M&E work has removed the discretion previously exercised by craftsmen, and so reduced their ability to restrain how much value is squeezed from their labour power. Finally, the commercialization of employment relations has generated fear and insecurity, which yields management the twin benefits of coercing workers into agreeing to the above changes and into working harder.

All of this has implications for models of the employment relation. The capitalist labour process is above all a valorization process, and surplus value can only be maximized by maximizing the difference between the value of labour power and the value that it produces. The value of labour power varies according to the social and technical setting in which it is consumed, and according to the subjective state of the worker. The problem of management is thus to address *both* elements of this variability of labour power; it must develop techniques for making the consumption process more efficient, *and* techniques for controlling subjective sources of variability. Sometimes, a single strategy can simultaneously embrace both sources of variability. Deepening the division of labour, for example, can lead to more efficient consumption of labour power and simultaneously reduce labour's subjective capacity to control how much value is pumped from labour power. But there is no automatic or necessary link between techniques for making the consumption process more efficient and techniques for controlling subjective sources of variability.

Taylorist strategies for pumping more value out of labour power by making the technical setting for consumption more efficient are not *automatically* accompanied by Taylorist strategies for restraining labour as a subjective force, as the example from wartime production organization shows. 'Flexible', non-Taylorist forms of work organization can increase the amount of value squeezed out of labour power by reducing waste and creating a new rhythm and pace of working, but such techniques are not *automatically* accompanied by attempts to secure greater efforts through progressive or integrationist policies. As the experience of Albion Water workers illustrates, management can abandon some of the specific details of Taylorism without relinquishing the desire or ability to constrain labour as a subjective force. Moreover, workers can be persuaded to offer up the full usefulness of their labour (or at least something approximating to this) by other means, such as the commercialization of employment relations.

All of this points to the fact that we need some way of conceptualizing employment relations and strategies for controlling the variability of labour power which allows for greater diversity. For if the significance of the technical content of work is overestimated, or if techniques for controlling both sources of the variability of labour power are taken as necessarily identical, the range of possible employment relations is conceptually limited. The following section attempts to articulate a model of employment relations which can accommodate diversity. It is at best merely a preliminary model.

Dimensions of the Employment Relation

The employment relation refers to the set of explicit and tacit bargains struck over the exchange of pay, benefits and conditions on the one hand, for work on the other (Brown, 1988, p. 54). Bargains over the content of work (i.e. what the worker is expected to do, whether he or she is expected to provide firm-specific or transferable skills, one skill or many, to conform to strict specifications or to innovate, problem-solve and take responsibility and so on) are therefore an important component of the employment relation. However, the employer wants the worker to agree not only to undertake certain tasks, but also to undertake to carry out these tasks at a reliable and predictable rate. Thus the employment relation is not solely concerned with what the employee is expected to do, but is also affected by the bargain struck about the pace, intensity, reliability and quality of work. It is concerned not just with the exchange of pay and conditions for work, but also with pay and conditions for working (i.e. *how* work is done). The pace, intensity, reliability and quality of work can be controlled in a variety of ways. It can be controlled internally, through direct supervision and/or a range of bureaucratically administered rewards or punishments. Alternatively, market forces can be allowed to exert a more direct control on working. Payment and other benefits such as job security can be made conditional upon output or performance.

These two sets of bargains cannot necessarily both be 'mapped out along the same continuum. Of course, firms can break work down into discrete, standard chunks and then try to control *working* internally. For instance, the pace and intensity of work can be controlled by the speed of an assembly line or by direct supervision. Reliability can be pursued through controlled daywork (Lupton, 1972, p. 152), and/or a variety of benefits accorded to long-standing employees, and supervisors can attempt to control the quality of work. But fragmented, standardized work can also be put out to homeworkers or subcontractors, for example. Here the pace, intensity, reliability and quality of work is primarily controlled impersonally, through market mechanisms. A homeworker stitching shirt sleeves works with a given degree of intensity not because a supervisor is standing at her shoulder driving her, nor because a new sleeve arrives at her 'station' every two minutes, but because she will only make a living wage this week, and she will only be offered work next week, if she completes a given number, to a given standard.

Similar possibilities exist for loosely specified work. The pace, intensity and quality of such work, which requires labour to engage more actively in the production process, can be controlled internally through various bureaucratic procedures, rewards and punishments. For example, lifetime employment deals, career ladders or packages of fringe benefits can serve as inducements to employees to work reliably and at a rate and intensity acceptable to their employer. But low-specification workers can also be exposed to market forces. Such work can be put out to specialist contractors, freelances, or the 'new homeworkers'.

No matter what the technical content of work, then, management can seek to control the pace, intensity, reliability and quality of work either through internal, bureaucratic measures, or through external, market forces. Furthermore, market mechanisms can be simulated within the firm. Various forms of profit centre management, competitive tendering for direct labour groups, and profit-related pay are examples of how market forces can be used to control the intensity, pace, quality and reliability of working. Pignon and Querzola describe how AT&T reorganized punch card operators' and checkers' work into geographically based, rather than functionally based, units in order to increase control over the quality and pace of work. Employees were made responsible for a given 'patch' and were directly accountable by name to individual customers. This meant that 'the employees [were] no longer confronted with the boss as the person they are responsible to but rather with their customers and with the market' (Pignon and Querzola, 1976, p. 75). Albion Water management has achieved much the same effect by transforming M&E and building maintenance into independently accountable units.

Rather than trying to include job content and modes of controlling effort, pace, reliability and quality of working along one single continuum, then, they should be conceptualized as operating simultaneously but independently. Figure 9.1 provides such a model of employment relations.

It is not, of course, strictly speaking possible to map job content along a single continuum. However, for presentational purposes, Figure 9.1 combines three dimensions of job content – the closeness of task specification, the degree of worker discretion and the degree of skill – along the horizontal axis. Such a model is better able to cope with the variety of capitalist employment relations. Within each square are different types of employment relation. For example, putting out standardized work to homeworkers, or organizing groups of relatively unskilled workers as DLOs, would be characteristic of A. Fordist-type employment relations would be characteristic of B. An idealized version of Japanese corporate paternalism would be characteristic of C, whilst D could embrace specialist freelances and cases where employers seek to insert market forces

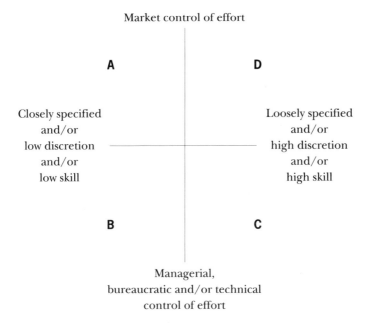

Market control of effort

A

Closely specified
and/or
low discretion
and/or
low skill

D

Loosely specified
and/or
high discretion
and/or
high skill

B

C

Managerial,
bureaucratic and/or technical
control of effort

Figure 9.1 *Dimensions of employment relations.*

into their relationship with highly skilled and or high-discretion direct employees. At Albion Water, privatization has led to employment relations being shifted from the lower to the upper segment of this model. The pace, intensity, reliability and quality of working are increasingly subject to market, as opposed to managerial, forms of control. More work is now put out to contractors, and direct employment relations are increasingly commercialized.

Using such a model it is possible to argue that the basic dynamic underpinning the employment relation is capital's need to control the variability of labour power, and yet to allow for a range of different employment relations which do not differ solely as a function of the technical content or organization of work. Once the emphasis is not exclusively upon job content, it also becomes easier to accommodate wider political, economic and institutional factors into the analysis of employment relations. For example, at Albion changes to employment relations and the pursuit of 'flexibility' have represented attempts not only to prevent workers as subjective beings from limiting the amount of value squeezed from their labour power, but also to improve techniques for consuming the commodity whole, and without waste. But achieving this end is not reducible to technical issues. Management's gains cannot be analytically separated from the political and institutional climate in which they have been won. How much value can be wrung from labour-power is also affected by the wider historical setting in which the transaction takes place.

In general, it can be argued that market control strategies are practical only in particular contexts. Where labour markets are tight, employers are taking a risk by adopting such tactics. If labour legislation was stringent, and if trade unions were powerful, market control of effort would be less effective. In the post-war years in Britain, which provided a context of rapid economic growth, tight labour markets, greater trade union power and so on, it is unsurprising that many employers chose to situate employment relations in the lower half of the model, and rely more heavily on managerial modes of controlling effort. In adopting this approach, employers did not resolve all the contradictions inherent in the capitalist employment relation, however. As Littler (1990, p. 67) observes, 'because of unionization, work-group influence and state agencies imposing regulations and minimum standards' employing labour directly does not necessarily enhance employer control.

In the political climate of Thatcherism in Britain, market control of effort became a more viable option for a greater number of employers, and for a wider range of workers. Littler (1990, p. 67) notes that 'remarketizing' employer–labour relations, e.g. through greater resort to contract labour, 'depends on high levels of unemployment in order to prevent contractual leap-frogging in terms of quoted job prices', and thus throughout most of the 1980s conditions were favourable to contracting out. The commercialization of employment relations within firms similarly becomes a more viable option where there is high unemployment and the threat of contractors is therefore perceived as more real, and where organized labour is weak, so that workers cannot readily defend their position. Once again, employers do not resolve the contradictions inherent in employment relations by commercializing or 'remarketizing' employment relations, as the case studies of BMU and M&E workers amply demonstrate. Albion Water may have found a way of pumping more labour out of labour power in this particular political and economic climate. The same techniques will not necessarily be effective when that climate changes.

It should be noted, however, that managerial solutions do not always represent concessions to labour, and that market solutions do not always represent a penalty. In some circumstances, self-employed or freelance status may be seen by certain highly skilled workers or professionals to be more lucrative and to offer greater autonomy. Shifting the employment relations that accompany such work to the upper half of the model could therefore represent an attempt to attract or retain labour. Conversely, if skilled work that was previously undertaken by highly paid freelances enjoying a high degree of discretion and autonomy is brought back in house to be controlled managerially, the shift to the lower half of the model would not necessarily represent a concession. For example, in the business information and publishing industries, some companies have responded to recession by replacing relatively highly paid freelances with directly employed, younger and less experienced workers, such as graduate trainees, in an attempt to cut costs. The point is that decisions over where to locate the employment relation are set in a particular legal and institutional context; they are influenced by wider economic conditions, and by the particular competitive pressures and labour market conditions in any given sector; they are affected by shifts to the balance of class forces, and are also the terrain of narrower contests between particular groups of workers and employers.

The above model is, of course, at best only a preliminary step towards explaining the variability of capitalist employment relations. But because it does not take job content to be the sole, or even necessarily the primary, determinant of employment relations, it could be developed to accommodate not only diversity over time and across countries, but also variations within and across sectors. Above all, the model suggests that it may be possible to retain an emphasis on capital's need to control the variability of labour power as the basic dynamic behind work organization and employment relations, without implying an ineluctable progression towards direct employment or Taylorist forms of work organization.

To the extent that capital does not buy in the product of labour, the problem of management is to try to exploit the labour power it purchases. When labour power is directly purchased, management must address both how to consume labour power efficiently and how to control labour as a subjective force, and both of these goals can be pursued in a number of ways: through the social organization of work, through the technical content of work, through a range of bureaucratically administered rewards and sanctions, through commercialization or marketization of employment relations. There is more than one way to skin a cat. No strategy can resolve, for once and for all, the basic contradiction between capital's need to control labour as a commodity like any other and its need to harness labour as a subjective force, and there is no one ideal or ultimate form of capitalist employment relation. Instead, particular forms of work organization and employment relations, like payment systems, 'cannot be abstracted from the historically specific struggle between capital and labour' (Nichols, 1980, p. 286).

Notes

1. It is important to note that the pursuit of flexibility can entail both contracting some types of work out and bringing other types back 'in house'. Both can represent stratagems for cutting costs and maximizing the return on capital employed.

2. This highlights a problem with Braverman's tendency to treat the distinction between the motive force of labour and labour itself, and that between conception and execution, as equivalent. The motive force of labour, its conscious and purposive element, is surely only the conscious will or intention to act in a particular way. When people obey the orders of others they act consciously and purposively, not automatically, just as much as when they carry out a plan they themselves have devised. To say that conception, in the sense of designing work, is hijacked by one class, so that one class designs and directs the labour of another class towards alien goals, does not mean that workers no longer act consciously and purposively. It is not possible to actually turn people into automatons, nor to design work that involves no conscious, mental activity at all, and this is precisely why the variability of human labour power will always remain a central problem for management. There must always be unity between the motive force of labour and labour itself, between mind and body. There need not, however, be unity between those who plan work and benefit from it, and those who undertake it.

REFERENCES

Abromeit, H. (1988) 'British privatisation policy', in *Parliamentary Affairs: A Journal of Comparative Politics*, Vol. 41, No. 1, pp. 68–85.

Amin, A. (1991) 'Flexible specialization and small firms in Italy: myths and realities', in A. Pollert (ed.), *Farewell to Flexibility?* Oxford: Basil Blackwell.

Aoki, M., Gustafsson, B. and Williamson, O. (eds) (1990) *The Firm as a Nexus of Treaties*, London: Sage.

Armstrong, P. (1982) 'If it's only women it doesn't matter so much', in J. West (ed.) *Work, Women and the Labour Market*, London: Routledge & Kegan Paul.

Ascher, K. (1987) *The Politics of Privatisation*, Houndmills: Macmillan Education.

Atkinson, J. (1984) 'Manpower strategies for flexible organizations', *Personnel Management*, August, pp. 28–31.

Atkinson J. (1985) 'Flexibility: planning for an uncertain future', *Manpower Policy and Practice*, Vol. 1 (Summer), pp. 26–9.

Batstone, E. (1984) *Working Order*, Oxford: Basil Blackwell.

Batstone, E., Gourlay, S. and Moore, H. (1987) *New Technology and the Process of Labour Regulation*, Oxford: Clarendon Press.

Beechey, V. (1985) 'The shape of the workforce to come', *Marxism Today*, August.

Beesley, M. and Littlechild, S. (1986) 'Privatisation: principles, problems and priorities', in J. Kay, C. Mayer and D. Thompson (eds) *Privatisation and Regulation: The UK Experience*, Oxford: Clarendon Press.

Bell, D. (1960) *The End of Ideology*, Illinois: Free Press of Glencoe.

Berg, M. (1985) *The Age of Manufactures 1700–1820*, London: Fontana.

Berger, S. and Piore, M. (1980) *Dualism and Discontinuity in Industrial Societies*, Cambridge: Cambridge University Press.

Beynon, H., Hudson, R. and Sadler, D. (1991) *A Tale of Two Industries*, Milton Keynes: Open University Press.

Blackburn, R. and Mann, M. (1979) *The Working Class in the Labour Market*, London: Macmillan.

Blauner, R. (1964) *Alienation and Freedom*, Chicago: Chicago University Press.

Blyton, P. and Morris, J. (1991) 'A flexible future: aspects of the flexibility debates and some unresolved issues', in P. Blyton and J. Morris (eds) *A Flexible Future?* Berlin: Walter De Gruyter.

Bottomore, T. (1985) *Theories of Modern Capitalism*, London: Unwin Hyman.

Braverman, H. (1974) *Labor and Monopoly Capital*, New York: Monthly Review Press.

Bray, M. and Littler, C. (1988) 'The labour process and industrial relations: review of the literature', *Labour & Industry*, Vol. 1, No. 3, pp. 551–87.

Bresnen, M., Wray, K., Bryman, A., Beardsworth, A., Ford, J. and Keil, E. (1985) 'The flexibility of recruitment in the construction industry: formalism or recasualisation?', *Sociology*, Vol. 19, pp. 108–24.

Brighton Labour Process Group (1977) 'The capitalist labour process', *Capital and Class*, No. 1.

Brown, R. (1988) 'The employment relationship in sociological theory', in D. Gallie (ed.) *Employment in Britain*, Oxford: Basil Blackwell.

Brusco, S. (1983) 'The Emilian model: productive decentralisation and social integration', *Cambridge Journal of Economics*, Vol. 6, pp. 167–84.

Burawoy, M. (1979) *Manufacturing Consent*, Chicago: University of Chicago Press.

Burawoy, M. (1985) *The Politics of Production*, London: Verso.

Campbell, I. (1989) 'New production concepts? The West German debates on restructuring', *Labour and Industry*, Vol. 2, No. 2, pp. 247–80.

Carsberg, B., Littlechild, S., McMillan, C. and Bonner, F. (1986) 'Water and the problem of price regulation in an age of privatisation', *Public Finance and Accountancy*, July 25, pp. 20–7.

Casey, B. (1987) 'The extent and nature of temporary employment in Great Britain', *Policy Studies*, Vol. 8:1.

Clarke, P. (1987) 'The argument for privatisation', in J. Neuberger (ed.) *Privatisation: Fair Shares for All or Selling the Family Silver?* London: Papermac.

Clawson, D. (1980) *Bureaucracy and the Labor Process*, New York: Monthly Review Press.

Coates, D. (1984) *The Context of British Politics*, London: Hutchinson.

Cockburn, C. (1983) *Brothers: Male Dominance and Technological Change*, London: Pluto Press.

Colling, T. (1987) Water works – keep it public, the trade union response to the threat of privatisation in the water industry, MA thesis, School of Industrial and Business Studies, University of Warwick.

Cook, J. (1989) *Dirty Water*, London: Unwin Hyman.

Cousins, C. (1990) 'The contracting out of ancillary services in the NHS', in G. Jenkins and M. Poole (eds) *New Forms of Ownership*, London: Routledge.

Creigh, S., Roberts, C., Gorman, A. and Sawyer, P. (1986) 'Self-employment in Britain: results from the Labour Force Surveys 1981–4', *Employment Gazette*, Vol. 94:6.

Cressey, P. and MacInnes, J. (1980) 'Voting for Ford: industrial democracy and the control of labour', *Capital and Class*, Vol. 11, pp. 5–33.

Cutler, A. (1978) 'The romance of labour', *Economy and Society*, Vol. 7, No. 1, pp. 74–95.

Cutler, A., Hindess, B., Hirst, P. and Hussain, P. (1977) *Marx's Capital and Capitalism Today*, Vol. 1, London: Routledge & Kegan Paul.

Dale, A. and Bamford, C. (1988) 'Temporary workers: cause for concern or complacency?', *Work, Employment and Society*, Vol. 2, No. 2, pp. 191–209.

Daniel, W. and Millward, N. (1983) *Workplace Industrial Relations in Britain*, London: Heinemann Educational Books.

Dearlove, J. and Saunders, P. (1984) *Introduction to British Politics*, Cambridge: Polity Press.

Department of the Environment (1973a) *The New Water Industry, Management and Structure*, London: HMSO.

Department of the Environment (1973b) *The Water Services: Economic and Financial Policies – First Report to the Secretary of State for the Environment*, London: HMSO.

Dex, S. (1985) *The Sexual Division of Work*, London: Harvester Wheatsheaf.

Doeringer, P. and Piore, M. (1971) *Internal Labour Markets and Manpower Analysis*, Lexington: Heath & Co.

Drucker, P.F. (1946) *The Concept of the Corporation*, New York: The John Day Company.

Du Gay, P. (1991) 'Enterprise culture and the ideology of excellence', *New Formations*, Spring, 13, pp. 45–61.

Durkheim, E. (1960) *The Division of Labour in Society*, Illinois: Free Press of Glencoe.

Edwards, P. (1985a) *Managing Labour Relations Through the Recession*, Mimeo, University of Warwick, Industrial Relations Research Unit.

Edwards, P. (1985b) 'Myth of the macho manager', *Personnel Management*, April, pp. 32–5.

Edwards, R.C. (1979) *Contested Terrain*, London: Heinemann.

Elger, A. (1979) 'Valorization and deskilling: a critique of Braverman', *Capital & Class*, No. 7, pp. 58–99.

Elger, A. (1982) 'Braverman, capital accumulation and deskilling', in S. Wood (ed.), *The Degradation of Work?* London: Macmillan.

Elger, A. (1990) 'Technical innovation and work reorganisation in British manufacturing in the 1980s: continuity, intensification or transformation?', *Work, Employment and Society*, May, pp. 67–101.

Elger, A. (1991) 'Task flexibility and the intensification of labour in UK manufacturing in the 1980s', in A. Pollert (ed.) *Farewell to Flexibility?* Oxford: Basil Blackwell.

Evan, W. (1963) 'Comment on Macauley's non-contractual relations in business', *American Sociological Review*, Vol. 28, No. l, pp. 67–9.

Fairbrother, P. (1991) 'In a state of change: flexibility in the Civil Service', in A. Pollert (ed.) *Farewell to Flexibility?* Oxford: Basil Blackwell.

Fairbrother, P. and Waddington, J. (1990) 'The politics of trade unionism: evidence, policy and theory', *Capital & Class*, Vol. 41, Summer, pp. 15–56.

Federation of Civil Engineering Contractors (1984) *Form of Sub-Contract*, Cowdray House, 6 Portugal Street, London WC2A 2HH: The Federation of Civil Engineering Contractors.

Ferner, A. (1987) 'Public enterprise and the politics of commercialism: changing industrial relations in British and Spanish railways', *Work, Employment & Society*, Vol. 1, No. 2, pp. 179–203.

Ferner, A. (1990) 'The changing influence of the personnel function: privatisation and organizational politics in electricity generation', *Human Resource Management Journal*, Autumn.

Fevre, R. (1986) 'Contract work in the recession', in K. Purcell *et al.* (eds) *The Changing Experience of Employment*, Houndmills: Macmillan.

Fevre, R. (1987) 'Subcontracting in steel', *Work, Employment and Society*, Vol. 1, No. 4, pp. 509–27.

Ford, H. (1922) *My Life and Work*, London: Heinemann.

Fox, A. (1974) *Beyond Contract: Work, Power and Trust Relations*, London: Faber & Faber.

Freeman, A. (1991) 'Diversifications: fewer than expected', *Financial Times*, Survey of the Water Industry, 22 November.

Friedman, A. (1977a), 'Responsible autonomy versus direct control over the labour process', *Capital & Class*, No. 1.

Friedman, A. (1977b) *Industry and Labour: Class Struggle at Work and Monopoly Capitalism*, London: Macmillan.

Friedman, A. (1990) 'Managerial strategies, activities, techniques and technology: towards a complex theory of the labour process', in D. Knights and H. Willmott (eds) *Labour Process Theory*, London: Macmillan.

Gallie, D. (1978) *In Search of the New Working Class*, Cambridge: Cambridge University Press.

Gamble, A. (1988) *The Free Economy and the Strong State*, London: Macmillan.

Geras, N. (1971) 'Essence and appearance: aspects of fetishism in Marx's Capital', *New Left Review*, No. 65.

Glynn, D. (1987) *The Economic Regulation of the Privatised Water Industry*, The Economist Conference Unit, London.

Goldthorpe, J. (1984) 'The end of convergence: corporatist and dualist tendencies in modern Western societies', in J. Goldthorpe (ed.) *Order and Conflict in Contemporary Capitalism*, Oxford: Clarendon Press.

Goldthorpe, J. (1987) 'Problems of political economy after the postwar period', in C. Maier (ed.) *Changing Boundaries of the Political*, Cambridge: Cambridge University Press.

Gordon, D., Edwards, R. and Reich, M. (1982) *Segmented Work, Divided Workers*, Cambridge: Cambridge University Press.

Hakim, C. (1987a) 'Homeworking in Britain', *Employment Gazette*, 95:2.

Hakim, C. (1987b) 'Trends in the flexible workforce', *Employment Gazette*, 95:3.

Hallet, R. (1990) 'Privatization and the restructuring of a public utility: a case study of British Telecom's corporate strategy and structure', in G. Jenkins and M. Poole (eds) *New Forms of Ownership*, London: Routledge.

Hassan, J. (1985) 'The growth and impact of the British water industry in the nineteenth century', *Economic History Review*, Vol. 38, pp. 531–47.

Haswell, C. and de Silva, D. (1989) *Civil Engineering Contracts: Practice and Procedure*, 2nd edn, London: Butterworth.

Heald, D. and Morris, G. (1984) 'Why public sector unions are on the defensive', *Personnel Management*, May, pp. 30–4.

Herrington, P. (1989) *Deep Water: Investors Beware*, WIUC, NALGO, 1 Mabledon Place, London WC1H 9AJ.

Herrington, P. and Price, C. (1987) *What Price Private Water?* Department of Economics, University of Leicester, Leicester LE1 7RH.

Hindess, B. and Hirst, P. (1975) *Mode of Production and Social Formation*, London: Macmillan.

HM Treasury (1990) 'Privatisation', *Economic Briefing*, No. 1, December.

Hobsbawm, E. (1964) *Labouring Men*, London: Weidenfeld & Nicolson.

Hyman, R. (1987) 'Strategy or structure: capital, labour and control', *Work, Employment and Society*, Vol. 1, No. 1, pp. 25–57.

Hyman, R. (1988) 'Flexible specialisation: miracle or myth?', in R. Hyman and D. Streek (eds) *New Technology and Industrial Relations*, Oxford: Basil Blackwell.

JAWS (1987) *Water under Pressure*, Joint Action for Water Services, 7th Floor, Centre City, 7 Hill Street, Birmingham 5.

JAWS (1989) *Tap Dancing: Water: The Environment and Privatisation*, Joint Action for Water Services, 7th Floor, Centre City, 7 Hill Street, Birmingham 5.

Jenson, J. (1989) 'The talents of women, the skills of men: flexible specialization and women', in S. Wood (ed.) *The Transformation of Work?* London: Unwin Hyman.

Katz, H. and Sabel, C. (1985) 'Industrial relations and industrial adjustment in the car industry', *Industrial Relations*, Vol. 24, pp. 295–315.

Kelly, J. (1982) *Scientific Management, Job Redesign and Work Performance*, London: Academic Press.

Kerr, C. (1960) *Industrialism and Industrial Man*, Cambridge, MA: Harvard University Press.

Kioke, K. (1990) 'Intellectual skill and the role of employees as constituent members of large firms in contemporary Japan', in M. Aoki, B. Gustafsson and O. Williamson (eds) *The Firm as a Nexus of Treaties*, London: Sage.

Kumar, K. (1986) *Prophecy and Progress: The Sociology of Industrial and Post-industrial Society*, Harmondsworth: Penguin.

Labour Research (1990) 'The nightmare of privatising power', *Labour Research*, No. 17.

Letwin, O. (1988) *Privatising the World: A Study of International Privatisation in Theory and Practice*, London: Cassell Educational.

Lever-Tracey, C. (1984) 'The paradigm crisis of dualism: decay or regeneration?' *Politics and Society*, Vol. 13, No. 1.

Littler, C. (1982) *The Development of the Capitalist Labour Process*, London: Heinemann.

Littler, C. (1985) 'Taylorism, Fordism, and job design', in D. Knights, H. Willmott and D. Collinson (eds) *Job Redesign: Critical Perspectives on the Labour Process*, Aldershot: Gower.

Littler, C. (1990) 'The labour process debate: a theoretical review 1974–88', in D. Knights and H. Willmott (eds) *Labour Process Theory*, London: Macmillan.

Littler, C. and Salaman, G. (1984) *Class at Work*, London: Batsford Academic and Educational.

Lupton, T. (1972) 'Methods of wage payment, organizational change and motivation', in T. Lupton (ed.) *Payment Systems*, Harmondsworth: Penguin.

Macauley, S. (1963) 'Non-contractual relations in business: a preliminary study', *American Sociological Review*, Vol. 28, No. 1, pp. 55–67.

MacInnes, J. (1987) *Thatcherism at Work*, Milton Keynes: Open University Press.

Mann, M. (1973) *Workers on the Move*, Cambridge: Cambridge University Press.

Marginson, P., Edwards, P., Martin, R., Purcell, J. and Sisson, K. (1988) *Beyond the Workplace*, Oxford: Blackwell.

Marglin, S. (1976) 'What do bosses do? The origins and functions of hierarchy in capitalist production', in A. Gorz (ed.) *The Division of Labour: The Labour Process and Class Struggle in Modern Capitalism*, Brighton: Harvester.

Marx, K. (1954) *Capital: A Critique of Political Economy*, Vol. 1, London: Lawrence & Wishart.

Marx, K. (1976) *Capital: A Critique of Political Economy*, Vol. 1, Harmondsworth: Penguin.

Marx, K. (1977) *Economic and Philosophical Manuscripts of 1844*, London: Lawrence & Wishart.

Massey, D. (1984) *Spatial Divisions of Labour*, London: Macmillan Education.

Meager, N. (1986) 'Temporary work in Britain', *Employment Gazette*, 94:1.

Millward, N. and Stevens, M. (1986) *British Workplace Industrial Relations 1980–1984*, London: ESRC/PSI/ACAS.

Mitchell, B. (1971) 'Water in England and Wales – supply, transfer and management', *Research Paper No. 9*, Department of Geography, University of Liverpool, Bemrose Press.

Moore, J. (1983) *Why Privatise?* London: Conservative Political Centre.

Moore, J. (1986) 'The success of privatisation', in J. Kay, C. Mayer and D. Thompson (eds) *Privatisation and Regulation: The UK Experience*, Oxford: Clarendon Press.

Murray, R. (1988) 'Life after Henry (Ford)', *Marxism Today*, October, pp. 8–13.

NALGO (1988) *Water down the Drain? The Case against Privatising the Water Industry*, NALGO, 1 Mabledon Place, London WC1H 9AJ.

NEDO (1986) *Changing Working Patterns: How Companies Achieve Flexibility to Meet New Needs*, London: National Economic Development Office.

Nichols, T. (1980) *Capital and Labour*, London: The Athlone Press.

Nichols, T. (1986) *The British Worker Question*, London: Routledge & Kegan Paul.

Nichols, T. and Beynon, H. (1977) *Living with Capitalism*, London: Routledge & Kegan Paul.

Nyland, C. (1987) 'Scientific management and planning', *Capital & Class*, No. 33.

O'Connell Davidson, J. (1990) 'The road to functional flexibility: white collar work and employment relations in a privatised public utility', *Sociological Review*, Vol. 38, No. 4.

O'Connell Davidson, J. (1994) 'The sources and limits of resistance in a privatised utility', in J. Jermier, W. Nord and C. Smith (eds) *Resistance and Power in Organizations: Agency, Subjectivity and the Labour Process*, London: Routlege (forthcoming).

O'Connell Davidson, J., Nichols, T. and Sun, W. (1991) *Privatisation and Change: Employee Attitudes in Two Privatised Utilities*, Department of Sociology, University of Leicester.

Ogden, S. (1990) 'The impact of privatization on industrial relations in the water industry', unpublished paper presented to the Cardiff Business School Annual Conference, September.

Perlman, N. (1972) Preface to I. Rubin, *Essays on Marx's Theory of Value*, Detroit: Black and Red.

Peters, T. and Waterman, R. (1982) *In Search of Excellence: Lessons from America's Best Run Companies*, New York: Harper & Row.

Phillips, A. and Taylor, B. (1980) 'Sex and skill: notes towards a feminist economics', *Feminist Review*, No. 6, pp. 79–88.

Pignon, D. and Querzola, J. (1976) 'Dictatorship and democracy in production', in A. Gorz (ed.) *The Division of Labour: The Labour Process and Class Struggle in Modern Capitalism*, Brighton: Harvester.

Piore, M. (1979) *Birds of Passage: Migrant Labor and Industrial Societies*, Cambridge: Cambridge University Press.

Piore, M. (1986) 'Perspectives on labor market flexibility', *Industrial Relations*, Vol. 25, No. 2, pp. 146-66.

Piore, M. and Sabel, C. (1984) *The Second Industrial Divide*, New York: Basic Books.

Pollard, S. (1965) *The Genesis of Modern Management*, London: Edward Arnold.

Pollert, A. (1988) 'Dismantling flexibility' *Capital & Class*, Vol. 34, pp. 42-75.

Pollert, A. (1991) *Farewell to Flexibility?* Oxford: Basil Blackwell.

Redwood, J. (1988) Foreword to O. Letwin, *Privatising the World*, London: Cassell Educational.

Rees, J. and Synott, M. (1988) 'The water industry', in C. Whitehead (ed.) *Reshaping the Nationalised Industries*, Oxford: Transaction Books.

Reeve, T. (1990) 'The firm as a nexus of internal and external contracts', in M. Aoki, B. Gustafsson and O. Williamson (eds) *The Firm as a Nexus of Treaties*, London: Sage.

Rose, M. (1988) *Industrial Behaviour*, Harmondsworth: Penguin.

Rubin, I. (1972) *Essays on Marx's Theory of Value*, Detroit: Black and Red.

Sabel, C. (1982) *Work and Politics*, Cambridge: Cambridge University Press.

Sako, M. (1988) 'Partnership between small and large firms: the case of Japan', unpublished paper presented to The Commission of the European Communities Conference, 'Partnership Between Small and Large Firms', Congress Centre, Brussels, June.

SCAT (1989) *Public Service Action*, No. 40, July.

SCAT (1990) *Public Service Action*, No. 43, August.

Schneiberg, M. and Hollingsworth, J. (1990) 'Can transaction cost economics explain trade associations?', in M. Aoki, B.Gustafsson and O. Williamson (eds) *The Firm as a Nexus of Treaties*, London: Sage.

Schott, K. (1983) 'The rise of Keynesian economics: Britain 1940-64', in D. Held (ed.) *States and Societies*, Oxford: Basil Blackwell.

Secretary of State for the Environment (1989) *Prospectus: The Water Share Offers*.

Sivanandan, A. (1990) 'All that melts into air is solid: the hokum of new times', *Race & Class*, Vol. 31, pp. 1-30.

Sloan, A. (1986) *My Years with General Motors*, Harmondsworth: Penguin.

Smith, A. (1986) *The Wealth of Nations: Books I–III*, Harmondsworth: Penguin Classics.

Smith, C. (1989) 'Flexible specialisation, automation and mass production', *Work, Employment and Society*, Vol. 3:2, pp. 203-20.

Stern, W. (1954) 'Water supply in Britain: the development of a public service', *Royal Sanitary Institute Journal*, Vol. LXXIV.

Stone, K. (1973) 'The origins of job structures in the steel industry', *Radical America*, Vol. 7:6.

Streek, W. (1987) 'The uncertainties of management in the management of uncertainty', *Work, Employment and Society*, Vol. 1, No. 3.

Taylor, F.W. (1947) *The Principles of Scientific Management*, New York: Harper & Row.

Therborn, G. (1984) 'Britain left out', in J. Curran (ed.) *The Future of the Left*, Oxford: Basil Blackwell.

Thompson, P. (1983) *The Nature of Work*, London: Macmillan.

Thompson, P. (1990) 'Crawling from the wreckage: the labour process and the politics of production', in D. Knights and H. Willmott (eds) *Labour Process Theory*, London: Macmillan.

Tomaney, J. (1990) 'The reality of workplace flexibility', *Capital & Class*, No. 40, Spring, pp. 29-61.

Ueno, H. (1980) 'The conception and evaluation of Japanese industrial policy', in K. Sato (ed.) *Industry and Business in Japan*, London: Croom Helm.

Upham, M. (1990) 'Passages on the path to privatization: the experience of British Steel', *Industrial Relations Journal*, 21:2, Summer, pp. 87-97.

Vickers, J. and Yarrow, G. (1988) *Privatization: An Economic Analysis*, London: MIT Press.

WAA (1988) *Waterfacts 88*, Water Authorities Association, 1 Queen Anne's Gate, London SW1H 9BT.

Walsh, K. (1989) 'Contracts and work organization: the case of local government', unpublished paper presented to the 1989 Cardiff Business School annual conference.

Water (1986) *White Paper for the Privatization of the Water Industry*, Cmnd. 9734, London: HMSO.

Watts, R. (1987) 'Prospects for water services PLCs', unpublished paper presented to The Economist Conference Unit, 'The Privatization of the Water Industry', Marriott Hotel, London, September.

West, J. (1990) 'Gender and the labour process', in D. Knights and H. Willmott (eds) *Labour Process Theory*, London: Macmillan.

Williams, K., Cutler, T., Williams, J. and Haslam, C. (1987) 'The end of mass production?' *Economy and Society*, Vol. 16, No. 3, pp. 405–39.

Williamson, O. (1985) *The Economic Institutions of Capitalism*, New York: Free Press.

Williamson, O. (1989) 'Transaction cost economics', in R. Schmalensee and R. Willig (eds) *Handbook of Industrial Organization*, Vol. 1, Amsterdam: North-Holland.

Williamson, O. (1990) 'The firm as a nexus of treaties: an introduction', in M. Aoki, B. Gustafsson and O. Williamson (eds) *The Firm as a Nexus of Treaties*, London: Sage.

Winterton, J. (1990) 'Private power and public relations: the effects of privatization upon industrial relations in the coal industry', in G. Jenkins and M. Poole (eds) *New Forms of Ownership*, London: Routledge.

Wood, S. (1988) 'Between Fordism and flexibility? The case of the US car industry', in R. Hyman and D. Streek (eds) *New Technology and Industrial Relations*, Oxford: Basil Blackwell, pp. 101–27.

Wood, S. (1989a) *The Transformation of Work?* London: Unwin Hyman.

Wood, S. (1989b) 'New wave management?', *Work, Employment and Society*, Vol. 3.

Wright, M. (1988) 'Redrawing the boundaries of the firm', in S. Thompson and M. Wright (eds) *Internal Organization, Efficiency and Profit*, Oxford: Philip Allan.

INDEX